Fodor's InFocus

P9-DED-964

CHARLESTON

13
TOP EXPERIENCES

Charleston offers terrific experiences that should be on every visitor's list. Here are Fodor's top picks for the most memorable trip.

1 Carriage Ride

Get your bearings the fun way with a carriage ride through the historic district. You'll soak up history, lore, and architectural tidbits all while enjoying amazing views. *(Ch. 1)*

2 White Point Gardens and the Battery

The tip of Charleston's peninsula has been home to everything from strolling ladies in hoopskirts to booming Civil War cannons. Today the stunning view of the harbor remains, along with a regal oak allée. *(Ch. 2)*

3 Old Slave Mart Museum

Charleston was the main point of entry into America for enslaved people in the 18th and 19th centuries. Visit this museum (and one-time slave auction house) for a detailed telling of their journey. *(Ch. 2)*

4 Sullivan's Island

Drive 20 minutes north of town to this slow-paced island. Family friendly and mellow, the beaches are edged in dunes and maritime forests. *(Ch. 6)*

5 Sweetgrass Baskets

"Sewn" from sweet-smelling plants that line the Lowcountry's marshes, these baskets were first made to winnow rice. The designs can be traced to West African countries. *(Ch. 7)*

6 USS *Yorktown*

Charleston's naval history is long, and Patriot's Point on the Charleston Harbor offers three amazing (and retired) ships for tours: the air carrier USS *Yorktown*, the destroyer USS *Laffey*, and the submarine USS *Clamagore*. *(Ch. 2)*

7 King Street

Shop for everything from antiques, artisan candy, fashion, jewelry, and homegoods at hip local boutiques and superior national chains on King Street. The two-mile mecca is Charleston's hottest shopping and dining area. *(Ch. 7)*

8 The Wreck of The Richard and Charlene

Named after an old shrimp boat, this seafood dive on Shem Creek is home to famed fried grits, red rice, okra, and fresh-off-the-docks crab, shrimp, and fish. *(Ch. 3)*

9 Drayton Hall

Head 40 minutes out of town to explore this rare, still-standing pre-Revolutionary plantation home on banks of the Ashley River. *(Ch. 2)*

10 Fort Sumter National Monument

Take the boat tour to this fort in the harbor to see where the first shots of the Civil War were fired in 1861. You can also learn about the lives of the Federal and Confederate troops that occupied it. *(Ch. 2)*

11 Regional Cuisine

A national culinary destination, Charleston has talented chefs who offer innovative twists on traditional Lowcountry cuisine. Pull up a chair at Husk, where James Beard Award-winning Sean Brock wows diners. *(Ch. 3)*

12 Spoleto Festival USA

Visit in late May and early June for Spoleto Festival USA's flood of indoor and outdoor performances by international luminaries in opera, music, dance, and theater. *(Ch. 5)*

13 Nathaniel Russell House Museum

Go behind closed doors at this mansion-turned-museum to wander grand parlors and drawing rooms, and learn how antebellum life carried on in Charleston. *(Ch. 2)*

CONTENTS

MAPS

ABOUT THIS BOOK

Fodor's Ratings

Everything in this guide is worth doing—we don't cover what isn't—but exceptional sights, hotels, and restaurants are recognized with additional accolades. **Fodor'sChoice★** indicates our top recommendations; ★ highlights places we deem highly recommended. Care to nominate a new place? Visit Fodors.com/contact-us.

Trip Costs

We list prices wherever possible to help you budget well. Hotel and restaurant price categories from **$** to **$$$$** are noted alongside each recommendation. For hotels, we include the lowest cost of a standard double room in high season. For restaurants, we cite the average price of a main course at dinner or, if dinner isn't served, at lunch. For attractions, we always list adult admission fees; discounts are usually available for children, students, and senior citizens.

Hotels

Our local writers vet every hotel to recommend the best overnights in each price category, from budget to expensive. Unless otherwise specified, you can expect private bath, phone, and TV in your room. For expanded hotel reviews, facilities, and deals visit Fodors.com.

Restaurants

Unless we state otherwise, restaurants are open for lunch and dinner daily. We mention dress code only when there's a specific requirement and reservations only when they're essential or not accepted. To make restaurant reservations, visit Fodors.com.

Credit Cards

The hotels and restaurants in this guide typically accept credit cards. If not, we'll say so.

Ratings
- ★ Fodor's Choice
- ★ Highly recommended
- ☾ Family-friendly

Listings
- ⊠ Address
- ⊠ Branch address
- ⌖ Mailing address
- ☎ Telephone
- 🖷 Fax
- ⊕ Website

- ✍ E-mail
- 🎫 Admission fee
- ☉ Open/closed times
- Ⓜ Subway
- �🗘 Directions or Map coordinates

Hotels & Restaurants
- 🏨 Hotel
- ⤵ Number of rooms
- ⦿ Meal plans

- ✕ Restaurant
- ⌕ Reservations
- 🏛 Dress code
- ⊟ No credit cards
- $ Price

Other
- ⇨ See also
- ☞ Take note
- 🏌 Golf facilities

Experience Charleston

WELCOME TO CHARLESTON

You hear it time and again from people you meet in Charleston: either they have been here for generations upon generations (happily so), or they came here from somewhere else and never left (happily so). There's just something about the city and its surrounding Lowcountry landscape that beguiles, from the pastel antebellum homes to the pedestrian-friendly downtown and the sprawling waters that wrap around the peninsula and pristine beaches that hug the outlying islands. Add culture in spades, history, shopping, and a foodie scene that's taken the nation by storm—James Beard Award winners and nominees are commonplace—and it's no wonder that Charleston is continually cited as one of America's top destinations.

Meet the Mayor

Much of the city's appeal is owed to Mayor Joseph Riley Jr., a visionary who transformed Charleston from a provincial and insular town into an energetic, forward-thinking city, one that is a model community for the entire country. First elected in 1975, Riley persuaded composer Gian Carlo Menotti to bring the famous Spoleto Festival to Charleston in 1977. Riley also inaugurated such tourism attractions as downtown's Waterfront Park, the South Carolina Aquarium, and the Old Slave Mart Museum. On the urban planning front, he played a vital role in the construction of the stunning Arthur Ravenel Jr. Bridge, one of the largest single-span bridges in North America, and the Shops at Charleston Place and the hotel itself. He has helped spearhead other major renovations, including the City Market, the White Point Gardens bandstand, the Memminger Auditorium, and the Gaillard Center project. Also on the list, not surprisingly, is an impressively renovated City Hall, where a gallery of famous presidential portraits remains a big draw for sightseers.

Tourism Reigns

Tourism, under Riley's guiding hand, has become the city's main industry. Star-studded hotels and restaurants are as run-of-the-mill as homey dives, both offering their spin on Lowcountry and seafood favorites. Add King Street, where stores range from Rodeo Drive names to mom-and-pop shops, and the city is a perfect mix of small-town charm, Southern grace, and world-class amenities. As popular among celebrities (many of whom wed or honeymoon here), former presidents, and the well-heeled as it is for regular families and couples looking to escape, Charleston has the nice manners to treat every visitor like what they are: guests of the "Holy City."

College Town

Charleston, in spite of its historic mantle and proper ways, is a youthful town, thanks to the College of Charleston (1770)—an institution that has seen booming growth in recent decades—and many grads now stay on after completing their education. As it has expanded, the "C of C" (to use its local nickname) has revitalized the Calhoun Street corridor. Other local institutions of higher learning are the Citadel Military College, Trident Technical College, and the Art Institute of Charleston. The latter two have culinary programs that have lured even more young people to the city's demographic mix and talent to its restaurants' kitchens.

Colonial Roots

The success the city enjoys today is built upon hundreds of years of effort. As part of "The Carolinas," South Carolina was the original Steel Magnolia of the original 13 colonies. No matter that fires, earthquakes, fearsome pirates, hurricanes, political scoundrels, smallpox epidemics, economic downturns, and major wars have all struck mighty blows—they only fortified the stalwart grande dame. Today, she is like a belle whose beauty has grown quieter but no less lovely with age. Her many historic landmarks and houses bear witness to her long and fascinating history.

War Time

After freedom in 1776, Charlestonians waited nearly a century before jumping into another fight, this one with the fledgling United States itself. Residents were adamant about defending states' rights (and the subsequent right of a state to keep slavery legal). With South Carolina the first state to secede from the Union, Charleston saw the start of the Civil War when Confederate soldiers at Fort Johnson fired upon the Union-occupied Fort Sumter. All that storied history can still be viewed today.

WHAT'S WHERE

1 North of Broad. The main part of the Historic District, where you'll find the lion's share of the Historic District's homes, bed-and-breakfasts, and restaurants, is the most densely packed area of the city and will be of the greatest interest to tourists. King Street, Charleston's main shopping artery, is also here.

2 The Battery and South of Broad. The southern part of the Historic District is heavily residential, but it has important sights and B&Bs, though fewer restaurants and shops than North of Broad.

3 Mount Pleasant and Vicinity. East of Charleston, on the other side of the Arthur Ravenel Jr. Bridge, which spans the Cooper River, is Mount Pleasant, an affluent suburb with some interesting sights (such as Boone Hall Plantation). There are several good hotels in Mount Pleasant itself.

4 West of the Ashley River. The area outside Charleston west of the Ashley River beckons to visitors with its three major historic plantations on Ashley River Road.

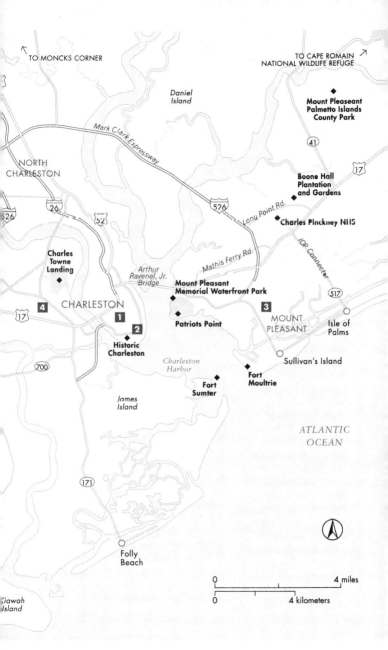

TO MONCKS CORNER

TO CAPE ROMAIN
NATIONAL WILDLIFE REFUGE

Daniel Island

Mount Pleaseant
Palmetto Islands
County Park

41

17

NORTH
CHARLESTON

Mark Clark Expressway

526

Boone Hall
Plantation
and Gardens

Long Point Rd.

Charles Pinckney NHS

26

52

Mathis Ferry Rd.

IOP Connector

Charles
Towne
Landing

*Arthur
Ravenel, Jr.
Bridge*

Mount Pleasant
Memorial Waterfront Park

517

CHARLESTON

3

17

4

1

Patriots Point

MOUNT
PLEASANT

Isle of
Palms

2

Historic
Charleston

700

*Charleston
Harbor*

Sullivan's Island

Fort
Sumter

Fort
Moultrie

*James
Island*

ATLANTIC
OCEAN

171

4 miles

0

0

4 kilometers

Folly
Beach

*Kiawah
Island*

CHARLESTON PLANNER

Visitor Resources

The **Charleston Area Convention & Visitors Bureau** (www.charlestoncvb.com) is the best place to start piecing together your trip, whether in person or via their website. Other great resources include the *Charleston City Paper* (www.charlestoncitypaper.com), a free weekly with events galore, and *Charleston* magazine (www.charlestonmag.com); check out both publications' online calendars for events. To find out more about Restaurant Week in this foodie city (January and September), look at the **Charleston Restaurant Association** website (www.charlestonrestaurantassociation.com). And to both browse options for home and garden tours and purchase tickets, head to the gift shops (or websites) of the **Charleston Preservation Society** (www.preservationsociety.org) and **Historic Charleston Foundation** (www.historiccharleston.org).

Getting Here and Around

Fly to Charleston: Flying into the Charleston International Airport is a pretty straightforward affair. American Airlines, United, Delta, US Airways, Southwest, and JetBlue all offer flights. Other options include the inexpensive Spirit Airlines, which flies into Myrtle Beach International Airport, 90 miles north of Charleston. Once you land, you'll have to take a taxi or shuttle into the city, about 15 minutes to downtown, unless you rent a car.

Hop a Train: Amtrak pulls into Charleston thanks to the Palmetto service, which spans New York City to Savannah, Georgia, with stops in Philadelphia, Washington, D.C., and other spots, including Charleston. The ride is pleasant, but the train station is on the rough side, so have a taxi or other ride waiting to take you the 15 minutes into town.

Drive in: Two main highways feed into Charleston—Highway 17 and Interstate 26.

In the City: A car isn't a must in this walkable city, but for those who prefer not to hoof it, there are bikes, pedicabs, tour buses, water taxis, ground taxis, and the CARTA trolley buses, plus buses that go to the burbs and beaches. Street parking is irksome, as meter readers are among the city's most efficient public servants. (But if you purchase a SmartCard from the Division of Motor Vehicles downtown, you can "deposit" meter money and credit it back to your card when you leave a metered spot.) Parking garages, both privately and publicly owned, charge approximately $1.50 an hour.

Planning Your Time

You can get acquainted with Charleston's Historic District at your leisure, especially if you can devote at least three days to the city, which will allow time to explore some of the plantations west of the Ashley River. With another day, you can explore Mount Pleasant, and if you have even more time, head out to the coastal islands.

Savings

You can pretty much bank on high season running year-round, with minor dips in the heat of late July through early September, and mid-January–Valentine's Day (February 14). But if you're motivated, there are deals to be found. Always look online to book hotel packages. Restaurant Week, where multi-course meals are offered at discounted prix fixe, hits twice, in January and September. Year-round, the DASH trolley service offers step-on, step-off free routes throughout downtown. If you must drive, know that metered parking is free from 6 pm to 9 am. And for those looking to hop on a carriage tour, be sure to raid hotel-lobby rack cards for coupons offering a few dollars off (discounts are also online). Freebie events include the City Farmers Market, where food vendors, farmers, and artisans offer their wares; Piccolo Spoleto (late May to mid-June), where artists sell their work and musicians give gratis performances; *Charleston City Paper's* Movies in Marion Square in April; Artwalk in the French Quarter, where galleries offer late-night viewing, cocktail nibbles, and drinks every first Friday of the month; and Second Sundays on King, when King Street closes to traffic from Calhoun to Broad streets, and sales hit the sidewalks along with restaurants offering Sunday specials.

Reservations

High season is pretty much any season in Charleston, aside from maybe the hottest stretch of the year, from mid-July through early September. That means reservations are always a good idea at restaurants, and a must for hotels downtown. Although you can call around a few days ahead for most tables, the top tier often require a week or more advanced booking for Friday or Saturday nights. And holidays (Thanksgiving, Christmas, New Year's Eve and Day, Valentine's Day, Mother's Day, or Easter brunch) demand reservations made a month or more prior. For those willing to fly by the seat of their schedules, same-day (and discounted) hotel reservations are available through the Lowcountry Reservation Service, operated at the Charleston Area Convention & Visitors Bureau, the Isle of Palms Visitor Center, and the North Charleston Visitors Center.

WHEN TO GO

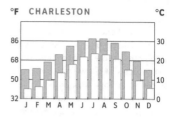

°F   CHARLESTON   °C

Spring and fall tend to be the most popular times to visit Charleston. The former sees courtyard gardens exploding in blooms and warm temperatures coaxing sundresses and seersucker suits out of local closets. The latter finds residents and tourists alike returning to the sidewalks to stroll, now that summer's most intense heat (and hair-curling humidity) is mellowing out. There are truly only two slightly slower times for tourism in Charleston (July to mid-September and January to mid-February), so those loath to brave crowds or vie for dinner reservations are best advised to visit during those months. Typically, airfare is pricey year-round, but discount airlines Southwest and JetBlue offer options that are easier on your bottom line. Book money-saving hotel packages online or make day-of reservations through Lowcountry Reservations Service at the Charleston Convention & Visitors Bureau.

Climate

Aside from the dog days of summer, where temperatures range from 80°F to 100°F, and the humidity nears a stifling 100% on a weekly basis, Charleston boasts mild temperatures and a semitropical climate. Expect afternoon rainstorms to blow in and out during summer months, but know that an umbrella is more than enough to keep you happily exploring outside. Come fall, pack light sweaters, and when winter rolls in from December to early February with low 50°F temps, pull on a coat if you're thin-blooded. Basically there are four seasons here, but summer and spring stretch out the longest.

Festivals and Events

The **Southeastern Wildlife Exhibition (SEWE)** in mid-February marks the first big annual event on Charleston's busy social calendar. Dog trials, birds-of-prey exhibits, and wildlife-art sales make it quite testosterone fueled, but it's fun for kids, too. Next up in March comes the **BB&T Wine & Food Festival** in Marion Square, where cook-offs, sampling, and special dinners reign. Spring home and garden tours hit in late March, and the catwalks are crawling with fashionistas for **Charleston Fashion Week**. The **Cooper River Bridge** run welcomes some 44,000 runners and walkers for the 10K the last weekend in March, and some 30,000 attendees catch the tennis matches at the **Family Circle Cup** in early April. **Spoleto Festival USA and Piccolo Spoleto** both offer live performances and art exhibitions (combined, they total more than 700 options) from late May to mid-June. Charleston's African-American and Caribbean heritage is celebrated with the **MOJA Arts Festival** in September and October, and fall home and garden tours rev up then as well.

PERFECT DAYS IN CHARLESTON

Here are a few ideas on how to spend a day in Charleston.

Tour Waterfront Park, South of Broad neighborhoods, the Battery, and the Market. To soak up Charleston best, you've either got to walk it, pedal it (via bike or pedicab), or cover it by carriage. The common thread: you've got to move slowly to see the intricate details in the gardens and architecture and to discover the sweet alleys. Start at Waterfront Park, and read the history markers there. Wander down to the Battery along East Bay and sit in White Point Gardens. Head up King or Church to gawk at the amazing antebellum residences, and then head over to the old City Market to shop for everything from sweets to sweetgrass baskets. Lunch at Husk is a good bet.

Shop King Street. King Street is Charleston's version of the Miracle Mile. On King Street, this amounts to antique, preserved storefronts that look much like they have for the past few hundred years. Start at Broad and King streets and work your way north for the most comprehensive experience. Try breakfast at Bull Street Gourmet & Market, and then wander from Broad to Market streets, checking out antiques shops and fancy clothing boutiques. Continue shopping in central King, where you'll find chic chains as well as locally born shops like Hampden Clothing. Get lunch at 39 Rue de Jean while heading into the Upper King Area. North of Calhoun, things get funkier. Here's where you'll find Blue Bicycle. Dinner at The MacIntosh makes a lovely end.

Explore the Plantations. Charleston started as a port city in the late 1600s and later dominated in the rice, indigo, and even cotton trade until the Civil War. Many of the large plantations still exist outside the city. Whether you opt to visit Boone Hall Plantation in Mount Pleasant or one or two of three other such properties along Ashley River Road in West Ashley you will get a better understanding of what built Charleston and helped the colonies break away from England so long ago.

Play at the Beach. Hit the shore at Folly Beach south of town if you like waves that you can surf, a rogue approach to living, a hopping village bar scene, and natural parks to wander. Head east from downtown to Sullivan's Island for kiteboarding and family-friendly beaches. And volleyball aficionados aim for Isle of Palms, where the sporting life and beach bars rule the surfside.

IF YOU LIKE

Exploring Living History

Time-travel to the 18th century with Charleston's wealth of markets, historic homes, and churches, and explore the agrarian side to the city via its outlying former plantations. Taken together, the sum tells the story of wars, wealth, collapse, and rebirth.

Nathaniel Russell House. Built in 1808, this remains one of the nation's finest surviving examples of Adam-style architecture.

Aiken-Rhett House. This downtown estate includes slave quarters, a stable, and a remarkable (and threadbare) mansion.

The City Market. See where whites and blacks shopped for produce, seafood, and meat from the late 1700s to the early 1900s. Shop the souvenir stalls that now thrive there.

Old Slave Mart Museum. Explore the slave history that's responsible for Charleston's grandeur and the eventual death of the Confederacy.

St. Philip's (Episcopal) Church. The namesake of famous Church Street, this graceful late-Georgian structure dates from 1838.

Boone Hall Plantation and Gardens. This still-working plantation is the oldest of its kind in the Charleston area.

Middleton Place. After viewing the house (once torched during the Civil War, its "gentlemen's wing" has been restored to its former glory), be sure to visit the estate's rolling green spaces, lively stableyard, and delightful Butterfly Lakes.

Magnolia Plantation and Gardens. The gardens and trolley tour of rice paddies, slave quarters, and the swamp is the main draw.

Drayton Hall. One of the few remaining plantation homes in the Lowcountry, Drayton Hall was completed in 1742 and lived in by descendants of original family until the 1970s.

Playing Outside

Water plays a major part in the recreation possibilities here, with the Atlantic Ocean and the Ashley and Cooper rivers, as well as myriad tidal creeks and estuaries. You can fish, especially in the Gulf Stream, go on dolphin-watching trips, and kayak. Back on land, tennis and golf are the top tickets.

Sullivan's Island. Head here for family-friendly beaches and a view of Charleston from across the harbor.

Shem Creek. Some of the area's best **kayak** and stand-up **paddleboard** outfitters are stationed here (**Coastal Expeditions**). Charters for **deep-sea fishing** (private and group boats) also depart from here.

Tennis. **Wild Dunes Resort** on Isle of Palms reigns for the best tennis camps in the area, and the **Family Circle Cup** takes place each spring on Daniel Island.

Golf. Golfers rave about the links both on **Kiawah Island** (the 2012 PGA Championship was played on the Ocean Course there) and at **Wild Dunes** on Isle of Palms.

Bike. Rent a bike from various outfitters downtown and beyond, and explore Charleston on two wheels. Consider biking the **Cooper River Bridge,** or taking your bike to the trails at **James Island County Park** or **Palmetto Island County Park, Charlestowne Landing,** or **Magnolia Plantation and Gardens.** Those looking to log miles loop **Hampton Park** with its new mile-long bike and pedestrian lane.

Run. Although all of downtown makes a great track, the **Cooper River Bridge** and Hampton Park's mile-long asphalt parcourse, half mile garden circle, and mile-long bike-pedestrian lane are where the locals go.

Learning Gullah and African-American History

"Gullah" is the name given to the descendants of slaves in the Lowcountry. The term can refer to the people themselves, to their language, or to their culture, now regarded as one of the most distinctive regional cultures of African-American history.

Gullah Tours. These tours cover Charleston, Beaufort, and Hilton Head, and give you a glimpse into the authentic history of the Gullah.

MOJA Arts Festival. During the last week of September and first week of October, African heritage and Caribbean influences on African-American culture are celebrated.

Avery Research for African American History and Culture. Part museum and part archive, this center began as a school in 1865, which trained freed slaves and people of color to be teachers. Today, see artifacts and documentation of the slave era here.

Middleton Place. Eliza's House, built in the 1870s for the freed slaves who stayed on at this plantation, has a fascinating *Beyond the Fields* exhibition that reveals how reliant this estate was on its former slaves.

Boone Hall Plantation. Take a self-guided tour through the *Black History in America* exhibition on view in eight original brick slave cabins, or attend a performance at the estate's outdoor Gullah Theater.

Shopping

Charleston has evolved into a shopper's haven. Most of the action happens on King Street, and Upper King has added the Design District, with a new wave of antiques, furniture, and home-fashion stores. Add to this more than 25 art galleries, predominantly in the French Quarter, and there's plenty to browse and buy.

City Market. Sweetgrass baskets, candies, T-shirts, bags, spices, and much, much more are for sale from the vendors here.

Heirloom Book Company. A foodie town deserves this bookstore specializing in vintage cookbooks.

Croghan's Jewel Box. This family-owned gem has sold wedding silver, engagement rings, anniversary presents, and jewelry galore to Charlestonians for more than 100 years.

Hamden Clothing. Find out why New York fashion editors consider this hipster paradise a must-see when they are anywhere in the South.

Magar Hatworks. Milliner Leigh Magar's toppers are tops with Barneys in New York, Martha Stewart, and celebrities galore.

Copper Penny. Designers like Diane Von Furstenberg, Trina Turk, and Millie are well represented on these racks.

Ben Silver. A Charleston institution, this provider of preppie blazers and polo shirts keeps locals looking snappy.

Blue Bicycle Books. The only bookstore downtown sells used, rare, and new books with local ties.

Geo. Birlant's & Co's Antiques. Silver, silver, and more silver abounds here.

City Gallery on Waterfront Park. It's worth a visit to admire the location alone. This gallery houses mainly South Carolina artists.

Getting Away from It All

Charleston itself is a little step off the beaten path, but for those looking to isolate and unwind further, there are options.

Wentworth Mansion. When celebrities want to stay downtown but out of the limelight, they head to this 1886 mansion with its spa, restaurant, and quiet neighborhood a few blocks from King Street.

The Inn at Middleton Place. A supermod-style hotel in the woodlands adjacent to Middleton Place, this inn affords private access to the plantation grounds.

The Sanctuary at Kiawah Island. Luxury knows no bounds at this hotel with its acclaimed restaurant, spa, and nearby golf courses.

Eating Out

You can't toss a plate for hitting a James Beard Award nominee or winner in Charleston these days. Take advantage of this and try some of these spots for fresh cuisine from Lowcountry farms and artisan purveyors.

Husk and McCrady's. Chef Sean Brock brought the Southern locavore movement into the mainstream with the former and treats you to top-end white-linen dining with the latter.

FIG. Mike Lata's impeccable Lowcountry-accented dishes are born of perfectly sourced, perfectly prepared, and perfectly honest ingredients.

Trattoria Lucca. Italian food never tasted so fine as it does at Chef Ken Vedrinski's neighborhood kitchen.

Peninsula Grill. Break out the fancy clothes for supreme service and gourmet decadence at the Charleston institution. Don't leave without trying the coconut cake.

Macaroon Boutique. Sweet treats that make for great gifts (or simple snacks) are the order of the day here.

Glazed. Find the world's best gourmet snacks before they sell out—usually by noon.

Market Street Sweets. Hit this confectionary to sample cinnamon-and-sugar crusted pecans or benne wafers—a Charleston original.

Ted's Butcherblock. One-stop-shopping for gourmet picnic provisions, Ted's is also a great place to hit for wine tastings.

KIDS AND FAMILIES

What kid wouldn't delight in a town that looks like a fairy tale, and has cobblestone streets and secret alleyways, horses pulling carriages, real-life pirate stories, and candy shops with free samples handed out daily? Charleston is made for kids, and exploring it is a great (and painless) way to get them to learn history, so bring on the family time.

Resorts

Kiawah Island Golf Resort and **Wild Dunes Resort** on Isle of Palms offer the most activities for kids. From tennis and golf lessons to swimming and crabbing and more, there are scores of ways to keep the junior set entertained. In town, **Embassy Suites** on Marion Square enchants with its castle-like appearance and sits in a primo location for all the events held on the square, from the Saturday Farmers' Market (with its jump castle and pony rides) to SEWE (with its dog trials), Piccolo Spoleto (with its children's arts activities), and more.

Dining

Kids are welcome everywhere in town—but they are expected to mind their manners. If your child needs a little schooling in that department, feel free to enroll them in etiquette camp or send them to a children's tea party for that purpose via the **Charleston School of Protocol and Etiquette** (www.charlestonschoolofprotocol.com). Manners aside, kids of all ages are especially welcome **Taco Boy**, and **Hominy Grill** (especially for weekend brunch).

Activities

As for entertainment, **carriage tours** (and the stables at Pinckney and Anson streets) captivate, as do rides on the **water taxis** and **pedicabs**. Rainy days are best passed in the **Children's Museum of the Lowcountry** (the interactive gravity and water exhibits and model shrimp boat are favorites), the **South Carolina Aquarium**, or at **Patriots Point** with its decommissioned destroyer, submarine, and aircraft carrier. Sunny days call for a visit to the blacksmith's shop and stable yard at **Middleton Place** or the petting zoo at **Magnolia Plantation and Gardens**, or a **Riverdogs** baseball game at the Joe downtown. If you're looking to cool off, any of the beaches are a good bet, or even the fountains at **Waterfront Park**. For shopping, try **Robot Candy Company** or **Charleston Candy Kitchen** for goodies, the **City Market** for souvenirs, or **Kapla Blocks by Tom's Toys**.

Exploring
Charleston

WORD OF MOUTH

"[Charleston] is one of the cities that should be on everyone's must-visit list. It has everything. It is historic, has great architecture, lots of fine restaurants with some of the best seafood you will ever find, a vibrant arts scene, interesting and beautiful places to visit nearby, friendly people, lots to do, good shopping, and is very tourist friendly as well without being over the top—it blends its tourism and everyday life very well."
—Basingstoke2

By Anna
Evans

Wandering through the city's famous Historic District, you would swear it is a movie set. Dozens of church steeples punctuate the low skyline, and horse-drawn carriages pass centuries-old mansions and town houses, their stately salons offering a crystal-laden and parquet-floored version of Southern comfort. Outside, magnolia-filled gardens overflow with carefully tended heirloom plants. At first glance, the city resembles an 18th-century etching come to life—but look closer and you'll see that block after block of old structures have been restored. Happily, after three centuries of wars, epidemics, fires, and hurricanes, Charleston has prevailed and is now one of the South's best-preserved cities.

Although home to Fort Sumter, where the bloodiest war in the nation's history began, Charleston is also famed for its elegant houses. These handsome mansions are show-cases for the "Charleston style," a distinctive look that is reminiscent of the West Indies, and for good reason. Before coming to the Carolinas in the late 17th century, many early British colonists first settled on Barbados and other Caribbean islands. In that warm and humid climate they built homes with high ceilings and rooms opening onto broad "piazzas" (porches) at each level to catch welcome sea breezes. As a result, to quote the words of the Duc de La Rochefoucauld, who visited in 1796, "One does not boast in Charleston of having the most beautiful house, but the coolest."

Preserved through the hard times that followed the Civil War and an array of natural disasters, many of Charleston's earliest public and private buildings still stand. Thanks to a rigorous preservation movement and strict Board of Architectural Review guidelines, the city's new structures blend in with the old. In many cases, recycling is the name of the game—antique handmade bricks literally lay the foundation for new homes. But although locals do dwell—on certain literal levels—in the past, the city is very much a town of today.

Take, for instance, the internationally heralded Spoleto Festival USA. For 17 days every spring, arts patrons from around the world come to enjoy international concerts, dance performances, operas, and plays at various venues citywide. Day in and day out, diners can feast at upscale restaurants, shoppers can look for museum-quality paint-ings and antiques, and lovers of the outdoors can explore

Charleston's outlying beaches, parks, and marshes. But as cosmopolitan as the city has become, it's still the South, and just beyond the city limits are farm stands cooking up boiled peanuts, the state's official snack.

EXPLORING CHARLESTON

Everyone starts a tour of Charleston in downtown's famous Historic District. Roughly bounded by Lockwood Boulevard on the Ashley River to the west, Calhoun Street to the north, East Bay Street on the Cooper River to the east, and the Battery to the south, this fairly compact area of 800 acres contains nearly 2,000 historic homes and buildings. The peninsula is divided up into several neighborhoods, starting from the south and moving north, including the Battery, South of Broad, Lower King Street, and Upper King Street ending near the "Crosstown," where U.S. 17 connects downtown to Mount Pleasant and West Ashley.

You'll see no skyscrapers in the downtown area, because building heights are strictly regulated to maintain the city's historic setting. In the 1970s, most department stores decamped for suburban malls, turning King Street buildings into rows of (architecturally significant) empty shells. Soon, preservation-conscious groups began to save these beauties, and by the mid-1980s the shopping district was revived with the addition of the Omni Hotel (now Charleston Place). Big-name retailers quickly saw the opportunity in this attractive city and settled in as well. Lower King thrives and Upper King has been revived in recent years, with many new businesses—hip bars and restaurants in particular—targeting the city's young, socially active population. Look up at the old-timey tile work at the entrances; inevitably it will have the names of the original businesses.

Beyond downtown, the Ashley River hugs the west side of the peninsula; the region on the far shore is called West Ashley. The Cooper River runs along the east side of the peninsula, with Mount Pleasant on the opposite side and Charleston Harbor in between. Lastly, there are outlying sea islands: James Island with its Folly Beach, John's Island, Wadmalaw Island, Kiawah Island, Seabrook Island, Isle of Palms, and Sullivan's Island. Each has its own appealing attractions, though John's and Wadmalaw have farms instead of beaches. Everything that entails crossing the bridges is best explored by car or bus.

NORTH OF BROAD

During the early 1800s, large tracts of land were available North of Broad—as it was outside the bounds of the original walled city—making it ideal for suburban plantations. A century later the peninsula had been built out, and today the resulting area is a vibrant mix of residential neighborhoods and commercial clusters, with verdant parks scattered throughout. The district comprises three primary neighborhoods: Upper King, the Market area, and the College of Charleston. Though there are a number of majestic homes and pre-Revolutionary buildings in this area (including the Powder Magazine, the oldest public building in the state), the main draw is the rich variety of stores, museums, restaurants, and historic churches.

As you explore, note that the farther north you travel (up King Street in particular), the newer and more commercial development becomes. Although pretty much anywhere on the peninsula is considered prime real estate these days, the farther south you go, the more expensive the homes become. In times past, Broad Street was considered the cutoff point for a coveted address. Those living in the area Slightly North of Broad were referred to as SNOBs, and, conversely, their wealthier neighbors South of Broad were nicknamed SOBs.

TOP ATTRACTIONS

☺ **Charleston Museum.** Although housed in a modern-day brick
★ complex, this institution was founded in 1773 and is the country's oldest museum. To the delight of fans of *Antiques Roadshow,* the collection is especially strong in South Carolina decorative arts, from silver to snuffboxes. There's also a large gallery devoted to natural history (don't miss the giant polar bear). Children love the permanent Civil War exhibition, with plenty of Confederate uniforms, and the interactive "Kidstory" area, where they can try on reproduction clothing in a miniature historic house. A recent addition is the Historic Textiles Gallery, featuring changing displays that showcase everything from couture gowns to antique quilts. Combination tickets that give you admission to the Joseph Manigault House and the Heyward-Washington House are a bargain at $22. ✉ *360 Meeting St., Upper King* ☏ *843/722–2996* ⊕ *www.charlestonmuseum. org* ⌑ *$10* ☉ *Mon.–Sat. 9–5, Sun. 1–5.*

Charleston Place. The city's most renowned hotel is flanked by upscale boutiques and specialty shops. Stop in for cocktails and tapas at the classy Thoroughbred Club. The city's finest public restrooms are downstairs near the shoeshine station. Entrances for the garage and reception area are just past the intersection of Hasell and Meeting streets. ✉ *205 Meeting St., Market area* ☎ *843/722–4900* ⊕ *www.charlestonplace.com.*

Charleston Visitor Center. A great stop to get your bearings and gather info. ✉ *375 Meeting St., Upper King* ☎ *843/853– 8000, 800/868–8118* ⊕ *www.charlestoncvb.com* ⛟ *Free* ⊙ *Apr.–Oct., daily 8:30–5:30; Nov.–Mar., daily 8:30–5.*

☾ ★ **Children's Museum of the Lowcountry.** Hands-on interactive environments at this top notch museum will keep kids— from toddlers on up to age eight—occupied for hours. They can climb aboard a Lowcountry pirate ship, drive an antique fire truck, race golf balls down a roller coaster, and create masterpieces in the art center. ✉ *25 Ann St., Upper King* ☎ *843/853–8962* ⊕ *www.explorecml.org* ⛟ *$7* ⊙ *Tues.–Sat. 9–5, Sun. noon–5.*

Circular Congregational Church. The first church building erected on this site in the 1680s gave bustling Meeting Street its name. The present-day Romanesque structure, dating from 1890, is configured on a Greek-cross plan and has a breathtaking vaulted ceiling. While the church is not open to drop-in visitors, guests are welcome to explore the graveyard, which is the oldest in the city, with records dating back to 1696. ✉ *150 Meeting St., Market area* ☎ *843/577–6400* ⊕ *www.circularchurch.org* ⊙ *Graveyard weekdays 8–6, Sun. 9–6.*

☾ **City Market.** Most of the buildings that make up this popular attraction were constructed between 1804 and the 1830s to serve as the city's meat, fish, and produce market. These days, you'll find the open-air portion packed with stalls selling jewelry, crafts, handmade clothing, jams and jellies, and regional souvenirs. In 2011, a major renovation transformed the market's indoor section, creating a beautiful backdrop for 20 desirable new stores and eateries. Local "basket ladies" weave and sell sweetgrass, pinestraw, and palmetto-leaf baskets—a craft passed down through generations from their West African and Caribbean ancestors. This shopping mecca's perimeters (North and South Market streets) are lined with restaurants and shops selling everything from pralines and other candies to high-end sportswear, hats, and Charleston gifts and collectibles. ✉ *N. and S. Market Sts. between Meeting and E. Bay Sts., Market area* ⊕ *www.thecharlestoncitymarket. com* ⊙ *Daily 9:30–dusk.*

9

TO FORT SUMTER

**Charleston
Maritime Center**

Downtown
Charleston

Cooper River

Aiken-Rhett House, **1**	French Protestant (Huguenot) Church, **21**
Avery Research Center for African American History and Culture, **11**	Gibbes Museum of Art, **15**
Battery, **29**	Heyward-Washington House, **26**
Charleston Museum, **3**	The *Hunley*, **7**
Charleston Place, **12**	Joseph Manigault House, **5**
Charleston Visitor Center, **2**	Market Hall, **13**
Children's Museum of the Lowcountry, **4**	Nathaniel Russell House, **27**
Circular Congregational Church, **16**	Old Citadel, **6**
City Hall, **23**	Old Exchange Building and Provost Dungeon, **25**
City Market, **14**	Old Slave Mart Museum, **22**
College of Charleston, **10**	Powder Magazine, **17**
Dock Street Theatre, **20**	St. Michael's Episcopal Church, **24**
Edmondston-Alston House, **28**	St. Philip's Church, **18**
Fort Sumter National Monument, **9**	South Carolina Aquarium, **8**
	Waterfront Park, **19**

0	1/4 mi
0	400 meters

College of Charleston. With a majestic Greek-revival portico, Randolph Hall—an 1828 building designed by Philadelphia architect William Strickland—presides over the college's central Cistern area. Draping oaks envelop the lush green quad, where graduation ceremonies and concerts, notably during the Spoleto Festival, take place. Scenes from films including *Cold Mountain* have been filmed on the historic campus of this liberal arts college, founded in 1770. ⊠ *Cistern Yard, 66 George St., College of Charleston Campus* ☎ *843/805–5507* ⊕ *www.cofc.edu.*

Dock Street Theatre. Incorporating the remains of the Old Planter's Hotel (circa 1809), this theater is hung with green velvet curtains and has wonderful woodwork, giving it a New Orleans French Quarter feel. After a three-year closure and a $20 million restoration, it reopened with fanfare in the spring of 2010 and now looks grand! ⊠ *135 Church St., Market area* ☎ *843/720–3968* ⊕ *www. charleston-sc.gov.*

QUICK BITES. **Bakehouse.** This popular bakery and café serves delicious desserts made on-site, including heavenly sweet 'n' salty brownies and cupcakes (the secret is in the frosting, which is light, fluffy, and always flavorful). Soft as a pillow, the homemade marshmallows make great take-away treats. Sandwiches and quiches are served, too, and can be washed down with craft beers, including a few local varieties. This Wi-Fi hotspot has roomy booths and community tables as well as a couple of sidewalk seats. ⊠ *160 E. Bay St., Market area* ☎ *843/577–2180* ⊕ *www.bakehousecharleston.com.*

★ Fodor'sChoice **Fort Sumter National Monument.** Set on a man-made island in Charleston's harbor, this is the hallowed spot where the Civil War began. On April 12, 1861, the first shot of the war was fired at the fort from Fort Johnson (now defunct) across the way. After a 34-hour battle, Union forces surrendered and Confederate troops occupied Sumter, which became a symbol of Southern resistance. The Confederacy managed to hold it, despite almost continual bombardment, from August 1863 to February of 1865. When it was finally evacuated, the fort was a heap of rubble. Today, the National Park Service oversees it, and rangers give interpretive talks and conduct guided tours. To reach the fort, you have to take a ferry or a private boat; ferries depart from the Fort Sumter Visitor

Education Center, downtown, and from Patriots Point in Mount Pleasant. There are six trips daily between mid-March and mid-August. The schedule is abbreviated the rest of the year, so call ahead for details. For those using a GPS to find the boat departure points for Fort Sumter, remember to use the address for Patriots Point and the Visitor Education Center, not the mailing address for the fort. ☎ *843/883-3123* ⊕ *www.nps.gov/fosu* ✉ *Fort free; ferry $17* ⊘ *Mid-Mar.–early Sept., daily 10–5:30; early Sept.–mid-Mar., daily 10–4 (11:30–4 Dec. 1–24, Jan., and Feb.).*

Fort Sumter Visitor Education Center. Next to the South Carolina Aquarium, the visitor center contains exhibits on the antebellum period and the causes of the Civil War. This is a departure point for ferries headed to Fort Sumter. ✉ *340 Concord St., Upper King* ☎ *843/577–0242* ⊕ *www. nps.gov/fosu* ✉ *Free* ⊘ *Daily 8:30–5*

HISTORY LESSON. **A ferry ride to Fort Sumter is a great way to sneak in a history lesson for the kids. For about the same price as a standard harbor cruise, you get a narrated journey that points out the historic sites and explains how the Civil War began.**

French Protestant (Huguenot) Church. The circa-1845 Gothic-style church is home to the only practicing Huguenot congregation in the nation. English-language services are held Sunday at 10:30. ✉ *136 Church St., Market area* ☎ *843/722–4385* ⊕ *www.frenchchurch.org* ⊘ *Mid-Mar.–mid-June and mid-Sept.–mid-Nov., Mon.–Thurs. 10–4, Fri. 10–1.*

★ Fodor'sChoice **Gibbes Museum of Art.** Experience Charleston's history through art. Housed in a beautiful Beaux-Arts building, the Gibbes boasts a collection of 10,000 works, principally American with a local connection. Each year a dozen special exhibitions, often of contemporary art, attract a more youthful audience. Different objects from the museum's permanent collection are always on view in "The Charleston Story," offering a nice overview of the region's history, and the gift shop is exceptional. The museum is slated to close for renovations in 2014, so call ahead before visiting. ✉ *135 Meeting St., Market area* ☎ *843/722–2706* ⊕ *www.gibbesmuseum.org* ✉ *$9* ⊘ *Tues.–Sat. 10–5, Sun. 1–5.*

WHAT'S IN A NAME. The Manigaults are descendants of the French Huguenots who fled Europe because of persecution, and are a golden example of the American dream fulfilled. They became a wealthy rice-planting family and are still prominent in Charleston; Manigaults own the daily newspaper, among other businesses.

★ **Fodor's**Choice **Joseph Manigault House.** Considered by many to be the finest example of Federal-style architecture in the South, this 1803 home was built for a rich rice-planting family of Huguenot heritage. Having toured Europe as a gentleman architect, Gabriel Manigault returned to design this residence for his brother Joseph as the city's first essay in neoclassicism. The house glows in red brick and is adorned with a two-story piazza balcony. Inside, marvels await: a fantastic "flying" staircase in the central hall; a gigantic Venetian window; elegant plasterwork and mantels; notable Charleston-made furniture; and a bevy of French, English, and American antiques, including some celebrated tricolor Wedgwood pieces. Outside, note the garden "folly." ⊠ *350 Meeting St., Upper King* ☎ *843/723–2926* ⊕ *www.charlestonmuseum.org* 🎟 *$10* ☉ *Mon.–Sat. 10–5, Sun. 1–5.*

Old Citadel. A fortresslike building on Marion Square became the first home of the Military College of South Carolina, now called The Citadel, in the 1840s. Today it is part of an Embassy Suites hotel, and you can stop into the lobby to see a case of artifacts found on-site. The present-day Citadel is near Hampton Park on the Ashley River. ⊠ *341 Meeting St., Upper King* ☎ *843/723–6900.*

FARMERS' MARKET. Set in Marion Square park, at the intersection of King and Calhoun streets, the market runs from 8 am to 2 pm every Saturday from April through mid-December. Here you can find organic produce, homemade jams, and handcrafted everything—from jewelry to decor and dog collars. Breakfast and lunch options are plentiful, too.

★ **Fodor's**Choice **Old Slave Mart Museum.** This is likely the only building still in existence in South Carolina that was used for slave auctioning, a practice that ended here in 1863. It was once part of a complex called Ryan's Mart, which also contained a slave jail, kitchen, and morgue. It is now a museum that recounts the history of Charleston's role in the slave trade, an unpleasant story but one that is vital to understand. Charleston once served as the center of commercial

JOHN JAKES'S BEST BETS IN CHARLESTON

Renowned historical novelist John Jakes, who lives in the Lowcountry, achieved the rare distinction of having 16 consecutive novels on the *New York Times* list of best sellers. Considered the contemporary master of the family saga, Jakes is best loved locally for his trilogy *North and South,* which was made into three miniseries for ABC in the 1980s and '90s. They focused on Charleston before and during the Civil War, with much of the filming done in the city. Less famous but equally entertaining and educational are his books and audiotapes, *Charleston* and *Savannah,* or a *Gift for Mr. Lincoln.* Jakes shared some suggestions for experiencing Charleston's historical sites with us:

"**Fort Sumter.** A boat ride to the famous Civil War fort is an attraction that shouldn't be missed by any visitor who appreciates history. Close your eyes just a bit and you can imagine Sumter's cannon blasting from the ramparts—maybe even spot a sleek, gray blockade-runner from Liverpool sneaking into the harbor at dusk.

Carriage Rides. We lived in the Lowcountry for years before I took one of the carriage rides that originate next to the outdoor market. I had a misguided scorn for such tours until I jumped impulsively into a vacant carriage one day. I found the young guide enormously informative, and learned a lot, even some years after writing the *North and South* trilogy. Caution: Carriage routes are determined by where they start from; try to avoid those that take you away from the real jewel featured in the others—the Historic District.

Boone Hall Plantation. This finely preserved property just a few miles north of the city stood in for Mont Royal, Patrick Swayze's home in the David L. Wolper miniseries *North and South.* The avenue of live oaks leading to the house is well worth the visit."

—John Jakes

activity for the South's plantation economy, and slaves were the primary source of labor both within the city and on the surrounding plantations. Galleries are outfitted with some interactive exhibits, including push buttons that allow you to hear voices relating stories from the age of slavery. The museum is on one of the few remaining cobblestone streets in town. ✉ *6 Chalmers St., Market area* ☎ *843/958–6467* ⊕ *www.charlestoncity.info* ✄ *$7* ⊙ *Mon.–Sat. 9–5.*

★ Fodor'sChoice **St. Philip's Church.** One of the three churches that gave Church Street its name, this graceful Corinthian-style building is the second one to rise on its site: the first one burned down in 1835 and was rebuilt in 1838. A shell that exploded in the churchyard while services were being held one Sunday during the Civil War didn't deter the minister from finishing his sermon (the congregation gathered elsewhere for the remainder of the war). Notable Charlestonians such as John C. Calhoun are buried in the eastern and western churchyards. If you want to tour the church, call ahead, as open hours depend upon volunteer availability. ✉ *142 Church St., Market area* ☎ *843/722–7734* ⊕ *www.stphilipschurchsc.org* ☉ *Churchyard weekdays 9–4.*

★ Fodor'sChoice **South Carolina Aquarium.** The 385,000-gallon
☺ Great Ocean Tank houses the tallest aquarium window in North America. Along with sharks, moray eels, and sea turtles, exhibits include more than 7,000 creatures, representing 350-plus species. In 2011, the 2,500-square-foot Saltmarsh Aviary opened, offering views of Charleston Harbor and allowing you to catch sight of herons, diamondback terrapins, puffer fish, and stingrays. The latest exhibit is Madagascar Journey, filled with exotic animals including ring-tailed lemurs—a favorite among visitors, who can step inside an observation bubble within the primates' habitat. The 4-D theater shows popular family films complete with special effects such as wind gusts and splashes of water. ✉ *100 Aquarium Wharf, Upper King* ☎ *800/722–6455, 843/720–1990* ⊕ *www.scaquarium.org* ☎ *$29.95* ☉ *Mar.–Aug., daily 9–5; Sept.–Feb., daily 9–4.*

☺ **Waterfront Park.** Enjoy the fishing pier's "front-porch"
★ swings, stroll along the waterside path, or relax in the gardens overlooking Charleston Harbor. Two fountains can be found here: the much acclaimed Pineapple Fountain and the Vendue Fountain, which children love to run around in on hot days. The park is at the foot of Vendue Range, along the east side of Charleston Harbor and the Cooper River. ✉ *Vendue Range at Concord St., Market area* ☎ *843/724–7321* ☎ *Free* ☉ *Daily 6 am–midnight.*

ON THE CHEAP. A $45.95 Charleston Heritage Passport, sold at the Charleston Visitor Center, gets you into the Charleston Museum, the Gibbes Museum of Art, the Nathaniel Russell House, the Edmondston-Alston House, the Aiken-Rhett House,

Drayton Hall, and Middleton Place (stableyards and grounds). It's good for two days.

WORTH NOTING

★ Fodor'sChoice **Aiken-Rhett House.** One of Charleston's most stately mansions, built in 1820 and virtually unaltered since 1858, has been preserved rather than restored, meaning visitors can see its original wallpaper, paint schemes, and some furnishings. Two of the former owners, Governor Aiken and his wife, Harriet—lovers of all things foreign and beautiful—bought many of the chandeliers, sculptures, and paintings in Europe. Out back, the kitchen, slave quarters, and work yard are much as they were when the original occupants lived here, making this the most intact mansion and accompanying outbuildings to showcase urban life in antebellum Charleston. Take the audio tour, as it vividly describes both the ornate rooms and the slaves', giving historical and family details throughout. ⊠ *48 Elizabeth St., Upper King* ☎ *843/723–1159* ⊕ *www.historiccharleston. org* ☎ *$10; $16 with admission to Nathaniel Russell House* ⊙ *Mon.–Sat. 10–5, Sun. 2–5; last tour at 4:15.*

Avery Research Center for African American History and Culture. Part of the College of Charleston, this museum, archive, and center for public programming was once a school for African Americans, training students for professional careers from approximately 1865 to 1954. The collections here focus on the civil rights movement but also include slavery artifacts such as badges, manacles, and bills of sale. The free tours include a brief film. ⊠ *125 Bull St., College of Charleston Campus* ☎ *843/953–7609* ⊕ *avery.cofc.edu* ☎ *Free* ⊙ *Weekdays 10–5, weekends by appointment.*

The *Hunley*. In 1864, the Confederacy's H. L. *Hunley* torpedoed the Union warship USS *Housatonic*, becoming the world's first successful submarine. But moments after the attack, it disappeared mysteriously into the depths of the sea. Lost for more than a century, it was found in 1995 off the coast of Sullivan's Island and raised in 2000. It is now being preserved and excavated in a 90,000-gallon tank, which you can view along with artifacts excavated from inside, facial reconstructions of the crew, and the National Geographic documentary *Raising the Hunley*. ⊠ *1250 Supply St., Old Charleston Naval Base, North Charleston* ☎ *843/743–4865, 877/448–6539 for tour reservations* ⊕ *www.hunley.org* ☎ *$12* ⊙ *Sat. 10–5, Sun. noon–5.*

Market Hall. Built in 1841, this imposing restored landmark was modeled after the Temple of Wingless Victory in Athens. The hall contains the **Confederate Museum** ($5), in which the United Daughters of the Confederacy mount displays of flags, uniforms, swords, and other Civil War memorabilia. ✉ *188 Meeting St., Market area* ☎ *843/723–1541* ⊕ *www.thecharlestoncitymarket.com* 🎫 *Free* ⊙ *Tues.–Sat. 11–3:30.*

Powder Magazine. Completed in 1713, the oldest public building in South Carolina is the only one that remains from the time of the Lords Proprietors. The city's volatile—and precious—gunpowder was kept here during the Revolutionary War, and the building's thick walls were designed to contain an explosion if its stores were detonated. Today it's a museum with a new permanent exhibit focusing on colonial warfare. ✉ *79 Cumberland St., Market area* ☎ *843/722–9350* ⊕ *www.powdermag.org* 🎫 *$3* ⊙ *Mon.–Sat. 10–4, Sun.1–4.*

BUILDING BOOM. Charleston grew apace with the plantation economy in the mid-1700s, thanks to the booming trade in South Carolina's rice, indigo, and cotton crops. Seeking a social and cultural lifestyle to match its financial success, the plantocracy entertained itself in style by using the talents of the local goldsmiths, silversmiths, gunsmiths, and cabinetmakers. More than 300 private residences were likely built between 1760 and 1770 alone, a surge reflective of Charleston's position as the wealthiest city in British North America at that time.

SOUTH OF BROAD

Locals jokingly claim that just off the Battery (at Battery Street and Murray Boulevard), the Ashley and Cooper rivers join to form the Atlantic Ocean. Such a lofty proclamation speaks volumes about the area's rakish flair. To observe their pride and joy, head to the point of the downtown peninsula. Here, handsome mansions and a large, oak-shaded park greet incoming boats and charm passersby.

The heavily residential area south of Broad Street brims with beautiful private homes, many of which have plaques bearing brief descriptions of the property's history. Mind your manners, but feel free to peek through iron gates and fences at the verdant displays in elaborate gardens. Although an open gate once signified that guests were welcome to venture inside, that time has mostly passed—residents tell stories of how they came home to find tourists sitting in their front-porch rockers. But you never know when an invitation to have a look-see might come from a friendly owner-gardener. Several of the city's lavish house museums call this famously affluent neighborhood home.

TOP ATTRACTIONS

★ Fodor'sChoice **Battery.** During the Civil War, the Confederate army mounted cannons in the Battery, at the southernmost point of Charleston's peninsula, to fortify the city against Union attack. Cannons and piles of cannonballs still line the oak-shaded park known as White Point Gardens—kids can't resist climbing them. Where pirates once hung from the gallows, strollers now take in the serene setting from Charleston benches (small wood-slat benches with cast-iron sides). Stroll the waterside promenades along East Battery and Murray Boulevard and you can enjoy views of Charleston Harbor, the Ravenel Bridge, and Fort Sumter on one side, with some of the city's most photographed mansions on the other. You'll find Gullah oldsters dangling their fishing lines, waiting for a catch. ✉ *E. Bay St. at Murray Blvd., South of Broad.*

OLD-FASHIONED WALK. In spring and summer, Charleston's gardens are in full glory. Then, in fall and winter, the homes are dressed in their holiday finest. Twilight strolls are a Dickensian experience, with houses lighted from within showing off one cozy scene after another.

Heyward-Washington House. Thomas Heyward, rice king, patriot leader, and signer of the Declaration of Independence, lived in this house, built in 1772. The city rented the house from Heyward for George Washington's use when Washington stayed in Charleston in May 1791. The salons have mid-18th-century Charleston furniture, notably the Withdrawing Room's Chippendale-style Holmes Bookcase, which is considered among the top 10 pieces of furniture in America. The original kitchen building is also significant, as it is the only such structure open to public view in Charleston. The three-story brick house is near Cabbage Row, a neighborhood central to Charleston's African American history and the setting for the book *Porgy* (and the Gershwin opera based on it), written by Heyward descendant DuBose Heyward. ✉ *87 Church St., South of Broad* ☎ *843/722–0354* 🌐 *www.charlestonmuseum.org* 🎫 *$10* ⏲ *Mon.–Sat. 10–5, Sun. 1–5.*

IF THE SHOE FITS. Wear good walking shoes, because the sidewalks, brick streets, and even Battery Promenade are very
uneven. Take a bottle of water, or take a break to sip from the
fountains in White Point Gardens, as there are practically no
shops south of Broad Street.

★ Fodor's Choice **Nathaniel Russell House.** One of the nation's finest examples of Federal-style architecture, the Nathaniel
Russell House was built in 1808, when Russell was 70
years old. Its grand beauty is proof of the immense wealth
he accumulated as one of the city's leading merchants. In
addition to the famous "free-flying" staircase that spirals
up three stories with no visible support, the ornate interior
is distinguished by fine, Charleston-made furniture as well
as paintings and works on paper by well-known American
and European artists, including Henry Benbridge, Samuel
F. B. Morse, and George Romney. The extensive formal
garden is worth a leisurely stroll. ✉ *51 Meeting St., South
of Broad* ☎ *843/724–8481* ⊕ *www.historiccharleston.org*
✆ *$10; $16 with admission to Aiken-Rhett House Museum*
☉ *Mon.–Sat. 10–5, Sun. 2–5.*

St. Michael's Episcopal Church. Topped by a 186-foot steeple,
Charleston's most famous, this is the city's oldest surviving
church. The first cornerstone was set in place in 1752 and,
through the years, other elements were added: the steeple
clock and bells (1764); the organ (1768); the font (1771);
and the altar (1892). The pulpit—original to the church—
was designed to maximize natural acoustics. Washington
worshipped here in 1791. ✉ *78 Meeting St., South of Broad*
☎ *843/723–0603* ⊕ *www.stmichaelschurch.net* ☉ *Weekdays
9–4:30, Sat. 9–noon.*

WORTH NOTING
City Hall. The intersection of Meeting and Broad streets is
known as the Four Corners of Law, representing the laws
of nation, state, city, and church. On the northeast corner is
the graceful City Hall, built in 1801. Visitors enjoy viewing
the historic portraits that hang in the second-floor council chamber (the second-oldest continuously used council
chamber in the country), with highlights including John
Trumbull's 1791 portrait of George Washington and Samuel
F. B. Morse's likeness of James Monroe. ✉ *80 Broad St.,
North of Broad* ☎ *843/577–6970, 843/724–3799* ✆ *Free*
☉ *Weekdays 8:30–5.*

FODOR'S FIRST PERSON:

PAT CONROY, WRITER

South Carolina's famed writer Pat Conroy describes Charleston in his 2009 novel, *South of Broad*: "I carry the delicate porcelain beauty of Charleston like the hinged-shell of some soft-tissued mollusk.... In its shadows you can find metal work as delicate as lace...it's not a high-kicking, glossy lipstick city."

"I know of no more magical place in America than Charleston's South of Broad," Conroy tells Fodor's. "I remember seeing this area near the Battery when I was a kid and I was stunned as to how beautiful it was. In meeting with my Doubleday publisher about writing this latest book, now entitled *South of Broad*, which is set there, she wanted to understand the big draw of this neighborhood. I said, 'It is the most beautiful area of this gorgeous city. It is what the Upper East Side is to Manhattan, what Pacific Heights is to San Francisco, or what Beverly Hills is to Los Angeles.' SOB is mysterious. It keeps drawing you back like a magnetic force. I am fortunate that my writer friend Anne Rivers Siddons lets me stay in her carriage house there when I come to town. As a cadet at The Citadel, I would walk along the Battery and watch the ships come in and out of port. They looked so close you thought you could touch them."

Conroy talks of other Charleston favorites: "When my children come to town, I go to the aquarium with my grandchildren. It is small enough to take in. Aquariums always make me believe in God. Why? You see the incredible shapes of things and the myriad capacity for different forms of animals. And there is that wonderful outdoor area where you can look at the fish tanks and then look out to the river and see porpoises playing.

"Thanks to Mayor Riley [the city's mayor for more than 35 years], who has been like Pericles for Charleston, there are so many parks and open spaces. Waterfront Park is a great example.

"And one of the true joys of Charleston in these last decades is its restaurant renaissance."

Edmondston-Alston House. In 1825, Charles Edmondston built this house in the Federal style, with Charles Alston transforming it into the imposing Greek-revival structure you see today beginning in 1838. Tours of the home—furnished with antiques, portraits, silver, and fine china—are informative. ✉ *21 E. Battery, South of Broad* ☎ *843/722–7171* 🌐 *www.edmondstonalston.com* 🎫 *$12; $44 with combination ticket for Middleton Place* ⏲ *Tues.–Sat. 10–4:30, Sun. 1–4:30.*

Old Exchange Building and Provost Dungeon. Originally a customs house with a waterside entrance, this building was used by the British to house prisoners during the Revolutionary War, an ordeal detailed in a new exhibit. Costumed interpreters bring history to life on guided tours, and kids are both fascinated and scared by the period mannequins on display in the dungeon. But happier events also occurred here: the state ratified the Constitution in 1788, and Washington attended a ball in 1791 (remarking in a letter on the 400 grand ladies that attended). ✉ *122 E. Bay St., South of Broad* ☎ *843/727–2165* 🌐 *www.oldexchange.com* 🎫 *$8* ⏲ *Daily 9–5.*

MOUNT PLEASANT AND VICINITY

East of Charleston, across the Arthur Ravenel Jr. Bridge—the longest cable-stay bridge in North America—is the town of Mount Pleasant, named not for a mountain but for a plantation founded there in the early 18th century. In its Old Village neighborhood are antebellum homes and a sleepy, old-time town center with a drugstore where patrons still amble up to the soda fountain and lunch counter for egg-salad sandwiches and floats. Along Shem Creek, where the local fishing fleet brings in the daily catch, several seafood restaurants serve the area's freshest (and most deftly fried) seafood. Other attractions in the area include military and maritime museums, plantations, and, farther north, the Cape Romain National Wildlife Refuge.

TOP ATTRACTIONS

★ Fodor's Choice **Boone Hall Plantation and Gardens.** A drive through a ½-mile-long live-oak alley draped in Spanish moss introduces you to this still-functioning plantation, the oldest of its kind. Tours take you through the 1935 mansion, the butterfly pavilion, and the heirloom rose garden. Eight slave cabins on the property have recently been transformed into the Black History in America exhibit, displaying life-size

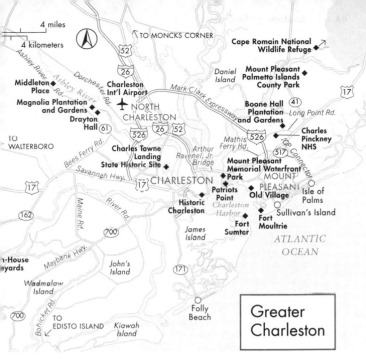

Greater
Charleston

figures, recorded narratives, audiovisual presentations, photos, and historical relics. Seasonal Gullah culture performances in the theater are perennial crowd favorites. Stroll along the winding river, or pick your own strawberries, pumpkins, or tomatoes in the fields. Across the highway is Boone Hall's Farm Market, with fresh local produce, a lunch café, and a gift shop. *North and South, Queen,* and Nicholas Sparks's *The Notebook* were filmed here. ■TIP→ Plan your visit to coincide with annual events like the Lowcountry Oyster Festival in January, the Strawberry Festival in the spring, and the Scottish Games & Highland Gathering in September. ⊠ *1235 Long Point Rd., off U.S. 17 N, Mount Pleasant* ☎ *843/884–4371* ⊕ *www.boonehallplantation.com* ⊐ *$19.50* ⊙ *Jan.–early Feb., Sat. 9–5, Sun. noon–5; early Feb.–mid-Mar. and Labor Day–Dec., Mon.–Sat. 9–5, Sun. noon–5; mid-Mar.–Labor Day, Mon.–Sat. 8:30–6:30, Sun. noon–5; call ahead to confirm hrs.*

�™ **Fort Moultrie.** A section of the Fort Sumter National Monument, this is the site where Colonel William Moultrie's South Carolinians repelled a British assault in one of the first patriot victories of the Revolutionary War. Completed in 1809, the fort is the third fortress on this site on **Sulli-**

van's Island (reached on Route 703 off U.S. 17 North, 10 miles southeast of Charleston). Set across the street, the companion museum is an unsung hero. Although much is made of Fort Sumter, this smaller, historical site is creatively designed, with mannequins in various uniforms and other creative visuals that make military history come alive. A well-done, 20-minute educational film that spans several major wars tells the colorful history of the fort. There's also an exhibit focusing on the slave trade and Sullivan's Island's role in it. ■TIP→Plan to spend the day bicycling through Sullivan's Island, which is characterized by its cluster of early-20th-century beach houses (fuel up at Dunleavy's Pub on Sullivan's, on Middle Street). ✉ *1214 Middle St., Sullivan's Island* ☎ *843/883–3123* ⊕ *www.nps.gov/fosu* ✑ *$3* ☾ *Daily 9–5.*

★ **Fodor's Choice** **Mount Pleasant Memorial Waterfront Park.** Sprawl-
☾ ing beneath the Ravenel Bridge, this beautifully landscaped green space invites lounging on the grass with views of Charleston Harbor (unless you want to take a path up to the bridge for a stroll). Find helpful info in the visitor center, chat with Gullah locals selling their traditional baskets in the Sweetgrass Cultural Arts Pavilion, and spend a quiet moment listening to the waterfall in the Mount Pleasant War Memorial. Kids love the playground modeled after the Ravenel Bridge, and parents appreciate that it's fenced, with benches galore. A 1,250-foot-long pier stretches into the water—grab a milk shake from the Snack Bar and Tackle Shop and a seat on one of the double-sided swings to watch locals fishing for their supper. ✉ *71 Harry Hallman Blvd., Mount Pleasant* ☎ *843/884–8517* ⊕ *www.comeonovermp. com* ☾ *Daily 6 am–11 pm.*

☾ **Patriots Point Naval and Maritime Museum.** Climb aboard
★ the USS *Yorktown* aircraft carrier—which contains the Congressional Medal of Honor Museum—as well as the submarine USS *Clamagore* and the destroyer USS *Laffey.* A life-size replica of a Vietnam support base camp showcases naval air and watercraft used in the military action. ✉ *40 Patriots Point Rd., Mount Pleasant* ☎ *843/884–2727* ⊕ *www.patriotspoint.org* ✑ *Museum $18, parking $5* ☾ *Daily 9–6:30; last tickets sold at 5.*

BASKET LADIES. Drive along U.S. 17 North, through and beyond Mount Pleasant, to find the "basket ladies" set up at rickety roadside stands, weaving the traditional sweetgrass, pine-straw, and palmetto-leaf baskets for which the area is known. Be braced for high prices, although baskets typically cost less on this stretch than in downtown Charleston. Each purchase supports the artisans, whose numbers are dwindling year by year.

WORTH NOTING

Cape Romain National Wildlife Refuge. A grouping of barrier islands and salt marshes, this refuge of 66,287 acres was established in 1932 as a migratory bird haven. The **Sewee Visitor & Environmental Education Center** has information and exhibits on the refuge and its trails, as well as an outdoor enclosure housing four red wolves. Currently, the refuge is aiding the recovery of the threatened loggerhead sea turtles, and a turtle-hatchling video details the work. ■TIP→ From the mainland refuge, take a ferry ride ($40) with Coastal Expeditions from Garris Landing to Bulls Island. There are also four scheduled tours each year to Lighthouse Island—call the Sewee Center for dates and cost. ⊠ *Sewee Center, 5821 U.S. 17 N, Awendaw* ☎ *843/928–3368* ⊕ *www.fws. gov/caperomain/* ☞ *Free* ☉ *Tues.–Sat. 9–5.*

Charles Pinckney National Historic Site. This site is comprised of the last 28 acres of the plantation of Charles Pinckney, a drafter and signer of the U.S. Constitution. You can tour an 1820s coastal cottage, constructed after Pinckney's death. It features interpretive exhibits about the man, the Constitution, and slave life. A nature trail includes the archaeological foundations of three slave houses. ⊠ *1254 Long Point Rd., off U.S. 17 N* ☎ *843/881–5516* ⊕ *www. nps.gov/chpi* ☞ *Free* ☉ *Daily 9–5.*

☾ **Mount Pleasant Palmetto Islands County Park.** With the "Big Toy" playground, paved trails, an observation tower, and boardwalks extending over the marshes, this 943-acre park offers a day full of outdoor fun. You can rent bicycles and pedal boats, or pay an extra fee ($7.99) for entrance to the small Splash Island water park (which is open 10–6 on weekends in May as well as mid-August through Labor Day, and daily from June through mid-August). ⊠ *444 Needlerush Pkwy., Mount Pleasant* ☎ *843/884–0832, 843/795–4386* ⊕ *www.ccprc.com/picp* ☞ *$1* ☉ *Jan., Feb., Nov., and Dec., daily 8–5; Mar., Apr., Sept., and Oct., daily 8–sunset; May–Labor Day, daily 8–8.*

Old Village. The historic nucleus of Mount Pleasant, this neighborhood is distinguished by white picket fences, storybook cottages, antebellum manses, tiny churches, and

Cruising from Charleston

For almost 300 years Charleston, queen of port cities, has been primarily known for its commercial activity, but it recently became a port of embarkation for cruises. It started with two cruise lines and two ports of call. On today's port of call calendar you will see such names as Norwegian, Seabourne, Aida, and Carnival. Charleston's most frequent visitor is the *Carnival Fantasy*, going out year-round on five-, six-, and seven-day cruises.

City officials have gone to great lengths to accommodate the needs of cruise-line passengers, opening a grand new cruise terminal in 2013. Prospective passengers are encouraged to start their planning by visiting *www.charlestoncruisepackages.com* for hotel discounts and special offers including dining, tours, and other attractions. Everyone should consider a pre- or post-cruise stay in Charleston, cited with several remarkable awards by cruisers, who have named the city one of the most romantic in the United States. Several hotels around the area offer free parking for the duration of their guests' cruise. For complete information on all ports of call, visit *www.scspa.com*.

waterfront homes. Prices run to the millions. It's a lovely area for a stroll or bike ride, and Pitt Street offers a couple of locally loved eateries and boutiques. Follow that street south until it ends in the Pickett Street Recreation Area (which residents call the Pitt Street Bridge), an old bridge-turned-greenway that's popular for picnicking, fishing, and enjoying sunset views. ⊠ *Pitt St. and Venning St.*

WEST OF THE ASHLEY RIVER

Ashley River Road, Route 61, begins a few miles northwest of downtown Charleston, over the Ashley River Bridge. Sights are spread out along the way, and those who love history, old homes, and gardens may need several days to explore places like Drayton Hall, Middleton Place, and Magnolia Plantation and Gardens. Spring is a peak time for the flowers, although many of them are in bloom throughout the year.

TOP ATTRACTIONS

☺ **Magnolia Plantation and Gardens.** Owner Thomas Drayton came from Barbados in 1671 and created this garden, the oldest public one in the country. The extensive informal garden, established in 1685, has evolved into an overflowing collection of plants, including a vast array of azaleas and camellias, along with some themed areas (a biblical garden, for example). Take a train or boat to tour the grounds, travel through the 125-acre Waterfowl Refuge (originally rice fields), or explore the 30-acre Audubon Swamp Garden by foot, compliments of a network of boardwalks and bridges. You can traverse more than 500 acres of trails, or bring your bike if you're inclined. Also here are a petting zoo, a nature center, and a reptile house. Five pre- and post-Emancipation cabins have been restored, and a new tour by interpreters is called From Slavery to Freedom. And be sure to tour the 19th-century plantation house, which originally stood in Summerville. The home was taken apart, floated down the Ashley River, and reassembled here. ☒ *3550 Ashley River Rd., West Ashley* ☎ *800/367–3517, 843/571–1266* ⊕ *www.magnoliaplantation.com* ☒ *Grounds $15; tram $8; boat $8; house tour $8; Audubon Swamp Garden $8; From Slavery to Freedom $8; combo ticket with Drayton Hall $24* ☉ *Apr.–Oct., daily 8–5:30; Nov.–Mar., daily 9–5.*

★ **Fodor's** Choice **Middleton Place.** This former plantation is home ☾ to America's oldest landscaped gardens, begun in 1741 by Henry Middleton, second president of the First Continental Congress. From camellias to roses, blooms of all seasons form floral *allées* (alleys) along terraced lawns and around a pair of ornamental lakes that are shaped like butterfly wings. As for the house, a large part of the three-building residential complex was destroyed during the Civil War, but the "flanker" that contained the gentlemen's guest quarters was restored. It now serves as a house museum, displaying impressive silver, furniture, paintings, and historic documents. In the Stableyards, craftspeople use authentic tools to demonstrate spinning, weaving, blacksmithing, and other skills from the plantation era. Heritage-breed farm animals, such as water buffalo and cashmere goats, are housed here, along with peacocks. If all this leaves you feeling peckish, head over to the Middleton Place Restaurant for excellent Lowcountry specialties for lunch and dinner. It has a cozy character and a real sense of history, and is a charming, tranquil spot. You do not have to pay admission to have dinner, and dinner guests can walk the grounds from 5 until dusk. There is also a high-end (but not overpriced) museum gift shop that carries local arts, crafts, and tasteful souvenirs, plus a wonderful garden shop with lunch café. Finally, you can stay overnight at the contemporary Middleton Inn, where floor-to-ceiling windows splendidly frame the Ashley River. Kayaking excursions depart from the inn, and the Middleton Equestrian Center offers trail rides in the surrounding woods. ✉ *4300 Ashley River Rd., West Ashley* ☎ *800/782–3608, 843/556–6020* ⊕ *www.middletonplace. org* ✍ *General admission $25, house tour $12, carriage tours $18; all-inclusive day pass $49; $45 combination ticket with Edmonston-Alston House* ⊙ *Gardens daily 9–5; house museum Mon. noon–4:30, Tues.–Sun. 10–4:30.*

WORTH NOTING

♻ **Charles Towne Landing State Historic Site.** This park commemo-
★ rates the site of the original 1670 settlement of Charles Towne, the first permanent European settlement in South Carolina. From a replica colonial common house to an experimental crop garden, it is filled with fascinating things to see. Begin with the 12-room, interactive museum in the Visitor Center, which includes a "digital dig" virtual archaeology exhibition. Kids will make a beeline for the Adventure, Charleston's only replica of the colonists' 17th-century tall ship (note that it is removed for maintenance for one to two weeks each summer). The park is threaded with paths through a preserved wooded area that lead to the marshes, creek, and Animal Forest, where you can view a black bear, bobcat, bison, and more. All in all, there are 80 acres of gardens, including an elegant live oak allée. To best experience the site, take the audio tour along the history trail. ✉ *1500 Old Towne Rd.* ☎ *843/852–4200* ⊕ *www. friendsofcharlestownelanding.org* ✍ *$7.50* ⊙ *Daily 9–5.*

★ **Fodor'sChoice Drayton Hall.** Considered the nation's finest example of unspoiled Palladian-inspired architecture, this mansion is the only plantation house on the Ashley River to have survived the Civil War intact. A National Trust Historic Site built between 1738 and 1742, it's an invaluable lesson in history as well as in architecture. The home has been left unfurnished to highlight the original plaster moldings, opulent hand-carved woodwork, and other ornamental details. Regular tours, with guides known for their in-depth knowledge, depart on the half hour and give wonderful insight into the people who once inhabited and built this fabled house. Visitors can also see the African-American graveyard and even take part in the 45-minute "Connections" program that uses maps, historic documents, and artifacts to trace the story of Africans from their journey to America, through slavery, and into the 20th century. ✉ *3380 Ashley River Rd., West Ashley*

CLOSE UP

Charleston Preserved

When the Civil War ended in 1865, Charleston was left battered and bruised—both physically and economically. And because locals had little money for building new homes and businesses in the coming decades, they made do with those they had, effectively saving from destruction the grand structures seen today. As development in the city began to pick up in the early 1900s, many of these historic buildings could have been lost were it not for the spirit of community activism that sprang into being in the 1920s.

According to Jonathan Poston, author of *Buildings of Charleston*, the preservation movement took off when an Esso gas station was slated to take the place of the Joseph Manigault House. Irate citizens formed the Society for the Preservation of Old Dwellings (the first such group in the nation), whose efforts managed to save what is now a vastly popular house museum. By 1931, Charleston's City Council had created the Board of Architectural Review and placed a designated historic district under its protection as a means of controlling unrestrained development—two more national firsts. The Historic Charleston Foundation was established in 1947, and preservation is now second nature (by law).

As you explore, look for Charleston single houses: one room wide, they were built with the narrow end streetside with multistory Southern porches (called piazzas) to catch prevailing breezes. Wide-open windows allow the cool air that drifts across these shaded porches to enter the homes.

You'll see numerous architectural vestiges of the past on homes situated along Charleston's preserved streets. Many houses have plaques detailing their history; some exhibit Carolopolis Awards, which were received for responsible stewardship of historic architecture. Old fire insurance plaques are rarer; they denote the company that insured the home and that would extinguish the flames if a fire broke out. Notice the "earthquake bolts"—some in the shape of circles or stars and others capped with lion heads—that dot house facades along the Battery. These are attached to iron rods installed in the house to reinforce it after the great earthquake of 1886. Note also the iron spikes along the top of residential gates, doors, walls, and windows. Serving the same purpose as razor wire seen today atop prison fences, most of these *chevaux de frises* (French for "Frisian horses") were added to deter break-ins— or escapes—after a thwarted 1822 slave rebellion.

☎ 843/769–2600 ⊕ *www.draytonhall.org* 🎟 *$18 (combination ticket with Magnolia Plantation, $24)* ☉ *Mon.–Sat. 9–3:30, Sun. 11–3:30.*

Irvin~House Vineyards. Located in idyllic countryside 40 minutes from downtown Charleston, Irvin~House—boasting 11 acres of vineyards—has evolved impressively from the first bottling of its muscadine wine in 2003. The owners have achieved notoriety in brewing circles thanks to their sweet-tea vodka, Firefly, deftly seasoned with tea from a Lowcountry plantation. Their mainstay remains muscadine wines, more in demand than ever thanks to their heart-healthy antioxidants. You can enjoy a $3 tasting ($6 for vodkas) at the retrofitted barn, which is also outfitted with everything country, from fried peanuts to preserves. ✉ *6775 Bears Bluff Rd., Wadmalaw Island* ☎ *843/559–6867* ⊕ *www.charlestonwine.com* 🎟 *Free* ☉ *Tues.–Sat. 10–5.*

SIDE TRIPS FROM CHARLESTON

Gardens, parks, and the great outdoors are good reasons to travel a bit farther afield for day trips. As Charleston and the surrounding suburbs—particularly Mount Pleasant—keep on growing, it is good to know that Southern country towns still exist right in the vicinity. Sit out on a screen porch after some good home cooking, paddle around a haunting cypress swamp, and take a hike through the towering pines of the Francis Marion National Forest. If the closest you have ever been to an abbey is watching *The Sound of Music,* you can visit Mepkin Abbey and see the simplicity of the religious life. Along the way, turn off the air-conditioning, breathe in the fresh air, and enjoy the natural beauty of these less-touristed parts of South Carolina.

MONCKS CORNER

30 miles northwest of Charleston on U.S. 52.

This town is a gateway to a number of attractions in Santee Cooper Country. Named for the two rivers that form a 171,000-acre basin, the area brims with outdoor pleasures centered on the basin and nearby Lakes Marion and Moultrie.

ESSENTIALS

Visitor Information Santee Cooper Counties Promotion Commission and Visitors Center. Contact this office for more information about area lakes and facilities. ✉ *9302 Old Hwy. 6, Santee* ☎ *803/854-2131* ⊕ *www.santeecoopercountry.org* ☉ *Daily 8:30–4:30.*

EXPLORING

Cypress Gardens. Explore the inky swamp waters of this natural area in a flat-bottom boat; walk along paths lined with moss-draped cypress trees, azaleas, camellias, daffodils, wisteria, and dogwood; and marvel at the clouds of butterflies in the butterfly house. The swamp garden was created from what was once the freshwater reserve of the vast Dean Hall rice plantation. The site is about 24 miles north of Charleston via U.S. 52, between Goose Creek and Moncks Corner. ✉ *3030 Cypress Gardens Rd.* ☎ *843/553–0515* ⊕ *www.cypressgardens.info* 🎟 *$10* ☉ *Daily 9–5; last admission at 4.*

Francis Marion National Forest. Pack a picnic and your fishing poles, or hit the hiking, biking, canoe, horseback-riding, and motorbike trails in 260,000 acres of swamps, lakes, oaks, and pines. The Buck Hall campsites, where tent camping is $15, are on the intracoastal waterway. Visit the Forest Service's website for directions to specific recreational areas. ✉ *Francis Marion Ranger District office, 2967 Steed Creek Rd., Huger* ☎ *843/336–2200* ⊕ *www.fs.usda.gov/scnfs* 🎟 *Free; $5 parking in some areas* ☉ *Hrs vary by area.*

Mepkin Abbey. This active Trappist monastery overlooking the Cooper River is on the site of the former plantation home of Henry Laurens. It was later the home of noted publisher Henry Luce and his wife Clare Boothe Luce. You can tour the gardens and abbey or even stay here for a spiritual retreat in the new facility with individual rooms and private baths (reservations are required). Hearing the monks sing during their normal daily routine and attending the annual Piccolo Spoleto Festival events here are peaceful and spiritual experiences. The simplicity of the abbey has a very grounding effect. The gift shop sells mushrooms and garden compost from the abbey's farm as well as candies, preserves, and creamed honey from other Trappist abbeys. ✉ *1098 Mepkin Abbey Rd., off Dr. Evans Rd.* ☎ *843/761–8509* ⊕ *www.mepkinabbey.org* 🎟 *Donations accepted, tours $5* ☉ *Tues.–Sat. 9–4:30, Sun. 1–4. Tours Tues.–Sat. at 11:30 and 3, Sun. at 3.*

ⓒ **Old Santee Canal Park.** Adventure into the Charleston area's past at Old Santee Canal Park. More than 3 miles of board-walks and unpaved paths take visitors through Biggin Swamp and along the last portion of the United States' first true canal. Prefer to explore by boat? Rent a canoe for $3 per half hour. An interpretive center details the history of the canal, which was used to transport goods from upstate South Carolina to the port of Charleston from around 1800 to 1850. The on-site Stony Landing Plantation House is furnished with period reproductions, offering a glimpse into what life would have been like for the merchant who built it in the 1840s. Adjacent to the park (and included in its admission) is the Berkeley Museum, which tells the story of Berkeley County's cultural and natural history. ✉ *900 Stony Landing Rd., off Rembert C. Dennis Blvd.* ☎ *843/899–5200* ⊕ *www.oldsanteecanalpark.org* 🖾 *$3* ⊗ *Daily 9–5; buildings close at 4:30.*

EDISTO ISLAND

44 miles southwest of Charleston via U.S. 17 and Rte. 174.

On rural Edisto (pronounced *ed*-is-toh) Island, find mag-nificent stands of age-old oaks festooned with Spanish-moss borders, quiet streams, and side roads; wild turkeys may still be spotted on open grasslands and amid palmetto palms. Twisting tidal creeks, populated with egrets and herons, wind around golden marsh grass. A big day on the island may include shelling and shark-tooth hunting.

The small "downtown" beachfront is a mix of public beach-access spots, restaurants, and old, shabby-chic beach homes that are a far cry from the palatial villas rented out on the other resort islands. The outlying Edisto Beach State Park is a pristine wilderness and camper's delight. There are a number of privately owned rental accommodations—condos, villas, and homes—and Wyndham Ocean Ridge Resort offers time-share units that can be rented when available. None are on the beach, however.

GETTING HERE AND AROUND
Edisto is connected to the mainland by a causeway. The only way here is by private car.

ESSENTIALS
Visitor Information Edisto Island Chamber of Commerce ✉ *430 Rte. 174* ☎ *843/869–3867, 888/333–2781* ⊕ *www.edistochamber. com* ⊗ *Weekdays 9–5.*

TOURS

Edisto Watersports & Tackle. Edisto Watersports & Tackle offers two-hour sunset river cruises through the beautiful Ace Basin with commentary on history and wildlife. The tour, on a 24-foot Carolina skiff, costs $40 per person. You can also charter a fishing boat, pick up an Otter Island shelling excursion, or take a kayak tour here. ✉ *3731 Docksite Rd.* ☎ *843/869–0663* ⊕ *www.edistowatersports.biz.*

The Pink Van Tour. An Edisto native leads tours full of history and facts entertainingly told. There are multiple stops of interest, from historic churches to a plantation, and the cost is $20 for 2½ hours. ✉ *Meets at Mains Market, 1084 Hwy. 174* ☎ *843/603–0967.*

EXPLORING

✪ **Edisto Island Serpentarium.** This is a top-notch operation where snake programs and alligator feedings are augmented by informative and educational commentary by naturalists. Children will likely want to buy the various reptilian stuffed animals and toys at the gift shop. ✉ *1374 Hwy. 174* ☎ *843/869–1171* ⊕ *www.edistoserpentarium.com* 💲 *$13.95* ⊙ *Thurs.–Sat. 10–6, but hrs vary by season.*

MYSTERY TREE. Truly unique, this tree across the highway (Route 174) from the entrance to Botany Bay Plantation is wildly decorated according to the season. A mystery person who prefers to be anonymous changes the tree's decorations during the night. Some people say that it is the work of a resident female artist.

WHERE TO EAT

$$ ✕ **Edisto Pavilion Restaurant.** *Seafood*. The water view at this oceanfront restaurant is reason enough to go. For lunch, try the fried oyster or shrimp po'boys. At dinnertime, you can't go wrong with the combination platter, which consists of broiled shrimp, oysters, flounder, fried soft-shell crab, and a crab cake. In addition to the main dining room, there's an oceanfront space with its own bar as well as Ping-Pong tables. You might start or finish your Pavilion experience at the Pier Pressure Lounge, whose bar scene is fueled by a tropical drink machine, pool tables, karaoke, and a deck for dining or smoking, with strong ocean breezes. ⑨ *Average main: $18* ✉ *102 Palmetto Blvd.* ☎ *843/869–4474* ⊙ *No lunch Tues. and Wed.*

SECRET OF THE ISLANDS. It is hard to keep a secret on an island for long. And so the word is getting out that a salt scrub that smells like coconut oil is a great salty souvenir of this island. The Sanders Brothers, who own the Edisto Pavilion Restaurant, have it in their restrooms with instructions to rub it into your hands for one minute. Voilà! Sun-parched, spotty skin becomes like a silk glove. Secret of the Islands is available in their gift shop. Try it on other extremities, too.

$$ ✕ **Old Post Office Restaurant.** *Seafood.* At this converted post office, the post-office boxes and metal cage remain, but instead of mail you'll find Southern-inspired fare from chef Cherry Smalls. Try the Atlantic black-cherrywood-smoked salmon with a sour-cream-and-mustardcaper sauce. The local shrimp in the savory shrimp 'n' grits are as white and delicate as porcelain. When there's a piano man in the upstairs bar, so much the better. $ *Average main: $20 ✉ 1442 Hwy. 174 ☎ 843/869–2339 ⊕ www.theoldpostofficerestaurant.com ⚓ Reservations essential ☉ Closed Sun. and Mon. No lunch.*

$ ✕ **Po' Pigs Bo-B-Q.** *Southern.* Step inside the Deep South at this restaurant, next door to a Horizon fillin' station, for pork barbecue that has South Carolinians returning and national media writing. Sample the different sauces (sweet, mustard, tomato, or vinegar) and wash it all down with a tall glass of sweet tea. The buffet line is all about down-home sides like squash casserole, pork skins, lima beans and ham, and red rice. The pulled turkey is a good option for those attempting to find something low-cal and heart healthy. If iced tea is not your beverage of choice, there is also beer and wine. $ *Average main: $9 ✉ 2410 Rte. 174 ☎ 843/869–9003 ☉ Wed.–Sat. 11:30–9, but hrs change seasonally.*

$$ ✕ **Whaley's.** *Seafood.* This 1940s-era filling station—the pumps are still outside—has been converted into a fun and eclectic bar and restaurant where you're sure to find some local color. While the interior is a bit rough around the edges, with concrete floors and bathrooms outside, the beer inventory consists of microbrews. The menu ranges from bar food like buffalo wings and burgers to local shrimp, crab cakes, and pan-seared mahimahi. For fine dining, look to the firefly flounder topped with mango chutney and a sweet-tea glaze. Nightly entertainment runs the gamut from karaoke to blues bands. $ *Average main: $19 ✉ 280 Myrtle St. ☎ 843/869–2161 ⊕ www.whaleyseb.com ☉ May only be open Tues.–Sat. off-season.*

WHERE TO STAY

For expanded hotel reviews, visit Fodors.com.

$ **Prudential-Kapp/Lyons Realty.** *Rental.* Prudential's inventory of privately owned beach homes ranges from a two-bedroom apartment over a gallery to one-bedroom condos and six-bedroom manses smack on the beach. **Pros:** excellent staff is known for their efficiency, caring, and Southern hospitality; sparkling-clean, well-maintained properties; wide diversity of offerings. **Cons:** properties do not have resort amenities; if you are a group of singles looking to rent a hard-core party house, go elsewhere; some units require that you empty your own trash and put away all dishes or be fined. [$] *Rooms from: $125* ✉ *440 Hwy. 174* ☎ *843/869–2516, 800/945–9667* 🌐 *www.kapplyons.com* 🛏 *160 units.*

$$ **Wyndham Ocean Ridge Resort.** *Resort.* If you're looking for high-end amenities in a get-away-from-it-all escape, you've found it here, at the only resort on the island. **Pros:** great choice for golfers rather than sun worshippers; only resort amenities on island; atmosphere is laid-back, unpretentious. **Cons:** no daily housekeeping services, nor will towels be switched out; as there are limited rental units, hard to book at peak times; many units come with two to three flights of stairs. [$] *Rooms from: $150* ✉ *1 King Cotton Rd., Edisto Beach* ☎ *843/869–4516, 843/869–2561 for reservations* 🌐 *www.wyndhamoceanridge.com* 🛏 *250 units* 🍴 *No meals.*

SPORTS AND THE OUTDOORS

BEACHES

★ **Fodor's Choice Edisto Beach State Park.** The park covers 1,255 acres and includes marshland and tidal rivers, a 1½-mile-long beachfront, towering palmettos, and a lush maritime forest with a 6-mile trail running through it. The trail is hard-packed shell sand, suitable for bikes and wheelchairs. The park has the best shelling beach on public property in the Lowcountry. Overnight options include rustic furnished cabins (with basic, no-frills decor) by the marsh and campsites by the ocean. This park stays extremely busy, so with only seven cabins (the park system struggles to maintain their livability), you have to reserve as far as 11 months in advance. The campsites (117) are another story: reservations are on a first-come, first-served basis. There are two campgrounds, one on the beach with 64 sites, another called Live Oak with 53 sites. Among those are five rustic, hike-in tent sites on the creek. The small ranger station has some fishing poles to lend and firewood for sale. Restrooms and showers are especially clean. Pets on leashes up to 6 feet long are allowed. The park's nearby Environmental Learning Center is worth a visit. **Amenities:** parking; showers; toilets. **Best for:** solitude; sunset; swimming; walking. ⊠ *8377 State Cabin Rd.* ☎ *843/869–2156* ⊕ *www.southcarolinaparks.com* 🖾 *$5* ⊙ *Early Apr.–late Oct., daily 8 am–10 pm; late Oct.–early Apr., daily 8–6.*

☾ ★ **Edisto Beach.** Edisto's south side has 4 miles of public beach. At its western end, the beach faces St. Helena Sound and has smaller waves. There is beach access at every block starting at the Pavilion Restaurant, as well as free public parking along the road. The beach itself has narrowed because of erosion, so it's best to time your visit for low tide. These clean coastal waters teem with both fish and shellfish, and it's common to see people throwing cast nets for shrimp. It's a great beach for beachcombing. Alcohol is allowed as long as it is not in glass containers. There is little shade, and there are no food stands, so be sure to pack snacks. This long stretch is home turf for individually owned beach cottages, nearly all of which are available for rent. **Amenities:** none. **Best for:** solitude; sunset; swimming. ⊠ *Hwy. 174 from Coral St. to Yacht Club Rd., Edisto Beach* ⊕ *www. townofedistobeach.com.*

BIKING

Island Bikes & Outfitters. For more than 25 years, Island Bikes & Outfitters has been renting bikes to vacationers. Owners Sonya and Tony Spainhour will arm you with a map, orient you to the bike trails, and advise you on how to reach the nearby entrance to the section of the park that has a boardwalk network for bikers and hikers. Delivery is available. In addition, you can rent golf carts, kayaks, canoes, paddleboards, and tackle, and buy bait. They sell beachwear, visors, boogie boards, beach chairs, and more. ⊠ *140 Jungle Rd.* ☎ *843/869–4444* ⊕ *islandbikesandout fitters.com* ⊙ *Mon.–Sat. 9–5, Sun. 9–noon.*

GOLF

The Plantation Course at Edisto. Sculpted from the maritime forest by architect Tom Jackson in 1974, this course mirrors the physical beauty of the island's Lowcountry-scape. Although located within the island's only resort, Wyndham Ocean Ridge, this totally renovated course was resurrected in 2005 by private owners, Edisto Golf, LLC. It operates as a public course with memberships. The moderate rates are the same for all seasons, with special three-day cards and weekly unlimited-rounds specials. It offers pick-up service within the resort and from the nearby marina. ✉ *19 Fairway Dr.* ☎ *843/869–1111* ⊕ *www.theplantationcourseatedisto.com* ⚑ *18 holes. 6200 yards. Par 70. Green Fee: $59* ⚐ *Facilities: putting green, golf carts, rental clubs, pro shop, restaurant, bar.*

WALTERBORO

44 miles west of Charleston via U.S. 17 and U.S. 64.

"Welcome Back to Let's Remember." This sleepy Southern town makes Charleston look like Manhattan. Its main drag, East Washington Street, still looks like it did in the 1950s. While continuing to embrace its endearing small-town ways, it is moving in a new, savvy direction. To wit, its marketing slogan is "Walterboro, the front porch of the Lowcountry," with a cherry-red rocking chair as its logo. Those rocking chairs can be found outside shops and restaurants, inviting passersby to sit awhile.

Walterboro has become a fun day trip for Charlestonians. The South Carolina Artisans Center has become a major draw, as have the moderately priced antiques and collectible stores. The annual events, which for decades included the Rice Festival on the last weekend in April and the Fall Tour of Plantation Homes in October, have been augmented by the Edisto Riverfest on the second weekend in June, the Walterboro Antiques, History & Arts Festival in mid-May, and the Downtown Walterboro Criterium USA Pro Cycling Classic in early May. A proliferation of inexpensive motels like Days Inn sprang up near the interstate, then limited-service chain hotels like Hampton Inn. Travelers wanting more local flavor opt for the homey bed-and-breakfasts in restored houses in the Historic District.

GETTING HERE AND AROUND
The downtown area is walkable and the town is great for bicycling, especially in the Great Swamp Sanctuary. There are no bike-rental shops, although some B&Bs do supply bikes.

ESSENTIALS
Welcome Center. Stop in for details on Walterboro's shopping, parks, museums, and more. ✉ *1273 Sniders Hwy.* ☎ *843/538–4353* ⊕ *www.walterborosc.org* ⊗ *Mon.–Sat. 9–5.*

Walterboro-Colleton Chamber of Commerce. Find friendly service and plenty of information on all of the area's attractions. ⊠ *109C Benson St.* ☎ *843/549–9595* ⊕ *www. walterboro.org* ⊙ *Daily 9–5.*

EXPLORING

Colleton Museum & Farmers Market. This museum chronicles the history of a small Southern town, displaying everything from butter churns to the first anesthesia machine used in the county. Particularly charming is the small reproduction chapel complete with stained glass, pews, and century-old wedding gowns. A farmers market takes place outside on Saturday. ⊠ *506 E. Washington St.* ☎ *843/549–2303* ⊕ *www.colletoncounty.org* ⊡ *Free* ⊙ *Tues. noon–6, Wed.– Fri. 10–5, Sat. 10–2.*

QUICK BITES. **Downtown Books and Espresso.** Stop in for java as well as sinful pastries and a great selection of new and used books, from local lore to history and Southern cookbooks. ⊠ *213 E. Washington St.* ☎ *843/849–2241* ⊙ *Weekdays 8:30–5:30, Sat. 9–4.*

Great Swamp Sanctuary. Boardwalks and hiking, biking, and canoe trails weave through this lovely 842-acre park. One of the paths traces the colonial-era Charleston-to-Savannah Stagecoach Road, where visitors can still see the cypress remnants of historic bridges. Serious hikers bring their gear and spend hours. It is a Southern swamp, so douse yourself with insect repellent and be on alert for reptiles. ⊠ *399 Detreville St.* ☎ *843/538–4353* ⊕ *www.thegreatswamp.org* ⊡ *Free* ⊙ *Daily dawn–dusk.*

★ Fodor'sChoice **South Carolina Artisans Center.** This lovely center is a showcase for the most talented artisans in the state. Mediums include jewelry, garden sculpture, glass, woodwork, and more. The loomed shawls and silk scarves make great gifts; the sweetgrass baskets are treasures. ⊠ *334 Wichman St.* ☎ *843/549–0011* ⊕ *www.scartisanscenter.com* ⊡ *Free* ⊙ *Mon–Sat. 10–6, Sun. 1–5.*

QUICK BITES. **Hiott's Pharmacy.** Hiott's Pharmacy is one of those delightful throwbacks—a drugstore with a soda fountain where the news of the day is discussed and young people share a Coca-Cola float. You can get a pimento cheese on white bread for $1.90. But if you want a malted milk to go with it, that'll cost you $2.50. ⊠ *373 E. Washington St.* ☎ *843/549–7222* ⊙ *Weekdays 9–6, Sat. 9–1.*

WHERE TO EAT AND STAY

For expanded hotel reviews, visit Fodors.com.

$ ★ 🍴 **Carmine's Trattoria.** *Italian.* Although some locals call it the "fancy place," the only high-end furnishing is a baby grand, which is tickled by a jazzman on Friday and Saturday nights. The littleneck clams appetizer comes in a white-wine sauce crossed with sticks of garlic bread, and the veal marsala with fresh mushrooms is tender. Lunch offerings include salads, panini, and pastas. [$] *Average main: $12* ✉ *242 E. Washington St.* ☎ *843/782–3248* ⏲ *Closed Sun. No lunch Fri. and Sat.*

$ **Fodor'sChoice** 🍴 **Main Street Grille.** *American.* Grab a window seat at this casual spot for a pleasant view of East Washington Street and dig into one of the two variations of shrimp and stone-ground grits, the Philly cheesesteak, or the juicy burgers on kaiser rolls. Baked goods such as Kentucky bourbon pecan pie are house made and served in generous portions. [$] *Average main: $12* ✉ *256 E. Washington St.* ☎ *843/782–4774* ⏲ *Closed Sun. No lunch Mon.–Wed.*

$ 🏨 **The Hampton House Bed & Breakfast.** *B&B/Inn.* Built in 1912 by the patriarch of the prominent Fishburne family, this B&B has all of the accoutrements of a Lowcountry mansion, from its high ceilings to the charming literary nook, as well as modern-day luxuries such as a crescent-shape pool, tennis court, gardens, and brickwork designed by the celebrated landscape architect Robert Marvin. **Pros:** pool and tennis court including racquets and balls; caring and hospitable owners; small dogs allowed. **Cons:** could have more rooms; some areas of the property could use a bit of freshening. [$] *Rooms from: $125* ✉ *500 Hampton St.* ☎ *843/542–9498* 🌐 *www.hamptonhousebandb.com* 🛏 *3 rooms* 🍽 *Breakfast.*

$ 🏨 **Nine O' Seven.** *B&B/Inn.* With high-quality construction, hardwood floors, high ceilings, a single floor with multiple rooms, and an elongated front porch, this classic, 1920s Walterboro cottage demonstrates excellent taste in its traditional decor, and everything is squeaky clean. **Pros:** good value for the money; exquisite interior decor; classy, intellectual proprietress. **Cons:** no credit cards; relatively small house; it would be a long walk to downtown Washington Street. [$] *Rooms from: $75* ✉ *907 Hampton St.* ☎ *843/542–2943* 🌐 *www.nineoseven.com* 🛏 *3 rooms, 1 suite* 💳 *No credit cards* 🍽 *Breakfast.*

SHOPPING

Bachelor Hill Antiques. David Evans displays an eclectic mix of fine furnishings, antiques, art, and '50s finds in inspiring room-like tableaux, while Jorge Ruiz runs a frame shop in the back. The fair prices mean items here move fast. ⊠ *255 E. Washington St.* ☎ *843/549–1300* ⊙ *Mon.–Sat. 9–6, Sun. 9–4.*

Choice Collectibles. On the site of the former Ritz Theater, Choice Collectibles is as retro as the sign for the theater's box office displayed over the cash register. You could get lost in time perusing the fascinating and inexpensive finds from decades past. ⊠ *329 E. Washington St.* ☎ *843/549–2617* ⊙ *Mon.–Sat. 9–5.*

DIG. An inspiring display of tabletop terrariums—with petite versions hanging from twine overhead—greet visitors to DIG, an acronym for "Design, Interiors, Gardens." In addition to outdoor statuary, fountains, and wind chimes, shop a selection of antiques, home accessories, and furniture made locally from reclaimed wood. Be sure to visit the back patio, lush with unique, easy-to-grow plants. ⊠ *225 E. Washington St.* ☎ *843/782–4322* ⊕ *www.digdesignshop. com* ⊙ *Tues.–Sat. 10–6.*

Where to Eat in Charleston

"There are many (MANY) places from which to choose. Not stuffy, but delicious, is FIG on Meeting St. Make a reservation. You won't get a table without one. Other favorites include High Cotton, SNOB, Anson, Tristan, McCrady's for trendy. . . . . Hank's is great for seafood, but all the places I listed have fresh seafood. It's a big deal around here."

—suewoo

Updated
by Rob
Young

Yes, to eat. Of course, to eat. This is, after all, Charleston, which is blessed with a bevy of Southern-inflected selections, from barbecue parlors to fish shacks, to traditional, white-tablecloth restaurants. The attention to Southern foods has increased in recent years, largely because of improved exposure, large food festivals like Big Apple Barbecue Block Party in New York, and regional emphases. Charleston, to its credit, rests at distinguished crossroads, benefiting from established stock, and newer flourishes, such as the nationally recognized Charleston Wine & Food Festival.

And the city's status continues to rise, boosted by a group of James Beard Foundation repeat award winners. Robert Stehling of Hominy Grill, Mike Lata of FIG, and Sean Brock of Husk each earned the designation of Best Chef in the Southeast, in successive years. But the city boasts other prodigious talents, too: Jeremiah Bacon of The Macintosh, Craig Diehl of Cypress, Michelle Weaver of Charleston Grill, Ken Vedrinski of Trattoria Lucca, Frank Lee of Slightly North of Broad, Nico Romo of Fish, and Josh Keeler of Two Boroughs Larder. It's the establishment of the New South, circa now.

As for attire, Charleston invites a casual atmosphere, appropriate for jeans or slacks, sundresses or skirts, and in many cases, even flip-flops. Don't forget, Charleston was recognized as the Most Mannerly City in the union by Marjabelle Young Stewart. Which means that residents are slow to judge (or, at the least, that they're doing so very quietly). But on the whole, the city encourages comfort and unhurried, easy pacing. The result is an idyllic setting in which to enjoy shrimp and grits, oysters on the half shell, and other homegrown delicacies from the land and sea that jointly grant the city its impressive culinary standing.

PRICES

Fine dining in Charleston can be expensive. One option to keep costs down might be to try several of the small plates that many establishments offer. To save money, drive over the bridges or go to the islands, including James and Johns islands.

NORTH OF BROAD

$$ ✕ **39 Rue de Jean.** *French.* With a backdrop of classic French-bistro style—gleaming wood, cozy booths, and white-papered tables—Charleston's trendy set wines and dines until the wee hours on such favorites as steamed mussels in a half dozen preparations. Order them with *pomme frites,* as the French do. Each night of the week there's a special, such as the bouillabaisse on Sunday. Rabbit with a whole-grain mustard sauce was so popular it jumped to the nightly menu, while Rue's burgers have a well-established following. If you're seeking quiet, ask for a table in the dining room on the right. It's noisy—but so much fun—at the bar, especially since it has the city's best bartenders. Ⓢ *Average main: $18* ✉ *39 John St., Upper King* ☎ *843/722–8881* ⊕ *www.39ruedejean.com* ⌂ *Reservations essential.*

$$ ✕ **Alluette's Cafe.** *Southern.* Alluette Jones has coined a new genre of cuisine—"holistic soul food"—which she fixes at her eponymously named restaurant. It's simple, fresh, local, and organic, drawing from Geechee-Gullah origins, and it has earned well-deserved praise. And guess what? You won't be able to find any pork products here. Her hearty soups (lima bean, for instance) contain nary a trace of the traditional Southern accoutrement: ham hock. Plus, Alluette cooks some of the city's best fried shrimp, which arrive butterflied and lightly battered after simmering in organic oil. It's a pleasant, newfound perspective on Southern food. Ⓢ *Average main: $15* ✉ *80 Reid St.Market Area* ☎ *843/577–6926* ⊕ *www.alluettes.com.*

$$$$ ✕ **Anson.** *Southern.* Nearly a dozen windows here afford picturesque views of the passing horse-drawn carriages. The softly lighted, gilt-trimmed dining room is ideal for romantic occasions, though some locals prefer the more casual scene downstairs. Cuisine is traditional Lowcountry, including shrimp with grits, and oysters fried in cornmeal (both served as appetizers). The she-crab soup is one of the best around. The chef takes liberties with some classics, including the whole crispy flounder in apricot sauce and the roasted red snapper with succotash and shrimp, giving them a more contemporary spin. Gooey, molten chocolate cake with house-made peanut butter ice cream is a favorite. Ⓢ *Average main: $27* ✉ *12 Anson St., Market area* ☎ *843/577–0551* ⊕ *www.ansonrestaurant.com* ◷ *No lunch.*

★ Fodors Choice ✕ **Basil.** *Asian.* This corner restaurant in the heart **$$** of downtown enjoys the best reputation for Thai food in the city. Need proof? Dinner hours generate extended wait

Where to Eat in Downtown Charleston

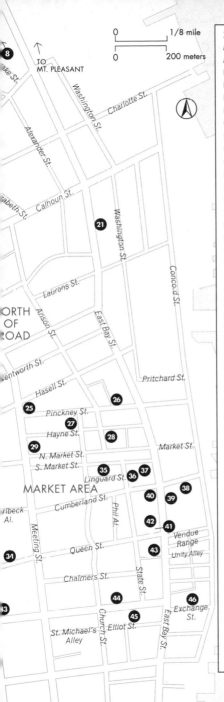

39 Rue de Jean, **19**	
Alluette's Cafe, **5**	
Anson, **28**	
Basil, **11**	
Blind Tiger, **44**	
Blossom, **42**	
Bull Street Gourmet & Market, **22**	
Carolina's, **46**	
Charleston Grill, **30**	
Circa 1886, **23**	
Coast Bar & Grill, **20**	
Cru Cafe, **26**	
Cupcake, **18**	
Cypress Lowcountry Grille, **41**	
Dixie Supply Bakery and Cafe, **36**	
FIG, **25**	
Fish, **14**	
Fulton Five, **31**	
Gaulart & Maliclet Café, **33**	
Glazed, **12**	
Grill 225, **37**	
The Grocery, **4**	
Hall's Chophouse, **15**	
Hank's Seafood, **27**	
High Cotton, **40**	
Hominy Grill, **9**	
Husk, **34**	
La Fourchette, **17**	
The Macintosh, **13**	
Martha Lou's Kitchen, **8**	
McCrady's, **43**	
Moe's Crosstown Tavern, **2**	
Moe's Downtown Tavern, **38**	
Monza, **16**	
Muse Restaurant & Wine Bar, **24**	
Oak Steakhouse, **45**	
Peninsula Grill, **29**	
Queen Street Grocery, **32**	
Recovery Room, **3**	
Slightly North of Broad, **39**	
Taco Boy, **7**	
The Tattooed Moose, **6**	
Ted's Butcherblock, **21**	
Trattoria Lucca, **1**	
Tristan, **35**	
Two Boroughs Larder, **10**	

CLOSE UP

Best Bets for Charleston Dining

With hundreds of restaurants to choose from, how will you decide where to eat? Fodor's writers and editors have selected their favorite restaurants by price, cuisine, and experience in the Best Bets lists below. The Fodor's Choice properties represent the "best of the best" in every price category. You can also search by neighborhood for excellent eats—just peruse our reviews on the following pages.

Fodor's Choice: Basil, Charleston Grill, Cupcake, Cypress Lowcountry Grille, FIG, Fish, The Grocery, Hall's Chophouse, Husk, The Macintosh, Martha Lou's Kitchen, McCrady's, Moe's Tavern, Peninsula Grill, Perfectly Frank's, Recovery Room, Sesame Burgers & Beer, Tattooed Moose, Tomato Shed Cafe, Trattoria Lucca, Tristan, Two Boroughs Larder, Voodoo Tiki Bar & Lounge, The Wreck of the Richard & Charlene

Best Budget Eats: Alluette's Cafe, Glazed, The Glass Onion, Hominy Grill, Jack's Cosmic Dogs, Martha Lou's Kitchen, Perfectly Frank's, The Tattooed Moose, Tomato Shed Cafe

Best American: The Grocery, Heart Woodfire Kitchen, Jack's Cosmic Dogs, Moe's Tavern, Ted's Butcherblock, Two Boroughs Larder

Best Asian: Basil

Best French: 39 Rue de Jean, Gaulart & Maliclet Café, La Fourchette

Best Italian: Fulton Five, Trattoria Lucca

Best Southern: Anson, FIG, Hominy Grill, Husk, McCrady's, Red Drum, Tristan

Best Brunch: The Glass Onion, High Cotton, Hominy Grill

Best Business Dining: Blossom, Slightly North of Broad

Child-friendly: Cupcake, Jack's Cosmic Dogs, Perfectly Frank's, The Wreck of the Richard & Charlene,

Great View: Bowen's Island, Fleet Landing, The Wreck of the Richard & Charlene

Hotel Dining: Charleston Grill, Tristan

Hot Spots: Basil, Hall's Chophouse, The Macintosh, Taco Boy,

Best Lunch: The Glass Onion, Poe's Tavern, Tomato Shed Cafe

Late-night Dining: Recovery Room, Voodoo Tiki Bar & Lounge

Most Romantic: Cypress Lowcountry Grille, Fulton Five, La Fourchette

Outdoor Seating: Blossom, Poe's Tavern

times—no reservations allowed—as patrons angle for an outdoor or window table. From the exposed glassed-in kitchen emerge popular specialties such as Tom Aban Talay, a hot-and-sour mixed seafood soup flavored with Kaffir lime leaves, lemongrass, and button mushrooms; red curry duck, a boneless half bird, deep-fried; and the tilapia served with shrimp and ginger sauce. And seriously, don't fret over the line. It's always worth the wait. But if you're farther afield, try hitting Basil's newest locations in Charlotte, N.C., and Mount Pleasant. [$] *Average main: $16* ✉ *460 King St., Upper King* ☎ *843/724–3490* 🌐 *www.eatatbasil.com.*

3

$$$ 🍴**Blossom.** *Southern.* Exposed white rafters and linenless tables make this place casual and yet upscale. The terrace has a view of St. Philip's majestic spire, and the dining room and bar are heavily populated with young professionals. The open, exhibition kitchen adds to the high-energy atmosphere. Lowcountry seafood is a specialty, and the small pizzas, particularly the lamb sausage, are unexpected finds. Special seasonal menus are provided and the bar menu is available as late as 1 am on Friday and Saturday nights. [$] *Average main: $22* ✉ *171 E. Bay St., Market area* ☎ *843/722–9200* 🌐 *www.magnolias-blossom-cypress.com.*

$ 🍴**Bull Street Gourmet & Market.** *American.* This gourmet market remains a distinguished purveyor of sandwiches, gourmet meats, cheeses, and wines. The King Street location opened in 2011, offering a more refined setting than its predecessor. Dean & Deluca is the favored comparison, as the exposed ceiling and ceramic tiling set the decor. Though the restaurant offers fillet and seared scallops for dinner, its lunchtime sandwiches served on local Normandy Farm breads earn top billing. Recommendations include the *bahn mi,* smoked salmon BLT, and smoked duck club. Another location in the historic Harleston Village neighborhood of downtown Charleston can be found at 60 Bull Street. [$] *Average main: $11* ✉ *120 King St., Lower King* ☎ *843/722–6464.*

★ $$$$ **Fodor'sChoice** 🍴**Charleston Grill.** *Southern.* Quite simply, this restaurant continues to provide what many think of as the city's highest gastronomic experience. Chef Michelle Weaver has succeeded her former boss, the estimable Bob Waggoner, and carries on the Grill's groundbreaking New South cuisine. The dining room is a soothing backdrop, highlighted by pale wood floors, flowing drapes, and elegant Queen Anne chairs. A jazz ensemble adds a hip, yet unobtrusive, element. As it was hoped, the Grill, which has been reborn in a more relaxed form, attracts a younger and more vibrant clientele than its original incarnation. The menu is now in four quadrants: simple, lush (foie gras and other delicacies), cosmopolitan, and Southern. A nightly tasting menu offers a way to sample it all. And don't skip the extra indulgences: Sommelier Rick Rubel has 1,300 wines in his cellar, with many served by the glass. And the pastry chef sends out divine creations like chocolate caramel ganache. [$] *Average main: $30* ✉ *Charleston Place Hotel, 224 King St., Market area* ☎ *843/577–4522* 🌐 *www.charlestongrill.com* ✍ *Reservations essential* ⏲ *No lunch.*

$$$$ 🍴 **Circa 1886.** *Southern.* Near Wentworth Mansion, in a former residential home full of hand-carved marble fireplaces and Tiffany stained-glass windows, rests the intimate Circa 1886 restaurant. The award-winning eatery sets a sophisticated tone with low lighting and a yellow rose atop each table. Executive chef Marc Collins emphasizes seasonal offerings, highlighted by the menu's heirloom-tomato salad, a deconstructed BLT made with bacon gelée, romaine *espuma* (foam), and white-grain toast. Collins also shows off his Texan extraction, serving an antelope dish, the free-range game procured from the Broken Arrow Ranch in Texas hill country. The tender variation spiced with horseradish is a must-eat for the adventurous. [$] *Average main: $28* ✉ *149 Wentworth St., Lower King* ☎ *843/853–7828* 🌐 *www.circa1886.com* ✍ *Reservations essential* ⏲ *Closed Sun. No lunch.*

$$$ 🍴 **Coast Bar & Grill.** *Seafood.* Tucked off a little alley in a restored indigo warehouse, Coast has a stripped-down look with exposed brick and raw-wood columns. Fried fare and heavy sauces are staples, but lighter dishes such as the fish tacos and ceviche make it a standout. The best dishes include oak-grilled fish and lobster served with pineapple-chili salsa, white-wine-and-lemon sauce, or rémoulade. Try the *cioppino*, too, a stew made from several varieties of fish and fresh tomatoes in a wine sauce. The room can be noisy, but it's always fun, especially if you like a festive atmosphere. You can watch the cooks in the heat of the open kitchen in the front room or go in the back dining room where it is cooler. There are usually half-price wine specials, and there's live music on Sunday evening. [$] *Average main: $20* ✉ *39D John St., Upper King* ☎ *843/722–8838* 🌐 *www.coastbarandgrill.com* ⏲ *No lunch.*

$$$ 🍴 **Cru Café.** *Southern.* The sunny wraparound porch in this 18th-century house lures people to lunch here, but it's the inventive menu that keeps them coming back. Fried chicken breasts are topped with poblano peppers and mozzarella, and the duck confit is served with caramelized pecans and goat cheese, topped with fried shoestring onions, and dressed with port-wine vinaigrette. Chef John Zucker likes to go heavy on the starches, and his flavorful whipped potatoes are made with cream. Meat dishes are laced with sauces featuring green peppercorns, port wine, pear sherry, chipotle peppers, and horseradish cream. The four-cheese mac is another favorite. [$] *Average main: $23* ✉ *18 Pinckney St., Market area* ☎ *843/534–2434* 🌐 *www.crucafe.com* 🕒 *Closed Sun. and Mon.*

★ Fodor'sChoice ✕**Cupcake.** *Bakery.* Better than Baskin-Robbins, this cute, small shop on upper King Street features 45 flavors of cupcakes. A daily flavor chart reveals the collection of pocket-size pleasures on offer here, covering various degrees of delicious. Flavors range from black-and-white to carrot cake, lemon-blueberry, peanut butter banana fluff, praline, pumpkin, red velvet, s'mores, strawberry cheesecake, and death by chocolate. If you're wandering on King, look for the pink Volvo station wagon parked outside the store, with the large, pink cupcake on top. [$] *Average main: $3* ✉ *433 King St., Upper King* ☎ *843/853–8181* 🌐 *www.freshcupcakes.com.*
$
👶

★ Fodor'sChoice ✕**Cypress Lowcountry Grille.** *Eclectic.* The owners of Magnolias and Blossom opened this restaurant in a renovated 1834 brick building with urban contemporary decor. Rust-color leather booths, a ceiling with light sculptures that change color, and a "wine wall" of 4,500 bottles add to the striking ambience. The cuisine is high-end Southern-American, with fresh local ingredients accented with exotic flavors, notably from the Pacific Rim. Executive chef Craig Deihl has gained recognition in the culinary world for his simple yet elegant fare. Try fabulous salads, like the hearts of palm and baby greens with local goat cheese topped with a walnut vinaigrette. The duck is a good entrée choice, as is the fillet cooked over hickory wood and topped with a Madeira wine sauce. And the charcuterie is a must-try for the table. [$] *Average main: $33* ✉ *167 E. Bay St., Market area* ☎ *843/727–0111* 🌐 *www.magnolias-blossom-cypress.com* ✍ *Reservations essential* 🕒 *No lunch.*
$$$$

$ ✕**Dixie Supply Bakery and Cafe.** *Southern.* It might be a lil' eatery buttressed by a Lil' Cricket convenience store, but don't be fooled by its size. Dixie Supply Bakery and Cafe belongs to an old Charlestonian family (and by old, we mean they arrived here in 1698 or so) that seeks to honor its roots through food. It's here you'll find Lowcountry and Southern classics: shrimp and creamy stone-ground

LOWCOUNTRY CUISINE

Although you can find Lowcountry cuisine along most of coastal South Carolina all the way down to Savannah, its foundation feeds off the Holy City of Charleston, where, centuries ago, European aristocrats would share kitchens with their African slaves. The result was a colonial European fusion with Caribbean and West African, otherwise known as Gullah, influences.

Shrimp and Grits. If you're not convinced that South Carolina is serious about grits, consider this: in 1976, it declared grits the official state food. To be truly decadent, you need to finish this starch off with heavy cream and a slab of butter. Each chef has his or her own guarded recipe, but traditionally, local wild shrimp is sautéed with onions, garlic, and fresh tomatoes. Today, foodies will delight in discovering the dish to be dressed up with everything from sausage, bacon, and Cajun seasoning to cheese, gravy, and tomato-based sauces.

She-Crab Soup. Rich and creamy, with lumps of crabmeat and a splash of dry sherry, she-crab soup is to the Lowcountry as chowder is to New England. The "she" of this signature dish actually comes from the main ingredient, a female crab's orange crab roe. It is delicious as an appetizer, and quite filling as an entrée.

Hoppin' John. This rice-and-bean concoction is not only a favorite Lowcountry dish but a lucky one at that. Families throughout the Lowcountry prepare hoppin' John on New Year's Day for lunch or dinner in hopes that it will provide them with a year's worth of good luck. It's all in the classic Lowcountry ingredients: black-eyed peas symbolize pennies (a side of collard greens adds to the wealth in the new year). Rice, chopped onions, bacon (or ham), and peppers are added to the peas. Add garnishes like a spoonful of salsa or a dollop of sour cream for an interesting Southwest spin.

Perlau. South Carolina takes great pride in its perlau (aka perloo), more lovingly known at the table as chicken bog. This rice-based dish is cooked with chunks of tender chicken and sausage slices, simmered in the chef's choice of Southern seasonings. For more than 30 years, in fact, the tiny town of Loris has been hosting its annual Loris Bog-Off Festival, where hundreds of chefs compete to be awarded with the best bowl of bog.

grits, fried chicken, and a mighty fine tomato pie. Daily alternating blue-plate specials abound, including fried green tomatoes, shrimp from nearby Wadmalaw Island, summer-squash-and-ricotta-cheese ravioli, and a steady assortment of locally plucked vegetables. $ *Average main: $7* ✉ *62 State St., Market area* ☎ *843/722–5650* ⊕ *www. dixiecafecharleston.com.*

★ **Fodor'sChoice** ✕**FIG.** *Southern.* Spend an evening here for fresh-off-the-farm ingredients cooked with unfussy, flavorful finesse. Chef and partner Mike Lata has won awards for keeping it simple at FIG. The menu changes frequently, but the family-style vegetables might be as simple as young beets in sherry vinegar placed in a plain white bowl. His dishes do get more complex: there's the pureed cauliflower soup with pancetta, incredible veal sweetbreads with smoked bacon and escarole, and grouper with a perfect golden crust accompanied by braised artichokes. Hit the lively bar scene for a nightcap. $ *Average main: $30* ✉ *232 Meeting St., Market area* ☎ *843/805–5900* ⊕ *www.eatatfig.com* ⊙ *No lunch*.

$$$$

★ **Fodor'sChoice** ✕**Fish.** *Eclectic.* Since European chef Nico Romo raised it to a high culinary level, Fish's popularity has soared. Savvy foodies have embraced the French/Asian cuisine, and others have followed suit. (In 2010, Romo became the youngest person to earn the title of Master Chef of France.) Start with the dim sum appetizer; it's more beautiful than a flower arrangement. Or try the sweet-chili calamari that gives the menu a new kick. The bouillabaisse with coconut-lemongrass broth and ginger croutons is one-of-a-kind. Increasing business has triggered a major renovation of the spaces, which blend antiqued mirrors and stainless steel, and a new dining room has gone into the adjacent building. The original bar has tripled in size, all the better for a pre-dinner cocktail. $ *Average main: $22* ✉ *440–442 King St., Upper King* ☎ *843/722–3474* ⊕ *www.fishrestaurant. net* ⌕ *Reservations essential* ⊙ *Closed Sun. No lunch Sat.*

$$$

$$$$ ✕**Fulton Five.** *Italian.* Tucked into the antiques district, this romantic restaurant is appropriately decorated in chartreuse walls and brass accents. In warm weather you can opt for a seat on the second-floor terrace. But wherever you sit, the northern Italian specialties are worth savoring. Mushroom risotto with sweet corn accompanies the beef with porcini mushrooms. There's pappardelle with rabbit, and spinach gnocchi with crabmeat and tarragon-laced butter. $ *Average main: $32* ✉ *5 Fulton St., Lower King* ☎ *843/853–5555* ⊕ *www.fultonfive.net* ⌕ *Reservations essential* ⊙ *Closed Sun. and late Aug.–early Sept. No lunch.*

$ ★ 🍴 **Glazed.** *Bakery.* Allison Smith and Mark Remi started their sweetheart of a store in August 2010, betting on an untapped enthusiasm for artisanal doughnuts. The verdict? Unqualified success. Glazed bakes 7 to 10 varieties daily, building its doughnuts with homemade dough, jam, fillings, and glaze. Just name your flavor. There's Chocolate Covered Cherry made from a merlot filling and dark chocolate glaze, the Charleston whipped up with bourbon cream filling, toffee glaze, and homemade pralines, or the uber-popular Maple Bacon, complete with maple glaze and bacon from Wisconsin's own Nueske's Applewood Smoked Meats. [$] *Average main: $3* ✉ *481 King St., Upper King* ☎ *843/577–5557* 🌐 *www.glazedgourmet.com.*

$$$$ 🍴 **Grill 225.** *Steakhouse.* This atmospheric establishment has been stockpiling accolades over the years, and it's never been better. The cuisine combined with a staggering array of excellent wines and professional, caring service make Grill 225 a popular special-occasion spot. Take the opportunity to dress up; the elegant wood floors, white linens, and red-velvet upholstery call for it. If you eat red meat, indulge in the prime USDA, wet-aged steaks; the fillet with foie gras with a fig demi-glace is equally excellent. But don't miss sharing a side or two, such as the mashed sweet potatoes with Boursin cheese. Presentation is at its best with appetizers like the tuna-tower tartare. Expect hefty portions, but save room for the pastry chef's shining creations, which include a contemporized version of baked Alaska with a nutty crust, flambéed table-side. [$] *Average main: $40* ✉ *Market Pavilion Hotel, 225 E. Bay St., Market area* ☎ *843/266–4222* 🌐 *www.marketpavilion.com.*

★ $$$ Fodor's Choice 🍴 **The Grocery.** *Modern American.* Executive chef and owner Kevin Johnson's new restaurant sits in impressive quarters near the corner of Cannon and King streets. Cast in dim lighting and painted concrete, the spacious Grocery projects an earthy, unassuming presence. The high wainscoting and tall shelving filled with jams, pickled vegetables, and vintage kitchenware match the restaurant's aim—and title. Similarly, the menu suggests a humble, considerate approach, as the dishes represent local flavors: liver mousse mixed with ripe persimmons provides a light, fluffy taste smeared on crunchy, buttered bread. Wood-roasted clams offer native appeal, emboldened with *merguez* sausage and a light chili. A rich pot roast is made from grass-fed beef, and the delicate scamp grouper crowns a bed of field peas, crab, and perlau (made from Charleston Gold rice). If you visit during the hot months, try the water-

WORD OF MOUTH

"I'm looking for a not crazy expensive but not cheap restaurant for a final dinner in Charleston. I've heard of Husk and Fig.... Any other recommendations?" —JoeTro

"You should also consider eating at the bar. You won't need a reservation for that and the bar at Husk is interesting. The bar at McCrady's is also memorable. If a place you like is booked, call and talk to them. Restaurant week is really busy." —suewoo

"We liked Blossom best of all and it fits your description of what you are looking for." —basingstoke2

"I had a good three course meal at Blossom: wedge salad, flounder with a great risotto and coconut cream pie (wish I'd have had the chocolate peppermint brownie). Took a cab back to my B and B for a whopping $6." —JoeTro

melon gazpacho with stone crab, too. It tastes like summer in a bowl. [$] *Average main: $22* ✉ *4 Cannon St., Market area* ☎ *843/302–8825* 🌐 *www.thegrocerycharleston.com.*

★ $$$$ **Fodor'sChoice** 🍴 **Hall's Chophouse.** *Steakhouse.* Hall's Chophouse set down in early 2009 in the old Artist and Craftsman Supply digs on upper King Street, plying a different brand of craftsmanship: 28-day aged fresh USDA steaks. In plush, two-story environs, the restaurant has swiftly made good, establishing itself as one of the top three steak houses in town (Oak and Grill 225 being the others). Recommended are the 28-ounce, long-bone Tomahawk rib eye, the New York strip, and the dry-aged, slow-roasted prime rib. A heads-up, too: Hall's service borders on excessive, or is it obsessive? Staff takes uncommon heed of its guests, though the lavishly prepared steaks offer the restaurant's greatest source of hospitality. [$] *Average main: $40* ✉ *434 King St., Upper King* ☎ *843/727–0090* 🌐 *www.hallschophouse.com* ✍ *Reservations essential.*

$$$$ 🍴 **Hank's Seafood.** *Seafood.* A lively spot with a popular bar and a community table flanked by paper-topped private tables, Hank's is an upscale fish house serving such Southern adaptations as Lowcountry bouillabaisse. Seafood platters come with sweet-potato fries and coleslaw. The atmosphere retains an authentic bistro air under longtime chef Frank McMahon, with waiters in long white aprons buzzing about. It's super-popular with the thirtysomething crowd and those who live inland and want the freshest seafood. With a location just off the Old Market, the sister restaurant

to the fancy-pants Peninsula Grill is a noteworthy landmark on Charleston's dining scene. [$] *Average main: $27* ✉ *10 Hayne St., at Church St., Market area* ☎ *843/723–3474* 🌐 *www.hanksseafoodrestaurant.com* 🕓 *No lunch.*

$$$$ ✕ **High Cotton.** *Southern.* The styling here remains unchanged by time: lazily spinning paddle fans, palm trees, and exposed brick walls. Clearly Joe Palma's appointment as chef has not affected the nature of this classic venue; rather, his selection has ramped up the restaurant to new heights. The picnic plate allows a pleasant introduction, displaying delicately fried green tomatoes, pillowy pimento cheese, pickled okra and peaches, a bit of the restaurant's housemade charcuterie, and a selection of BBQ Lowcountry peanuts. Smothered in a sticky sauce, the peanuts seem a modernized, much improved version of Cracker Jack. If you want a traditional dinner, the restaurant still offers thick cuts of steaks and chops with choice of sauce and side dishes like fried brussels sprouts and the timeless creamy white corn grits. Then for dessert: a Southern-style pecan pie baked with bourbon brown sugar caramel, or a high-rising peanut butter pie. Choose both if you feel bold. They're like rich Southern blessings. [$] *Average main: $27* ✉ *199 E. Bay St., Market area* ☎ *843/724–3815* 🌐 *www.mavericksouthernkitchens.com/highcotton* ✍ *Reservations essential* 🕓 *No lunch weekdays.*

$ ✕ **Hominy Grill.** *Southern.* The wooden barber poles from the last century still frame the door of this small, homespun café. Chalkboard specials are often the way to go here, whether you are visiting for breakfast, lunch, or dinner. Chef Robert Stehling is a Carolina boy who lived in New York; that dichotomy shows in his "uptown" comfort food. Here, you can have the perfect soft-shell-crab sandwich with homemade fries, but leave room for the tangy buttermilk pie or the chocolate peanut butter pie. The bottom line: whatever Stehling cooks tastes good. Renovations in recent years include a new patio and roomier indoor seating. Both are lovely improvements. [$] *Average main: $13* ✉ *207 Rutledge Ave., Canonboro* ☎ *843/937–0930* 🌐 *www.hominygrill.com* 🕓 *No dinner Sun.*

★ $$$$ **Fodor's Choice** ✕ **Husk.** *Southern.* Welcome to Husk, home to celebrated chef Sean Brock, a host of ingredients indigenous to the region, and an abundance of accolades. Named Best New Restaurant in America by *Bon Appetit* magazine in 2011, Husk serves an ambitious menu steeped in the South—and the South alone. Seriously. Brock forbids the inclusion of items from other regions or provinces, even

Fodor's Interview with Holly Herrick

Holly Herrick is a classically trained chef, former restaurant critic at Charleston's *Post and Courier*, and author of the book *The Charleston's Chef's Table*. Here, she talks with Fodor's about some of her favorite places in the Holy City.

Q: She-crab soup is probably the most iconic Charleston dish. Where do you go for the best version?

A: My personal favorite is at **Virginia's on King** (⊠ *412 King St.* ☎ *843/735–5800*). What I love about it is that they use the blue crab, which is local and seasonal. To me it's just really delicious. It's a perfect dish to make for New Year's Eve or for the holidays. There are several good variations around town, but that's my personal favorite.

Q: Where do you go for the best shrimp and grits?

A: I happen to love the shrimp and grits at **Hominy Grill** (⊠ *207 Rutledge Ave.* ☎ *843/937–0930*). In fact I love Hominy Grill in general. [Chef Robert Stehling] uses local shrimp. There's really a difference in taste in Lowcountry shrimp, unlike any other. It's got a real, briny sweetness to it that makes it exceptional. It's fabulous.

Q: Are there any new places that you're excited about?

A: There's a place that I'm just over-the-moon crazy about. It's a patisserie called **Macaroon Boutique** (⊠ *45 John St.* ☎ *843/577–5441* ⊕ *www. macaroonboutique.com*). It's just this cool, boutique-y place with glass counters and the most beautiful pastries and breads, and then the *macaron* case, which looks too beautiful to eat. The pastry crème and the ganache that fill the *macarons* are just impeccable. It's impossible not to feel happy when you go there. It feels like you are in Paris the second you open the door.

Q: Do you have a favorite local's joint?

A: My current favorite is **The Glass Onion** (⊠ *1219 Savannah Hwy., West Ashley* ☎ *843/225–1717* ⊕ *www.ilovetheglassonion.com*). It's about 12 to 14 minutes from the heart of downtown, so it's really easy to get to. It's just casual and they just do amazing, hearty, Southern food, like a really great oyster po'boy or really fabulous meat loaf. It's just a feel-good place. The people are really friendly and there are a lot of local regulars.

olive oil. A large chalkboard inside the restaurant accounts for an offering of ever-changing artisanal foods, as the menu sometimes varies twice daily. Supper favorites include seafood such as snapper, catfish, and flounder, frequently paired with heirloom vegetables. Try the Southern fried chicken skins or skillet of smoky bacon corn bread, too—both are terrifically popular. The building itself, balcony intact, dates to the late 19th century, and the freestanding bar beside the restaurant is lined with 100-year-old exposed brick and several Kentucky bourbons and whiskeys. Ⓢ *Average main: $26* ✉ *76 Queen St., Market area* ☎ *843/577-2500* ⊕ *www.huskrestaurant.com.*

$$$ ✕ **La Fourchette.** *French.* French owner Perig Goulet moves agilely through the petite dining room of this unpretentious bistro. With back-to-back chairs making things cozy (and noisy), this place could easily be in Paris. Kevin Kelly chooses the wines—predominantly French and esoteric—and they befit the authentic fare. Goulet is especially proud of his country pâté, from a recipe handed down from his *grand-mère.* Other favorites include duck salad, scallops sautéed in cognac, and shrimp in a leek sauce. Dieters may be shocked by the golden *frites* fried in duck fat and served with aioli, but they keep putting their hands in the basket. Check the blackboard for fish straight off the boats. Ⓢ *Average main: $22* ✉ *432 King St., Upper King* ☎ *843/722-6261* ⊕ *www.lafourchettecharleston.com* ⊘ *Closed Sun. No lunch Aug.–Mar.*

★ Fodor'sChoice ✕ **The Macintosh.** *American.* Here's another
$$$ name to tuck into your sweetgrass basket filled with great Charleston chefs: Jeremiah Bacon. And what a perfect name, right? As the former chef at Carolina's and Oak Steakhouse, Bacon enjoys free reign at The Macintosh, named one of *Bon Appetit*'s 50 Best New Restaurants in America in 2012. The Macintosh continues in the traditions of restaurants like FIG, offering comfy quarters and homespun victuals to a stylish crowd. Here, Bacon shows off his fondness for the little-regarded deckle, a highly-marbled, delicious piece of rib eye, as well as local cobia, clams, and grouper, and bone marrow bread pudding. Already exceedingly popular, The Mac's aiming to take its place among Charleston's best. Ⓢ *Average main: $24* ✉ *478 King St., Upper King* ☎ *843/788-4299* ⊕ *www.the macintoshcharleston.com.*

CHITTERLINGS. Do not be afraid, be informed. Chitterlings, better known as chitlins (and sometimes chit'lins), can be sampled from several soul food establishments in Charleston, including Martha Lou Gadsden's eponymously named restaurant. A quick primer: Chitterlings are made up of the small intestines of a pig, and usually served fried or steamed after being boiled for several hours. They're not for everyone, but try to withhold judgment before tasting (possibly with cider vinegar or hot sauce).

★ $ Fodor'sChoice 🍴 **Martha Lou's Kitchen.** *Southern.* You may not delight in the decor—vinyl booths repaired with duct tape and walls muddled with old photographs—but for those venturing inside Martha Lou's Kitchen, a bit of Charleston heritage awaits. Of course, the chicken, perfectly cooked to golden brown, and those fried pork chops aren't bad, either. Martha Lou Gadsden has made her pink cinder-block building into a palace of soul food, serving some of the city's finest. The tireless octogenarian works all day, preparing collard greens, giblet rice, lima beans, and, yes, even chitterlings. Just a chat with Miss Martha Lou is enough to make the trip worthwhile. [$] *Average main: $8* ✉ *1068 Morrison Dr.* ☎ *843/577–9583* 💳 *No credit cards* 🕒 *Closed Sun.*

★ $$$$ Fodor'sChoice 🍴 **McCrady's.** *American.* Executive chef Sean Brock may spend the majority of his time at his new enterprise, Husk, but the unswerving McCrady's still delivers thanks to talented chef de cuisine Jeremiah Langhorne and his crackerjack restaurant staff. Originally constructed in 1788, the structure features heart pine flooring, two fireplaces, exposed brick walls, and a pair of handsome brick archways. Its impressive legacy is supported by cuisine still ranking among Charleston's best. Bear witness to the short rib, set with sweet corn and green tomatoes, or the beef tartare featuring small discs of egg yolk, ramps, and frisée. Or enjoy fresh fish from local waters, such as grilled cobia or flounder crusted with green peppercorn. Meats include Berkshire pork so tender your fork leaves indentions, and aged duck roasted on the bone. A four-course menu featuring smaller dishes allows diners to taste several items. The only trouble: it may leave you craving more. [$] *Average main: $30* ✉ *2 Unity Alley, Market area* ☎ *843/577–0025* 🌐 *www.mccradysrestaurant.com* ✍ *Reservations essential* 🕒 *No lunch.*

★ Fodor's Choice 🍴 **Moe's Tavern.** *American.* First things first: No,
$ it's not a burrito joint—far from it. Moe's Tavern is decidedly old-school, earning a perennial place on the area's best-burger list. The big, half-pound, Angus beef chuck patties are cooked to order. And they're not even the best things on the menu. Give it up for Moe's BLT, containing a sizable disc of mozzarella cheese, fried tomato, and, of course, plenty of bacon. Visit the original location on Rutledge Avenue near Hampton Park, or the newer, downtown installation at 5 Cumberland Street. The former is preferable, as much for its nostalgic charm as its heady selection of beers. [$] *Average main: $8* ✉ *714 Rutledge Ave., Hampton Park* ☎ *843/722–3287* 🌐 *www.moestaverns.com* [$] *Average main: $8* ✉ *Moe's Downtown Tavern:, 5 Cumberland St., Market area* ☎ *843/577–8500.*

$ 🍴 **Monza.** *Pizza.* An homage to the Italian city of the same name, Monza provides genuine Neapolitan-style pizza and an introduction to one of the world's most historic motor-sport racing circuits: the Autodromo Nazionale Monza. The restaurant takes its cue after several Formula One greats, naming its pizzas for Emilio Materassi, Felice Nazzaro, Giuseppe Campari, Wolfgang Von Trips, Ronnie Peterson, and "El Maestro," Juan Manuel Fangio. Like the sport the restaurant celebrates, service is quick-paced, the setting modish. As for the pizza, baked in a wood-fired oven, all specialties boast a thin, crisp crust, and toppings such as house-made sausage, pepperoni, eggplant, roasted red peppers, and locally farmed eggs. [$] *Average main: $13* ✉ *451 King St., Upper King* ☎ *843/720–8787* 🌐 *www.monzapizza.com.*

$$$ 🍴 **Muse Restaurant & Wine Bar.** *Mediterranean.* Set in an older, pale yellow home on Society Street, Muse lays bare Mediterranean stylings in sophisticated, relaxed quarters. The bar functions as a drawing room, permitting easy introductions and closer inspection of the restaurant's impressive, 100-plus-bottle wine list. Nature provides ideal lighting, as sunlight spills into the dining rooms during evenings in spring and summer. The restaurant serves standout plates, such as tuna carpaccio, sweetbreads, swordfish, and its signature dish: a delicious, scarcely fried sea bass, served with head and tail intact, over saffron rice and roasted-pepper puree. [$] *Average main: $24* ✉ *82 Society St., Lower King* ☎ *843/577–1102* 🌐 *www.charlestonmuse.com* ✍ *Reservations essential* ⏲ *No lunch.*

$$$$ 🍴 **Oak Steakhouse.** *Steakhouse.* Inside a 19th-century bank building, this dining room juxtaposes antique crystal chan-

deliers with contemporary art. Reserve a table on the third floor for the full effect and the best vistas. It's pricey, but the filet mignon with a foie-gras-black-truffle butter is excellent, and the side dishes, such as creamed spinach, are perfectly executed. Favorite appetizers include beef carpaccio and Gorgonzola fondue. Service is professional and cordial under the leadership of executive chef Jeremiah Bacon and chef de cuisine Joseph Jacobson. $ *Average main:* $40 ⊠ *17 Broad St., Market area* ☎ *843/722–4220* ⊕ *www.oaksteakhouserestaurant.com* ⊗ *No lunch.*

3

COLD-PRESSED COFFEE. Though not exclusive to Charleston, cold-pressed coffee is considered more potent than regular coffee. The basis: Cold-pressed coffee requires extended brewing times, which removes some of the bite or acidity while ramping up natural caffeine levels. **Queen Street Grocery** (⊠ *133 Queen St.*) supplies the hooch downtown.

★ **Fodor**'s Choice ✕ **Peninsula Grill.** *Southern.* Graham Dailey has
$$$$ successfully filled the post formerly occupied by longtime chef Bob Carter, incorporating Lowcountry produce and seafood into traditional Peninsula dishes, at once eyeing the past and the future. The dining room looks the part: the walls are covered in olive-green velvet and dotted with 18th-century-style portraits, and the ceiling supports black-iron chandeliers. These fixtures serve as an excellent backdrop for "sinfully grilled" Angus steaks, as well as jumbo sea scallops, and Berskhire pork chops. Palate-cleanse with the homemade sorbet, or try the signature three-way chocolate dessert that comes with a shot of ice-cold milk. The servers, who work in tandem, are pros; the personable sommelier makes wine selections that truly complement your meal, anything from bubbly to clarets and dessert wines. The atmosphere is animated and convivial, and Carter's famous coconut cake still graces the menu. $ *Average main: $35* ⊠ *Planters Inn, 112 N. Market St., Market area* ☎ *843/723–0700* ⊕ *www.peninsulagrill.com* ⚅ *Reservations essential* ⊗ *No lunch.*

$ ✕ **Queen Street Grocery & Café.** *American.* For crepes and cold-pressed coffee, most folks turn to a venerable Charleston institution: Queen Street Grocery. Established in 1922, the corner shop and café has endured several guises through the years: butchery, candy shop, and late-night convenience store. Back in 2008, new owners returned the store to its roots as a neighborhood grocery store, sourcing much of the produce and other goods from local growers. It's a great preservation act, improved upon by QSG's newest offerings: sweet and savory crepes named for the islands surrounding Charleston. [$] *Average main: $9* ✉ *133 Queen St., Market area* ☎ *843/723–4121* 🌐 *www.qsg29401.com.*

★ Fodor's Choice 🍴 **Recovery Room.** *American.* The graffiti-splashed
$ walls and tongue-in-cheek title make the Recovery Room a favorite for hipsters and college kids. In addition to cans of Pabst Blue Ribbon, the watering hole, set underneath the U.S. Highway 17 bridge, serves up brunch, lunch, a late-night menu, and even amateur pole dancing on Monday night. Go for the tater tachos, tater tots covered in shredded cheeses, jalapeños, tomatoes, and onions, or the wings in 12 sauces. The windows may be few and the view muted, but look at it this way: at least nobody will see you scarf down an order of "chicken biscuits"—fried chicken tenders sopping with honey or gravy over a homemade biscuit. [$] *Average main: $6* ✉ *685 King St., Upper King* ☎ *843/722–4220* 🌐 *www.recoveryroomtavern.com.*

$$$$ 🍴 **Slightly North of Broad.** *Southern.* This former warehouse with brick-and-stucco walls has a chef's table that looks directly into the open kitchen. It's a great place to perch if you can "take the heat," as chef Frank Lee, who wears a baseball cap instead of a toque, is one of the city's culinary characters. He is known for his talent in prepping game, and his venison is exceptional. Many of the items come as small plates, which makes them perfect for sharing. The braised lamb shank with a ragout of white beans, arugula, and a red demi-glace is divine. Lunch can be as inexpensive as $9.95 for something as memorable as mussels with spinach, grape tomatoes, and smoked bacon. [$] *Average main: $28* ✉ *192 E. Bay St., Market area* ☎ *843/723–3424* 🌐 *www.mavericksouthernkitchens.com/snob* ⏲ *No lunch weekends.*

$ 🍴 **Taco Boy.** *Mexican.* Accommodating visitors and locals alike, Taco Boy delivers tasty Mexican treats to a bustling patio crowd. The restaurant belongs to Revolutionary Eating Ventures (REV), the talented gang behind Monza and Moe's Tavern, two other restaurants found in this guide. REV casts an eye toward sustainability at Taco Boy, constructing the restaurant (in its previous life an old bread-distribution warehouse) with rehabbed or reclaimed materials—right down to the bar counter, carved from a fallen North Carolina walnut tree. It's a forward-thinking and fun joint, perfect for downing margaritas and *micheladas* (beer with lime juice, tomato juice, and chilies) or sharing a sampler trio of house-made guacamole and salsas. For beach-bound travelers, Folly Beach—south of downtown

Charleston—boasts the original Taco Boy restaurant on Center Street. [$] *Average main: $7* ✉ *217 Huger St., North of Broad* ☎ *843/789–3333* 🌐 *www.tacoboy.net* [$] *Average main: $7* ✉ *15 Center St., Folly Beach* ☎ *843/588–9761.*

★ **Fodor'sChoice** 🍴 **The Tattooed Moose.** *American.* It only seems
$ like a cross between a veterans' hall and a dive bar, but the Tattooed Moose's decidedly unpretentious look was thoughtfully put together by the owners of the Voodoo Tiki Bar in West Ashley. With 90-plus beers on the menu, and a large moose head behind the counter, the Tattooed Moose cuts a distinctive figure. The bar's famous duck club is a menu showstopper. Priced at twice the amount as the other sandwiches, it relies on duck confit, apple-smoked bacon, garlic aioli, and ripened tomatoes bounded by sweet, Hawaiian bread. Homey eats like house-smoked barbecue brisket, chicken salad, jumbo chicken wings, and fried turkey breast round out the offerings. [$] *Average main: $10* ✉ *1137 Morrison Dr., Market area* ☎ *843/277–2990* 🌐 *www.tattooedmoose.com.*

$ 🍴 **Ted's Butcherblock.** *American.* Land at Ted's on a lucky evening (or lunch break), and you'll likely be conferred a memorable greeting: the scent of smoked meats drifting from a grill perched near the restaurant entrance. Happy day, indeed. Ted's operates as a one-stop butcher shop, supplying beef, game, seafood, and homemade sausages to complement its selection of artisanal cheeses, wine, and other specialty foods. But the shop also maintains a first-rate deli counter, drawing praise from *Bon Appetit* and other publications. Among the favored offerings: the house-roasted Wagyu beef panini, and the ever-changing bacon-of-the-month BLT. [$] *Average main: $8* ✉ *334 E. Bay St., Market area* ☎ *843/577–0094* 🌐 *www.tedsbutcherblock.com.*

MUSTARD SAUCE. So, you've sampled rich, tomato-based sauces in Kansas City or Memphis, spiked your barbecue with vinegar-flavored concoctions in eastern North Carolina, and maybe even tried the white, mayonnaise-based sauce of Alabama. Now, about that mustard sauce . . . It can be traced to the state's German forebears, and is often called Orangeburg mustard in deference to the city of the same name, situated about 80 miles north of Charleston. Colored golden, the sauce is made up of mustard (naturally), brown sugar, and molasses and is certainly worth pouring over pulled pork or smoked chicken.

★ $$$ Fodor's Choice ✕ **Trattoria Lucca.** *Italian.* The naysayers scoffed when chef Ken Vedrinski opened Trattoria Lucca back in 2008. Not because of Vedrinski; the well-heeled chef manned the kitchen of the bygone Sienna restaurant on Daniel Island. Rather, the whispers were from Lucca's unlikely location, deep on the peninsula in a neighborhood in need of TLC. And now, well, now they flock, visiting Lucca for his warm cauliflower *sformatino* (with soft organic egg, pancetta, and *parmigiano* cheese), organic Mezze Maniche and Chitarra pastas, and, on Sunday evening, family-style suppers with communal seating. [$] *Average main: $24* ✉ *41 Bogard St., North of Broad* ☎ *843/973–3323* 🌐 *www.luccacharleston.com* ✍ *Reservations essential.*

★ $$$$ Fodor's Choice ✕ **Tristan.** *Southern.* Within the French Quarter Inn, this fine dining room has a sleek, contemporary style with lots of metal, glass, contemporary art, and fresh flowers. The menu has been purposely tailored to complement the decor: it's ultrachic, innovative, and always evolving. The banquettes that line the wall are sought after, so ask for one when you reserve. Chef Nate Whiting emphasizes market-fresh fish, artisanal pasta, and Lowcountry comforts such as she-crab soup. Pastry chef Amanee Nierouz also tantalizes with sorbets, pudding cakes, and parfaits. After dark, the prices escalate—it's a status place with a sophisticated bar scene. On Sunday there's a fab brunch with a jazz trio, and residents of the Holy City reserve for after church. [$] *Average main: $29* ✉ *French Quarter Inn, 55 S. Market St., Market area* ☎ *843/534–2155* 🌐 *www.tristandining.com.*

★ $$$ Fodor's Choice ✕ **Two Boroughs Larder.** *American.* Husband and wife Josh and Heather Keeler ventured down from Philadelphia to open up their restaurant and market in the Cannonborough-Elliotborough neighborhoods. The menu changes daily, featuring an eclectic but irrepressible mix. You can opt for a breakfast sandwich any time of the day, only with *pepperonata* and egg, Neueske's bacon, or pork scrapple—a traditional heap of pork mush from Pennsylvania Dutch and Amish descent. But the restaurant supplies other pleasing mains, too, like grouper *brodetto*, oven-roasted trout, and veal sweetbreads along with plentiful sides such as marrow-roasted cauliflower, braised heirloom beans, and buffalo pig tails. The restaurant is already prized by the community, so much so that Josh Keeler nabbed one of the seven seats at the 2012 Critics' Dinner, an annual event affiliated with the Charleston Wine & Food Festival. [$] *Average main: $20* ✉ *186 Coming St., Cannonborough* ☎ *843/637–3722* 🌐 *www.twoboroughslarder.com.*

SOUTH OF BROAD

$ 🍴 Blind Tiger. *American.* The old fella's still got it. As one of Charleston's oldest speakeasies, the Blind Tiger can go toe-to-toe with any newcomer. Name the beer, name the backdrop, and the Tiger can deliver in spades, starting with two indoor bars and a historic, handsome outdoor patio. The kitchen also turns out brilliant, cooked-to-temp, Angus beef cheeseburgers, elk burgers, and ground alligator. Also available: chorizo, *banh mi* sandwiches, and gyros. It might be unexpected, but it's still rewarding. [$] *Average main: $10* ✉ *36–38 Broad St., South of Broad* ☎ *843/577–0088* 🌐 *www.blindtigercharleston.com.*

$$$$ 🍴 Carolina's. *Southern.* On a quiet side street between East Bay Street and Waterfront Park, this longtime favorite occupies a former wharf building. The smartened up decor includes romantic banquettes, and an evolving menu under chef Jill Mathias has a strong emphasis on healthful ingredients. (Owner Richard Stoney also owns Kensington Plantation, where most of the produce is grown.) Lowcountry favorites stand next to original dishes like scallops with roasted cauliflower. Local grouper works amazingly well with a port-wine broth. Ask about the special prix-fixe dinners, including ones with beer pairings. On Sunday and Monday bottles of wine are half price. The free valet parking is another nice touch. [$] *Average main: $30* ✉ *10 Exchange St., South of Broad* ☎ *843/724–3800* 🌐 *www.carolinasrestaurant.com* ✍ *Reservations essential* ⏲ *No lunch weekends.*

$$ 🍴 Gaulart and Maliclet Café. *French.* Sharing high, family-style tables for breakfast, lunch, or dinner leads to camaraderie at this bustling bistro also known as Fast 'n' French. Thursday brings a crowd for fondue. The cheese version can be disappointing, but the seafood, which you cook in broth yourself, is better. Opt to get your cheese fix with the wonderful Bucheron cheese salad. Nightly specials, such as bouillabaisse or couscous, are reasonably priced and come with a petite glass of wine. And a subtly sweet chocolate-mousse cake is the best way to end your meal. The service is often imperfect but fun, and prices have stayed reasonable (while others downtown have soared). Although not as popular as it once was, the restaurant still has a loyal following. [$] *Average main: $15* ✉ *98 Broad St., South of Broad* ☎ *843/577–9797* 🌐 *www.fastandfrenchcharleston.com* ⏲ *Closed Sun. No dinner Mon.*

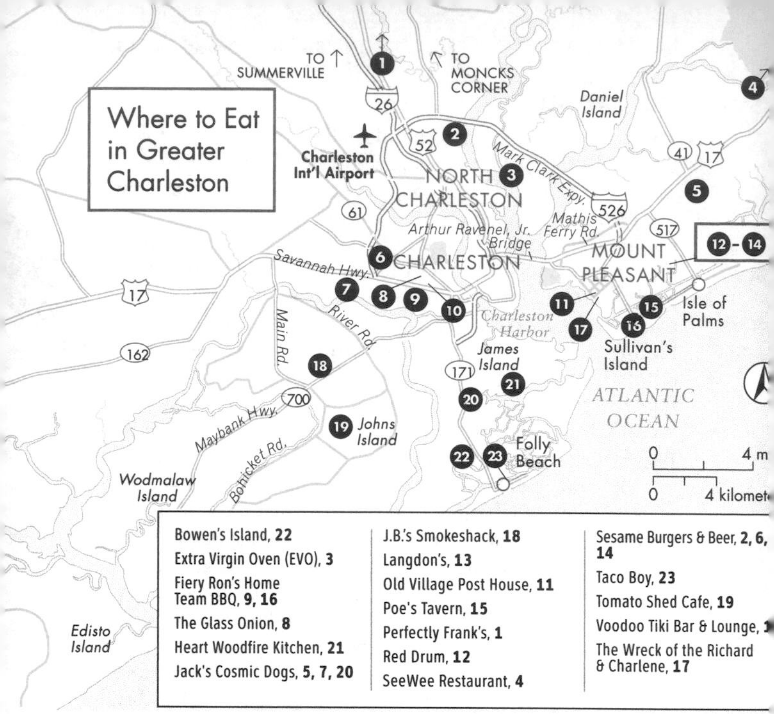
Where to Eat in Greater Charleston
TO SUMMERVILLE
TO MONCKS CORNER
Daniel Island
Charleston Int'l Airport
NORTH CHARLESTON
Mark Clark Expy.
Mathis Ferry Rd.
Arthur Ravenel, Jr. Bridge
CHARLESTON
MOUNT PLEASANT
Savannah Hwy.
River Rd.
Main Rd.
Charleston Harbor
James Island
Isle of Palms
Sullivan's Island
ATLANTIC OCEAN
Johns Island
Maybank Hwy.
Bohicket Rd.
Folly Beach
Wodmalaw Island
Edisto Island
Bowen's Island, 22
Extra Virgin Oven (EVO), 3
Fiery Ron's Home Team BBQ, 9, 16
The Glass Onion, 8
Heart Woodfire Kitchen, 21
Jack's Cosmic Dogs, 5, 7, 20
J.B.'s Smokeshack, 18
Langdon's, 13
Old Village Post House, 11
Poe's Tavern, 15
Perfectly Frank's, 1
Red Drum, 12
SeeWee Restaurant, 4
Sesame Burgers & Beer, 2, 6, 14
Taco Boy, 23
Tomato Shed Cafe, 19
Voodoo Tiki Bar & Lounge,
The Wreck of the Richard & Charlene, 17

MOUNT PLEASANT AND VICINITY

$$$$ 🍴 **Langdon's.** *Modern Hawaiian.* Langdon's only drawback: it's inside a nondescript strip mall across the Cooper River Bridge from Charleston. Otherwise, the restaurant and wine bar belonging to Mount Pleasant native son Patrick Owens triumphs, earning a teetering pile of awards. Owens merges local cuisine with Asian and worldly flavors, exacting a rich menu composed of Hawaiian tuna, lamb racks, black skillet beef tenderloins, local shrimp and grouper, and sides like succotash, smoked-tomato-and-Brie grits, and leek-and-corn risotto. [$] *Average main: $30* ✉ *778 S. Shelmore Blvd., Mount Pleasant* ☎ *843/388–9200* 🌐 *www.langdonsrestaurant.com.*

$$$$ 🍴 **Old Village Post House.** *Southern.* If you've been on the road too long, this circa 1888 inn will provide warmth and sustenance. Many residents of this tree-lined village consider this their neighborhood tavern. The second, smaller dining room is cozy, and the outdoor space under the market umbrellas is open and airy. Expect contemporary takes on Southern favorites like lump crab cakes, shrimp and grits, and especially the fresh vegetables, like a butter beans mélange. From the open kitchen, the chefs can perfectly sauté the catch of the day. Here, pork tenderloin may have a ginger-peachy glaze. In season, plump softshell crabs are deftly fried. Frank Sinatra serenades as you cleanse your palate with a tart, key lime pie with a crunchy crust and passion-fruit coulis. $ *Average main: $25* ✉ *101 Pitt St., Mount Pleasant* ☎ *843/388–8935* 🌐 *www.mavericksouthernkitchens.com* 🕒 *No lunch Mon.–Sat.*

$$$$ ★ 🍴 **Red Drum.** *Southwestern.* Vacationers and locals alike tend to overlook the Mount Pleasant restaurant Red Drum in favor of the choicer, more stylish picks downtown. That's their loss. Chef Berryhill leans on his Texas roots to formulate a South-by-Southwest approach, cooking quail, double-cut pork chops, venison sausage, New York strips, and rib-eye steaks on a wood-burning grill he calls "The Beast." Also sample savory beef empanadas or large "fork and knife" tacos from the bar, and head out to the outdoor patio for a beer or beverage. The nightlife here is lively. $ *Average main: $25* ✉ *803 Coleman Blvd., Mount Pleasant* ☎ *843/849–0313.*

$$ 🍴 **SeeWee Restaurant.** *Southern.* A throwback to the 1950s (or earlier), this spot was once a general store. It's some 20 minutes from downtown, but worth the trip for this Southern-style flashback. You pull open the screen door, and the shelves are still lined with canned goods, with a few tables for four. Outdoors on the screened porch is more seating, and that is also where the bands play (really good blues, bluegrass, and so on) come Saturday night in warm weather. The veteran waitresses will call you "hon" and caringly recommend their favorites, a lot of which are Southern-fried: pickles, green tomatoes, chicken, oysters, and fresh local shrimp. Look on the blackboard to find the more contemporary, less caloric (and more expensive) dishes. For breakfast or lunch, opt for the lovely traditional shrimp and grits. $ *Average main: $18* ✉ *4808 Hwy. 17 N, Awendaw* ☎ *843/928–3609* 🕒 *No dinner Sun.*

★ $$$ **Fodor's Choice** 🍴 **The Wreck of the Richard & Charlene.** *Seafood.* At first glance the name appears to refer to the waterfront restaurant's look, topped off with a shabby, screened-in porch. (In actuality, the *Richard and Charlene* was a trawler that slammed into the building during a hurricane in 1989.) But looks aren't the thing here—it's all about the food. Located in the old village of Mount Pleasant, the kitchen serves up Southern tradition on a plate: boiled peanuts, fried shrimp, and stone-crab claws. The best option is the most expensive: the mixed-seafood platter with fried flounder, shrimp, oysters, and scallops. Know that it closes by 8:30 Tuesday through Thursday, and at 9:15 on Friday and Saturday night. [$] *Average main: $22* ✉ *106 Haddrell St., Mount Pleasant* ☎ *843/884–0052* 🌐 *www.wreckrc.com* ✍ *Reservations not accepted* 💳 *No credit cards* 🕓 *Closed Sun. and Mon. No lunch.*

GREATER CHARLESTON

$$ 🍴 **Bowen's Island.** *Seafood.* This landmark seafood shack has survived hurricanes, fires, and the onslaught of trendy restaurants hitting downtown. Littered with oyster shells and graffiti, the funky spot serves dinner in an enclosed dock house, on the covered deck, and inside the recently renovated main building. The menu is the constant: big ol' shrimp, fried or boiled; shrimp and grits; Frogmore stew; hush puppies; and the biggie—all the steamed oysters you can eat for about $20. At this "fish camp," you might be entertained by musician Smokin' Weiner or Juke Joint Johnny. It's on an island just before Folly Beach, off Folly Road, about 15 minutes from downtown; there's a big sign. Go down the dirt road until you see water. [$] *Average main: $16* ✉ *1871 Bowen's Island Rd., James Island* ☎ *843/270–7050* 🌐 *www.bowensislandrestaurant.com* 💳 *No credit cards* 🕓 *No lunch. No dinner Sun. and Mon.*

$ 🍴 **Extra Virgin Oven (EVO).** *Pizza.* Make way to the Park Circle neighborhood of North Charleston for the area's top pizzeria, which doles out Neapolitan-style pies with super-thin and crunchy crusts. The Food Network chose this restaurant's pistachio pesto pie—containing goat, mozzarella, and Parmesan cheese on a pesto base whipped up with olive oil, salt, and pistachios—as the state's best slice. As for the locals, they tend to go for the pork trifecta pizza, a meat-tastic dish made with house-made sweet sausages, pepperoni, and smoked bacon. EVO also relies on local and regional purveyors for produce like grape and heirloom tomatoes and lettuce. [$] *Average main: $12* ✉ *1075 E. Montague Ave., North Charleston* ☎ *843/225–1796* 🌐 *www.evopizza.com* 🕓 *Closed Mon. No lunch Sat.*

$ 🍴 **Fiery Ron's Home Team BBQ.** *Southern.* Home Team, as the bar and restaurant is called, has swiftly earned the endorsement of even the old-school barbecue set (the restaurant's newfangled pork tacos notwithstanding). And they've done so with time-honored adherence to the oft-preferred technique of low-and-slow grilling, producing St. Louis–style ribs, and traditional smoked pork and chicken. Dress up your meal with three table-side sauces, including vinegar flavored, tomato tinged, and a mustard-based concoction, befitting South Carolina's German heritage. Side offerings are a good measuring stick for any barbecue joint, and Home Team delivers with mashed potatoes, mac 'n' cheese, collards, red rice, baked beans, Brunswick stew, poppy-seed slaw, and potato salad. A second location is on Sullivan's Island at 2209 Middle Street. $ *Average main: $8* ✉ *1205 Ashley River Rd., West Ashley* ☎ *843/225–7427* 🌐 *www.hometeambbq.com* ✉ *2209 Middle St., Sullivan's Island* ☎ *843/883–3131.*

$ 🍴 **The Glass Onion.** *Southern.* Established by a trio of New Orleans ex-pats, the Glass Onion fashions a taut bond between Charleston and its sister city, dishing up *beaucoup* seasonable, Southern eats. Take a peek at the menu: deviled eggs, overstuffed pimiento-cheese sandwiches, meat loaf, and fried catfish po'boys, and sweets like bread pudding with whiskey sauce. Yep, it's decidedly Southern, and decidedly dreamy. The Saturday brunch (10–3) is a must, with fluffy buttermilk biscuits and gravy, and pork tamales, but get there early, as they often sell out. The meals are set on sheets of brown paper that drape the restaurant's wooden tabletops, another clever touch. $ *Average main: $12* ✉ *1219 Savannah Hwy., Johns Island* ☎ *843/225–1717* 🌐 *www.ilovetheglassonion.com.*

$$ ★ 🍴 **Heart Woodfire Kitchen.** *American.* Over on James Island, Heart fires up grilled skewers, flatbreads, four-cheese pastas, and roasted vegetables aboard its large open-flame rotisserie grill and wood-fired oven. Housed inside a remodeled burrito joint, the restaurant's best feature is its outdoor patio. The pricing—cocktails included—checks in at a reduced rate compared with the rest of downtown, allowing a stylish but affordable night out. Heart's heavenly cheeseburger, the roll baked in-house, remains one of the best around. The sides, too, are considerably tasty and seasonal, including kale, apple-celery root, grits, and creamed mustard greens. $ *Average main: $15* ✉ *1622 Highland Ave., James Island* ☎ *843/718–1539* 🌐 *www.heartkitchenji.com.*

$ 🐤 🍴 **Jack's Cosmic Dogs.** *American.* Searching for a good hot dog? Jack's Cosmic has traversed the outer reaches of space to procure its Galactic, Krypto, Orbit City, and Neutron varieties. They're otherworldly excellent, with blue-cheese slaw, spicy mustard, sauerkraut, zippy onion relish, and Jack's own sweet-potato mustard, all swaddled in Pepperidge Farms split-top buns. Akin to a diner, Jack's serves milk shakes and sundaes, real custard soft-serve ice cream, draft root beer, and hand-cut fries. Kids love it here. It's the perfect intersection of the '50s—the 1950s and 2050s. Two other Jack's locations are on Johns Island at 817 St. Andrews Boulevard and James Island at 1531 Folly Road. [$] *Average main: $5* ✉ *2805 N. Hwy 17, Mount Pleasant* ☎ *843/225–1817* 🌐 *www.jackscosmicdogs.com* ✉ *1531 Folly Rd., James Island* ☎ *843/884–7677.*

🍴 **JB's Smokeshack.** *Southern.* When you come to the sign of the pig (not to mention other rudimentary signs stuck in the ground like "Catfish"), turn in for one of the area's best barbecue joints. At this funky find, you will see evidence of the diverse crowd, beat-up pickup trucks to new BMWs—the latter often driven by guests at nearby Kiawah Island. (JB's will deliver out there for $35.) Most people have the buffet, which consists of barbecue pork, apple-wood-smoked chicken, and all of the Southern veggies—usually including okra gumbo, butter beans, and coleslaw—plus desserts like banana pudding; it's all for one (very) low price. Barbecue connoisseurs know that JB's takes the big prizes at the competitions and that the ribs and the Angus beef brisket are top-shelf. To further flavor the smoky meats, sauces are served on the side. Just come early, because dinner is over by 8:30. [$] *Average main: $9* ✉ *3406 Maybank Hwy., Johns Island* ☎ *843/577–0426* 🌐 *www.jbssmokeshack.com* 🕒 *Closed Sun.–Tues.*

★ **Fodor'sChoice** 🍴 **Perfectly Frank's.** *Hot Dog.* Former Summerville High quarterback Perry Cuda and ex-Atlanticville chef Billy Condon make a dynamic duo at Perfectly Frank's. As owner/operators of this hot dog eatery, the two serve up a catalog of famous franks and other fun creations, and fame has followed. The Food Network's Guy Fieri stopped by in recent months, sampling several items for a segment on his television show. Among the choice offerings: the house-ground bison Sloppy Joe with chorizo sausage, Guinness-battered onion rings, fish tacos, sea salt and vinegar fries, and crunchy, vinegary "icebox" pickles. But best, the menu lists 35 hot dogs, the ingredients ranging from fried spinach, bacon, and crispy onions to black-peppered bacon and bleu cheese. [$] *Average main: $5* ✉ *118 N. Main St., Johns Island* ☎ *843/871–9730.*

$

$ 🍴 **Poe's Tavern.** *American.* Sullivan's Island has played host to history, accommodating an important battle of the American Revolution and, in the late 1820s, a certain author named Edgar Allan Poe. The writer enlisted in the army and wound up at Fort Moultrie, situated at the western end of the island. His stint inspired "The Gold Bug," a short story about a magical beetle, and then much later, Poe's Tavern. The bar and restaurant is beloved among visitors and residents for its fish tacos and gourmet burgers, all named after Poe stories. To wit: the Tell-Tale Heart, containing fried eggs, apple-wood bacon, and cheddar cheese; the Amontillado, with guacamole, jalapeño jack cheese, *pico de gallo,* and chipotle sour cream; and naturally, the Gold Bug Plus, done up in a variety of cheeses. [$] *Average main: $8* ✉ *2210 Middle St., Sullivan's Island* ☎ *843/883–0083* 🌐 *www.poestavern.com.*

★ Fodor's Choice 🍴 **Sesame Burgers & Beer.** *American.* Sesame's
$ secret? The burger-and-beer joint makes just about everything on the premises—from its house-ground burgers right down to the mustard, ketchup, and mayonnaise. Sample the South Carolina, topped with homemade pimiento cheese; the Southwestern, with guacamole and chipotle sour cream; or the Park Circle, with cheddar cheese, coleslaw, barbecue sauce, and tomatoes. Also garnering special mention: Blue's Corn on the cob, which is charred on the grill, then slathered in chipotle butter and Cotija cheese. Sesame's devotion to beer is strong, too, with selections running at least 30-deep. Two other locations can be found in North Charleston at 4726 Spruill Avenue and in Mount Pleasant at 675-E Johnny Dodds Boulevard. [$] *Average main: $8* ✉ *2070 Sam Rittenberg Blvd.* ☎ *843/766–7770.*

★ Fodor's Choice 🍴 **Tomato Shed Cafe.** *Southern.* Open only for lunch on weekdays and Saturdays, the Tomato Shed Cafe presents a banquet of locally raised delicacies. Owners and farmers Pete and Babs Ambrose maintain a 135-acre farm on Wadmalaw Island, sourcing grounds for the restaurant. The menu emphasizes seasonal choices, allowing for fresh butter beans, cabbage, collards, cucumber salad, and rutabaga casserole. These veggies sit well with the Tomato Shed's other offerings, such as peel-and-eat shrimp from local waters, barbecue, crab cakes, and roast pork. Be sure to grab a bag of boiled peanuts on your way out. [$] *Average main: $10* ✉ *842 Main Rd., Johns Island* ☎ *843/599–9999* 🌐 *www.stonofarmmarket.com/tomatoshedcafe.html* ⏲ *Closed Sun. No dinner.*

★ Fodor's Choice 🍴 **Voodooo Tiki Bar & Lounge.** *Eclectic.* Pop (cul-
$ ture) quiz: Who would you rather share a mai tai with—Bruce Lee, Elvis, or Wile E. Coyote? At Voodoo, no choice is needed. All three are set in velvet portraits and framed in the dining room, directly opposite the portholes and gold curtains. The decor helps doll up this fantastical tiki hut and lounge, situated in Charleston's Avondale neighborhood, west of the Ashley River. Of course, the Pu Pu

Platter—lobster corndogs, teriyaki Spam kabobs, cheeseburger spring rolls, et al—adds a bit of Polynesian flair. Try an order of tacos: flavors range from bacon cheeseburger to BBQ duck, Baja shrimp, and cashew-and-*panko*-encrusted tuna, and they're offered for half price on Sunday. [$] *Average main: $8* ✉ *15 Magnolia Rd., West Ashley* ☎ *843/769–0228* 🌐 *www.voodootikibar.com.*

Where to Stay in Charleston

WORD OF MOUTH

"We loved our room at the Mills House. It looked down on a little court-yard and over the pool, but more, it looked out over rooftops to the stee-ple of St. Michael's Church, [whose] steeple, along with the bells, figured so prominently in the [John] Jakes book that I felt I knew it."

—Bo2642

By Anna
Evans

Charleston has gained a reputation, both nationally and internationally, not only as one of the most historic and beautiful cities in the country but also as one that offers superior accommodations. It is a city known for its lovingly restored mansions that have been converted into atmospheric bed-and-breakfasts, as well as deluxe inns, all found in the residential blocks of the Historic District. Upscale, world-class hotels are in the heart of downtown as are boutique hotels that provide a one-of-a-kind experience. Most are within walking distance of the shops, restaurants, and museums housed within the nearly 800-acre district.

Chain hotels pepper the busy, car-trafficked areas (like Meeting Street). In addition, there are chain properties in the nearby areas of West Ashley, Mount Pleasant, and North Charleston, where you'll find plenty of Holiday Inns, Hampton Inns, Marriott Courtyards, and La Quinta Inns. Mount Pleasant is considered the most upscale suburb; North Charleston is the least, but if you need to be close to the airport, are participating in events in its Coliseum, or aim to shop the outlet malls there, it is a practical, less expensive alternative.

Overall, Charleston is a lifetime memory, and to know it is to love it. The city's scorecard for repeat visitors is phenomenal. Now Charleston is a port of embarkation for cruise ships, and most cruisers wisely plan on a pre- or post-cruise stay. The premier wedding and honeymoon destination also draws many couples back for their anniversaries.

ResortQuest. For condo and house rentals on Kiawah Island or Seabrook Island, call the Kiawah Island branch of ResortQuest. ⊠ *2 Beachwalker Dr., Kiawah Island* ☎ *800/544–8222* ⊕ *www.resortquestcharleston.com.*

ResortQuest. For rentals on Isle of Palms, Sullivan's Island, or Wild Dunes Resort, call the Isle of Palms branch of ResortQuest. ⊠ *1400 Palm Blvd.* ☎ *800/247–5050* ⊕ *www. resortquestcharleston.com.*

BED-AND-BREAKFAST AGENCIES

Historic Charleston Bed & Breakfast. Rent a carriage house behind a private home in downtown's Historic District through this reservation service. Handsomely furnished, these properties can be less expensive than commercial operations. Each one has a private entrance and is required to offer free parking. ☎ *800/743–3583* ⊕ *www.historic-charlestonbedandbreakfast.com.*

PRICES

Charleston's downtown lodgings have three seasons: high season (March–May and September–November), mid-season (June–August), and low season (late November–February). Prices drop significantly during the short low season, except during holidays and special events. High season is summer at the island resorts; rates drop for weekly stays and during the off-season. Although prices have gone up at the B&Bs, don't forget that a good breakfast for two is generally included, as well as an evening reception, which can take the place of happy hour and save on your bar bill. You should factor in, however, the cost of downtown parking; if a hotel offers free parking, that is a huge plus. In the areas "over the bridges," parking is generally free. Depending on when you arrive—such as a Saturday night, staying Sunday—you can try to find on-street metered parking, as there is no charge after 6 pm and all day Sunday.

■ TIP→ If you're on a budget, consider lodgings outside the city limits, which tend to be less expensive. Also try booking online, where you can often find good deals and packages. A longer stay sometimes translates to a better per-night price.

LODGING REVIEWS

Listed alphabetically within neighborhoods. The following reviews have been condensed for this book. Please go to Fodors.com for full reviews of each property.

DOWNTOWN CHARLESTON

NORTH OF BROAD

$$ 🏨 **1837 Bed & Breakfast.** *B&B/Inn.* A hospitable staff helps give you a sense of what it would be like to live in one of Charleston's grand old homes. **Pros:** a very good concierge will help you plan your days; a nice piazza where guests can relax after touring the town. **Cons:** cell reception not great in the three carriage-house rooms because of the brick walls; there are only seven small parking spaces on-site, with two additional spots at a private lot five houses down. [$] *Rooms from: $175* ✉ *126 Wentworth St., Market area* ☎ *843/723–7166, 877/723–1837* 🌐 *www.1837bb.com* 🛏 *8 rooms, 1 suite* 🍴 *Breakfast.*

$$$ 🏨 **Andrew Pinckney Inn.** *B&B/Inn.* Nestled in the heart of Charleston, this West Indies–inspired inn offers charming rooms as well as two-story town-house suites that

CLOSE UP

Best Bets for Charleston Lodging

Fodor's offers a selective listing of high-quality lodging experiences in every price range, from the city's best budget beds to its most sophisticated luxury hotels. Here, we've compiled our top recommendations by price and experience. The very best properties—those that provide a particularly remarkable experience in their price range—are designated in the listings with the Fodor's Choice symbol.

Fodor's Choice: Ansonborough Inn, Charleston Place, Kiawah Island Golf Resort, Market Pavilion Hotel, Mills House, Planters Inn, Restoration on King, Wentworth Mansion, Wild Dunes Resort

Best Budget Stay: Aloft Charleston Airport & Convention Center, Old Village Post House

Celebrity Retreat: Charleston Place, Market Pavilion Hotel

Best Beds: Restoration on King, Wentworth Mansion

Great Concierge: Courtyard by Marriott Charleston Historic District, Francis Marion Hotel, Mills House

Best Hotel Bars: Charleston Place, Market Pavilion Hotel, Vendue Inn

Best Gym: Charleston Place, The Sanctuary at Kiawah Island (at Kiawah Island Golf Resort)

Best Beaches: Kiawah Island Golf Resort, Wild Dunes Resort

Best for Kids: DoubleTree by Hilton Hotel & Suites Charleston–Historic District, Wild Dunes

Resort, Charleston Harbor Resort & Marina

Best for Romance: John Rutledge House Inn, Wentworth Mansion

Best B&Bs: The Governor's House Inn, John Rutledge House Inn

Best Grand Dame Hotels: Francis Marion Hotel, Wentworth Mansion

Best Pools: Charleston Place, Market Pavilion Hotel

Best Service: Charleston Place, Planters Inn

Business Travel: Charleston Place, HarbourView Inn

Best Views: HarbourView Inn, Two Meeting Street Inn

Pet-Friendly: Charleston Place, Indigo Inn

Hipster Hotels: Aloft Charleston Airport & Convention Center, Restoration on King

Best Interior Design: Restoration on King, The Sanctuary at Kiawah Island (at Kiawah Island Golf Resort)

Remarkable Architecture: Wentworth Mansion, William Aiken House Cottage and Lowndes Grove

Best Location: Charleston Place, Francis Marion Hotel

Best for Jogging Buffs: Charleston Marriot, HarbourView Inn

Best-Kept Secret: Restoration on King, William Aiken House Cottage and Lowndes Grove

sleep four. **Pros:** the town houses are ideal for longer stays; afternoon gourmet tea and coffee service with fresh-baked cookies; iPod docks in each room. **Cons:** elevator accesses regular rooms only, not town houses; near the horse stables, which can smell; can tend toward the loud side due to the bustling neighborhood. [$] *Rooms from: $229* ✉ *40 Pinckney St., Market area* ☎ *843/937–8800, 800/505–8983* 🌐 *www.andrewpinckneyinn.com* ⇆ *37 rooms, 3 town houses, 1 suite* 🍴 *Breakfast.*

★ $$ Fodor'sChoice 🏨 **Ansonborough Inn.** *B&B/Inn.* At this boutique hotel boasting a number of large, comfortable suites, you can indulge in evening wine and cheese on the rooftop terrace while enjoying views of the city and Cooper River. **Pros:** great pub downstairs; large, 24-hour upscale supermarket with Charleston products across the street; easy walking distance to the Market. **Cons:** not that close to King Street shops; street noise can be a problem for ground-floor rooms [$] *Rooms from: $169* ✉ *21 Hasell St., Market area* ☎ *843/723–1655, 800/522–2073* 🌐 *www.ansonboroughinn.com* ⇆ *45 suites* 🍴 *Breakfast.*

★ $$$$ Fodor'sChoice 🏨 **Charleston Place.** *Hotel.* Even casual passersby enjoy gazing up at the immense handblown Murano glass chandelier in the hotel's open lobby, clicking across the Italian marble floors, admiring the antiques from Sotheby's, and browsing the gallery of upscale shops that completes the ground-floor offerings of this hotel with deluxe day spa. **Pros:** three fantastic restaurants; on the best shopping street in the Historic District; pet-friendly. **Cons:** rooms aren't as big as one would expect for the price; much of the business is conference groups in shoulder seasons; built in 1986, it lacks the charm of area historic properties. [$] *Rooms from: $375* ✉ *205 Meeting St., Market area* ☎ *843/722–4900, 888/635–2350* 🌐 *www.charlestonplace.com* ⇆ *435 rooms, 48 suites* 🍴 *No meals.*

$$ 🏨 **Courtyard by Marriott Charleston Historic District.** *Hotel.* Step off the historic streets of Charleston into the high-tech, modern lobby of this hotel that opened in 2011 after a down-to-the-studs renovation. **Pros:** concierge Kevin McQuade gets rave reviews for his excellent recommendations; families will be right at home in the suites with comfortable seating and kitchenettes; bar service is available at the pool. **Cons:** in many of the rooms, views are obstructed by other buildings; breakfast not included; at the corner of a very busy intersection. [$] *Rooms from: $159* ✉ *125 Calhoun St., Upper King* ☎ *843/805–7900* 🌐 *www.marriott.com* ⇆ *168 rooms, 8 suites* 🍴 *No meals.*

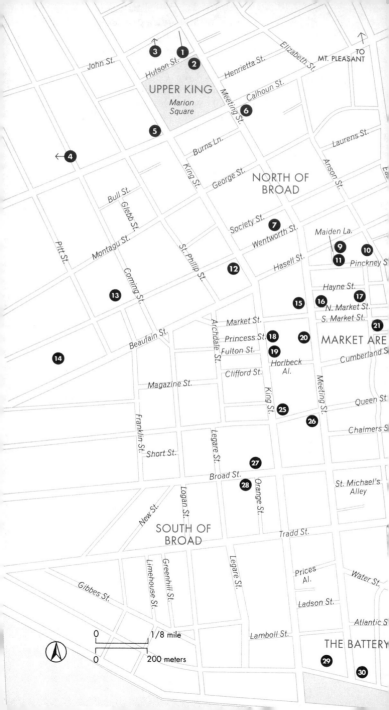

Where to Stay in Downtown Charleston

1837 Bed and Breakfast, **13**

1843 Battery Carriage House Inn, **29**

Andrew Pinckney Inn, **10**

Ansonborough Inn, **8**

Charleston Place, **15**

Courtyard by Marriott Charleston Historic District, **6**

DoubleTree by Hilton Hotel & Suites—Charleston Historic District, **17**

The Elliott House Inn, **25**

Embassy Suites Historic Charleston, **2**

Francis Marion Hotel, **5**

French Quarter Inn, **21**

Fulton Lane Inn, **18**

The Governor's House Inn, **28**

Hampton Inn–Historic District, **1**

HarbourView Inn, **23**

Indigo Inn, **11**

Jasmine House Inn, **9**

John Rutledge House Inn, **27**

Kings Courtyard Inn, **19**

Lowndes Grove, **4**

Market Pavilion Hotel, **22**

Meeting Street Inn, **20**

Mills House, **26**

Planters Inn, **16**

Renaissance Charleston Historic District Hotel, **7**

Restoration on King, **12**

Two Meeting Street Inn, **30**

Vendue Inn, **24**

Wentworth Mansion, **14**

William Aiken House Cottage , **3**

$$$ **DoubleTree by Hilton Hotel & Suites Charleston–Historic District.** *Hotel.* Housed in a onetime bank with a restored entrance portico from 1874, this property has clean, spacious suites with nice touches like antique reproductions and canopy beds. **Pros:** in the Market; it's an easy walk to King Street shopping and a charming one to the South of Broad residential area. **Cons:** no breakfast; Internet is expensive; can be noisy because of the location. [$] *Rooms from: $209* ✉ *181 Church St., Market area* ☎ *843/577–2644* 🌐 *www.doubletree.com* 🛏 *47 rooms, 165 suites* 🍴 *No meals.*

$$$$ **The Elliott House Inn.** *B&B/Inn.* Listen to the chimes of St. Michael's Episcopal Church as you sip wine in the lovely courtyard of this inn, then retreat to a cozy room with period furniture, including canopied four-posters and Oriental carpets, or bubble away some social time in the whirlpool tub that can and often does hold a dozen people. **Pros:** the helpful staff is generous with recommendations and advice; free bikes and Wi-Fi; nightly wine-and-cheese reception. **Cons:** ground-floor, street-view rooms can be noisy; kids are allowed but there's only one bed in each room; the complimentary breakfast offerings are limited. [$] *Rooms from: $269* ✉ *78 Queen St., Market area* ☎ *843/518–6500* 🌐 *www.elliotthouseinn.com* 🛏 *25 rooms* 🍴 *Breakfast.*

$$ **Embassy Suites Historic Charleston.** *Hotel.* In this contemporary hotel, a courtyard where cadets once marched is now an atrium, complete with skylights, palm trees, and a fountain, and the restored brick walls of the breakfast room and some guest rooms contain original gun ports, reminders that the 1822 building was the Old Citadel. **Pros:** on Marion Square, where the Saturday farmers' market, Charleston Fashion Week, Wine & Food Festival, and more take place; close to Upper King's hip business and retail district; complimentary manager's reception nightly in the bar and lobby. **Cons:** the suites are chain-hotel standard, not handsome and atmospheric like the public spaces; some rooms have little or no natural light. [$] *Rooms from: $199* ✉ *337 Meeting St., Upper King* ☎ *843/723–6900, 800/362–2779* 🌐 *www.embassysuites.com* 🛏 *153 suites* 🍴 *Breakfast.*

$$ **Francis Marion Hotel.** *Hotel.* Wrought-iron railings, crown moldings, and decorative plasterwork speak of the elegance of 1924, when the Francis Marion was the largest hotel in the Carolinas, and in the guest rooms—many of which have views of Marion Square—bountiful throw pillows and billowy curtains add flair. **Pros:** architecturally and historically significant building; in the midst of the peninsula's best shopping, yet still near the College of Charleston; some

PROPERTY TYPES IN CHARLESTON

B&Bs: Bed-and-breakfasts conjure up the image of a mom 'n' pop operation with Mother at the stove flipping pancakes. In Charleston, the concept has been taken to a higher level; although they may be owned by a couple, most B&Bs also employ a small staff. Most are within the Historic District and often were former grand residences, such as the Governor's House Inn or the John Rutledge House Inn.

Inns. In this town, a fine line divides true inns from B&Bs. They are usually larger than B&Bs and often have more professional staff, including a concierge (as at the Planters Inn). The breakfast and evening offerings are often a step above those of B&Bs, and they may even have a restaurant, as does the Wentworth Mansion.

Boutique Hotels: Though small by international hotel standards, Charleston's boutique hotels offer a pampering staff in a small setting. Those who stay here can experience the good life by day and at night slumber in a sumptuous bed dressed with Egyptian-cotton sheets and cashmere blankets. The Market Pavilion Hotel is per-

haps the city's best-known boutique hotel, but a newer kid on the boutique hotel block, Restoration on King, is quickly gaining notoriety and a solid fan base as well.

Full-Service Hotels: In a city known for atmospheric B&Bs, there are visitors who prefer the amenities and privacy of a large, world-class property (Charleston Place) or a well-known American chain hotel (such as the Charleston Marriott). And in a city where the temperatures trend high during the summer months, a hotel pool and vigorous air-conditioning may be worth trading for historic charm.

Island Resorts: The barrier islands surrounding the city of Charleston are the sites for three major, self-contained resorts: Kiawah Island Golf Resort, its neighbor Seabrook Island, and the Wild Dunes Resort on the Isle of Palms. All three have 18-hole golf courses, with Kiawah's being the most famous and most costly (the PGA Championship was played there in 2012), and each has excellent tennis facilities. Seabrook has no hotel accommodations (just villas and condos); Wild Dunes is the most family-friendly.

of the best city views. **Cons:** rooms are small, as is closet space; on a busy intersection. [$] *Rooms from: $169* ✉ *387 King St., Upper King* ☎ *843/722–0600, 877/756–2121* 🌐 *www.francismarioncharleston.com* 🛏 *217 rooms, 16 suites* 🍴 *No meals.*

SOMETHING EXTRA. Charleston isn't regularly voted among the most romantic cities in the country for nothing. When you book your room, ask about special packages. Extras that are often available include romantic carriage rides, dinners, interesting guided tours, and champagne or other goodies delivered to your room. This goes for most properties downtown.

$$ 🏨 **French Quarter Inn.** *B&B/Inn.* Guests appreciate the lavish seasonal breakfasts, the afternoon wine-and-cheese reception, and evening cookies and milk at this boutique hotel, where the first architectural detail you'll notice is the circular staircase with a wrought-iron banister embellished with iron leaves that were made by a local blacksmith. **Pros:** in the heart of the Market area yet is a quiet haven; excellent restaurant (Tristan) that takes up the ground floor; champagne at check-in. **Cons:** no pool or fitness area; being smack in the busy Market has its downside when it comes to noise, crowds, and tourists. [$] *Rooms from: $199* ✉ *166 Church St., Market area* ☎ *843/722–1900, 866/812–1900* 🌐 *www.fqicharleston.com* 🛏 *31 rooms, 19 suites* 🍴 *Breakfast.*

$$$ 🏨 **Fulton Lane Inn.** *B&B/Inn.* This inn is both lovely and quirky: its Victorian-dressed rooms (some with four-poster beds, fireplaces, and spa baths) are laid out in a bit of a floor-creaking maze, but it adds to the inn's individuality. **Pros:** location is tops; Room 317 is a cute spot off an alley; privately owned. **Cons:** what's character to one guest can be annoying to another; street noise does seep in; the free breakfast can be paltry. [$] *Rooms from: $219* ✉ *202 King St., Lower King Street* ☎ *843/720–2600* 🌐 *www.fultonlaneinn.com* 🛏 *45 rooms* 🍴 *Breakfast.*

$$ 🏨 **Hampton Inn–Historic District.** *Hotel.* Hardwood floors, a fireplace, and cozy new furnishings in the lobby of what was once an 1800s warehouse help elevate this chain hotel a bit above the rest. **Pros:** hot breakfast; located near the business and retail district of Upper King and near a couple of really good restaurants. **Cons:** a long walk to the Market area; rooms are smallish; no views. [$] *Rooms from: $199* ✉ *373 Meeting St., Upper King* ☎ *843/723–4000, 800/426–7866* 🌐 *www.hamptoninn.com* 🛏 *170 rooms* 🍴 *Breakfast.*

$$$$ 🏨 **HarbourView Inn.** *B&B/Inn.* This is the only hotel on the harbor, and if you ask for a room facing the harbor, you can gaze out onto the kid-friendly fountain and 8 acres of Waterfront Park. **Pros:** continental breakfast can be delivered to the room or the rooftop; service is notable. **Cons:** rooms are off long, modern halls; rooms are not particularly spacious. [$] *Rooms from: $279* ✉ *2 Vendue Range, Market area* ☎ *843/853–8439, 888/853–8439* 🌐 *www.harbourviewcharleston.com* 🛏 *52 rooms* 🍴 *Breakfast.*

$$ 🏨 **Indigo Inn.** *B&B/Inn.* Repeat guests are the norm thanks to the convenient setting and the particularly welcoming and helpful front desk staff at this smoky-teal, family-owned hotel in a former indigo warehouse. **Pros:** excellent location; pets allowed in some rooms; mini-bottles of liquor and good bottles of wine can be purchased from front desk. **Cons:** rooms are not large and some are dark; since the inn opened in 1981, the rooms are a little tired; parking is $12. [$] *Rooms from: $189* ✉ *1 Maiden La., Lower King* ☎ *843/577–5900* 🌐 *www.indigoinn.com* 🛏 *40 rooms* 🍴 *Breakfast.*

$$ 🏨 **Jasmine House Inn.** *B&B/Inn.* Walking down the quiet, tree-lined street and coming upon this glorious Greek-revival mansion—yellow with white columns—you simply want inside, and a stay here is like living in a grand Charleston home without the real-estate closing. **Pros:** complimentary beverages (hot and cold in the kitchen); evening wine-and-cheese spreads on the sideboard; several rooms have working fireplaces. **Cons:** property is well appointed but not swanky; children are not allowed. [$] *Rooms from: $199* ✉ *64 Hassell St., Market area* ☎ *843/577–5900* 🌐 *www.jasminehouseinn.com* 🛏 *8 rooms, 2 suites, 1 apartment* 🍴 *Breakfast.*

$$$ 🏨 **Kings Courtyard Inn.** *B&B/Inn.* The two cozy courtyards at this centrally located circa-1853 inn invite guests—from couples to families—to take their continental breakfast, afternoon sherry, or evening wine and cheese in the open air. **Pros:** ideal location for walking to shops and restaurants; pets are allowed in some rooms; double-paned windows muffle street noise. **Cons:** walls are thin; guests from sister property Fulton Lane Inn share in the evening wine-and-cheese receptions, creating a sometimes-bustling atmosphere. [$] *Rooms from: $219* ✉ *198 King St., Lower King Street* ☎ *800/845–6119* 🌐 *www.kingscourtyardinn.com* 🛏 *37 rooms, 4 suites* 🍴 *Breakfast.*

★ $$$$ **Fodor'sChoice** 🏨 **Market Pavilion Hotel.** *Hotel.* The melee of one of the busiest corners in the city vanishes as soon as the uniformed bellman opens the lobby door to reveal dark, wood-paneled walls, antique furniture, and chandeliers hung from high ceilings; it resembles a European grand hotel from the 19th century, and you feel like you're visiting royalty. **Pros:** opulent furnishings; architecturally impressive, especially the tray ceilings; conveniently located for everything. **Cons:** the gym is small; those preferring a minimalist or understated decor may find the interior over the top and perhaps a touch nouveau riche. [$] *Rooms from: $279* ✉ *225 E. Bay St., Market area* ☎ *843/723–0500, 877/440–2250* 🌐 *www.marketpavilion.com* 🛏 *61 rooms, 9 suites* 🍴 *Breakfast.*

$$$ 🏨 **Meeting Street Inn.** *B&B/Inn.* Rooms in this 1870s stucco house with porches on the second, third, and fourth floors overlook a lovely courtyard with fountains and a garden as well as a large, heated spa tub. **Pros:** all rooms have free Wi-Fi, and some of the more expensive rooms have desks and piazza access; bathrooms sport nice marble fixtures. **Cons:** rooms have 19th-century-style reproductions but could use some updated decor; parking in a nearby lot is $12 a day. [$] *Rooms from: $239* ✉ *173 Meeting St., Market area* ☎ *843/723–1882, 800/842–8022* 🌐 *www.meetingstreetinn.com* 🛏 *56 rooms* 🍴 *Breakfast.*

★ **$$** **Fodor's Choice** 🏨 **Mills House.** *Hotel.* A favorite local landmark, from which several historic tours depart, the Mills House is the reconstruction of an 1853 hotel where Robert E. **Pros:** convenient to business district, Historic District, and art galleries; a popular Sunday brunch spot; a concierge desk so well regarded that locals have long called on the Mills House for neighborly assistance and advice. **Cons:** rooms are rather small, which is typical of hotels of this time period; it's on a busy street. [$] *Rooms from: $179* ✉ *115 Meeting St., Market area* ☎ *843/577–2400, 800/874–9600* 🌐 *www.millshouse.com* 🛏 *199 rooms, 16 suites* 🍴 *No meals.*

★ **$$$$** **Fodor's Choice** 🏨 **Planters Inn.** *B&B/Inn.* Part of the Relais & Châteaux group, this boutique property with well-appointed and beautifully maintained rooms is a stately sanctuary amid the bustle of Charleston's Market. **Pros:** double-pane and interior shuttered windows render the rooms soundproof; the same front-desk people take your initial reservation and know your name upon arrival; exceptional full breakfast (included only as part of a package). **Cons:** no pool; no fitness center. [$] *Rooms from: $399* ✉ *112 N. Market St., Market area* ☎ *843/722–2345, 800/845–7082* 🌐 *www.plantersinn.com* 🛏 *64 rooms, 2 penthouse king suites, 6 governor suites* 🍴 *No meals.*

$$$$ **Renaissance Charleston Historic District Hotel.** *Hotel.* If you want to park your car and enjoy the rest of your vacation exploring Charleston by foot, this upscale property operated by the Marriott chain is the place for you. **Pros:** the rooms were renovated in 2008, as was the lobby; located in the King Street shopping district; friendly and helpful staff. **Cons:** rooms have the feel of a chain hotel and no mini-fridges; pool is small. [$] *Rooms from: $299* ✉ *68 Wentworth St., Ansonborough* ☎ *843/534–0300* 🌐 *www.renaissancecharlestonhotel.com* ↩ *163 rooms, 3 suites* 🍴 *No meals.*

★ **Fodor's Choice** **Restoration on King.** *Hotel.* Charleston architect Neil Stevenson is known for his modern buildings and
$$$$ streamlined interiors, so it makes sense that the luxury boutique hotel he designed in 2010 would be swank and suave to the hilt, even featuring a rooftop terrace with sleek sofas and prime views. **Pros:** wine and water when you arrive is a nice touch, as is the stock-the-refrigerator option; room service comes via neighboring restaurants; iHome stations and Blu-ray players help technophiles feel at home; the location is ideal for those who want to explore all aspects of the city. **Cons:** no gym on the premises, but there are complimentary passes to nearby workout facilities within easy walking distance; prices are steep; no on-site restaurant. [$] *Rooms from: $299* ✉ *75 Wentworth St., Market area* ☎ *877/221–7202* 🌐 *www.restorationonking.com* ↩ *16 suites* 🍴 *Breakfast.*

DOGGIE DAY CARE. Zen Dog. If you have brought your dog along but don't want to leave him in your room all day, call Zen Dog, run by Pet Vet Animal Hospital. Services are $20 a day. ✉ ***307 Mill St., Mount Pleasant*** ☎ ***843/884–7387.***

$$$$ **Vendue Inn.** *B&B/Inn.* Two 19th-century warehouses have been transformed into an inn with nooks and crannies filled with antiques. **Pros:** soundproofing masks street noise; pets allowed for a $50 fee; the Library Restaurant on the first floor is well regarded. **Cons:** popular local hangouts nearby can be noisy; $250 fine for smoking in rooms; complimentary breakfast is only for those who book directly through the inn. [$] *Rooms from: $355* ✉ *19 Vendue Range, Market area* ☎ *843/577–7970, 800/845–7900* 🌐 *www.vendueinn.com* ↩ *31 rooms, 35 suites* 🍴 *Breakfast.*

★ **Fodor's Choice** **Wentworth Mansion.** *B&B/Inn.* Guests at the
$$$$ most grand inn in town admire the Second Empire antiques and reproductions, the rich fabrics, inset wood paneling,

and original stained-glass windows, as well as the views from the roofop cupola. **Pros:** luxury bedding, including custom-made mattresses, down pillows, and Italian linens; each room has a whirlpool tub and iPod docking station. **Cons:** Second Empire style can strike some people as forbidding; the building has some of the woes of an old building, including loudly creaking staircases; location deems pedicab, bike, or car advisable to reach tourist areas. Ⓢ *Rooms from: $379* ✉ *149 Wentworth St., College of Charleston Campus* ☎ *888/466–1886* ⊕ *www.wentworthmansion.com* ⌧ *21 rooms* ⦿ *Breakfast.*

$$ ⊡ **William Aiken House Cottage and Lowndes Grove.** *Rental.* Two of the most picturesque, historic, and popular wedding sites in Charleston (operated by the same company) also have overnight rooms and suites on-site. **Pros:** both are true Charleston experiences in historic treasures; ideal for those who crave privacy. **Cons:** neither is for guests who want or need a lot of attention; you'll need a car if you opt for Lowndes Grove; there's no kitchen there. Ⓢ *Rooms from: $175* ✉ *William Aiken, 456 King St., Upper King* ✉ *Lowndes Grove, 266 St. Margaret St.* ☎ *843/853–1810* ⊕ *www.pphgcharleston.com* ⌧ *7 suites* ⦿ *No meals.*

SOUTH OF BROAD

$$$ ⊡ **1843 Battery Carriage House Inn.** *B&B/Inn.* Visitors can find out what it would be like to live on the Battery by booking a room in this home across the street from White Point Gardens. **Pros:** great location that is quiet and romantic; high level of service; each room is individually decorated. **Cons:** most rooms are small, modest, and on the dark ground floor; children staying here must be at least 12 years old; no full breakfast (light continental instead). Ⓢ *Rooms from: $229* ✉ *20 S. Battery, South of Broad* ☎ *843/727–3100* ⊕ *www.batterycarriagehouse.com* ⌧ *10 rooms, 1 suite.*

$$$$ ⊡ **The Governor's House Inn.** *B&B/Inn.* The stately archi-
★ tecture of this quintessential Charleston lodging radiates the grandeur, romance, and civility of the city's bountiful colonial era. **Pros:** you can take breakfast on the piazza, in the dining room, or have it delivered; pets are allowed in some rooms; free bicycles make exploring the centrally located area a breeze. **Cons:** older children are welcome in the former kitchen-house rooms, but the main house is not the appropriate environment; busy commercial and government street location. Ⓢ *Rooms from: $265* ✉ *117 Broad St., South of Broad* ☎ *843/720–2070, 800/720–9812* ⊕ *www. governorshouse.com* ⌧ *11 rooms* ⦿ *Breakfast.*

$$$$ **John Rutledge House Inn.** *B&B/Inn.* In 1791, George Washington visited this elegant, grand mansion, then residence of one of South Carolina's most influential politicians, John Rutledge, and now a National Historic Landmark with spacious accommodations within the main house. **Pros:** at night, when you "go home" and pour a sherry, it's like being a blue-blood Charlestonian; nice, quiet back courtyard; friendly staff. **Cons:** you can hear some street and kitchen noise in the first-floor rooms; the two carriage houses are not as grand as the main house. [$] *Rooms from: $279* ✉ *116 Broad St., South of Broad* ☎ *800/476–9741* 🌐 *www.johnrutledgehouseinn.com* *16 rooms, 3 suites* 🍴 *Breakfast.*
★

$$$ **Two Meeting Street Inn.** *B&B/Inn.* As pretty as a wedding cake, this 1892 Queen Anne–style mansion wears overhanging bays, colonnades, balustrades, and a turret; Tiffany-stained-glass windows, carved-oak paneling, and a crystal chandelier dress up the public spaces inside. **Pros:** free on-street parking; community refrigerator on each floor; ringside seat for a Battery view and horse-drawn carriages clipping by. **Cons:** no credit cards accepted; some rooms have thick walls and make Wi-Fi spotty; the decor is on the grandmotherly side. [$] *Rooms from: $225* ✉ *2 Meeting St., South of Broad* ☎ *843/723–7322* 🌐 *www.twomeetingstreet.com* *9 rooms* 💳 *No credit cards* 🍴 *Breakfast.*
★

MOUNT PLEASANT

$$ **Charleston Harbor Resort & Marina.** *Resort.* Mount Pleasant's finest hotel sits on Charleston Harbor, so you can gaze at the city's skyline, just a 10-minute water-taxi ride away from the marina. **Pros:** the most accessible hotel to downtown that's not in downtown (approximately 6 miles away); a "trolley" runs to the Market from 10 am to 10 pm daily; some rooms have fireplaces. **Cons:** no gym onsite (guests are offered complimentary use of an area gym 10 minutes away); the lobby and the restaurant are not memorable. [$] *Rooms from: $129* ✉ *20 Patriots Point Rd., Mount Pleasant* ☎ *843/856–0028, 888/856–0028* 🌐 *www.charlestonharborresort.com* *127 rooms, 6 suites.*

WORD OF MOUTH. **"I love, love, love Kiawah for family vacations, golfing, and bike rides on the beach. Top it all off with a nice trip into Charleston for some seafood or barbecue and you are in heaven." —BradleyK**

4

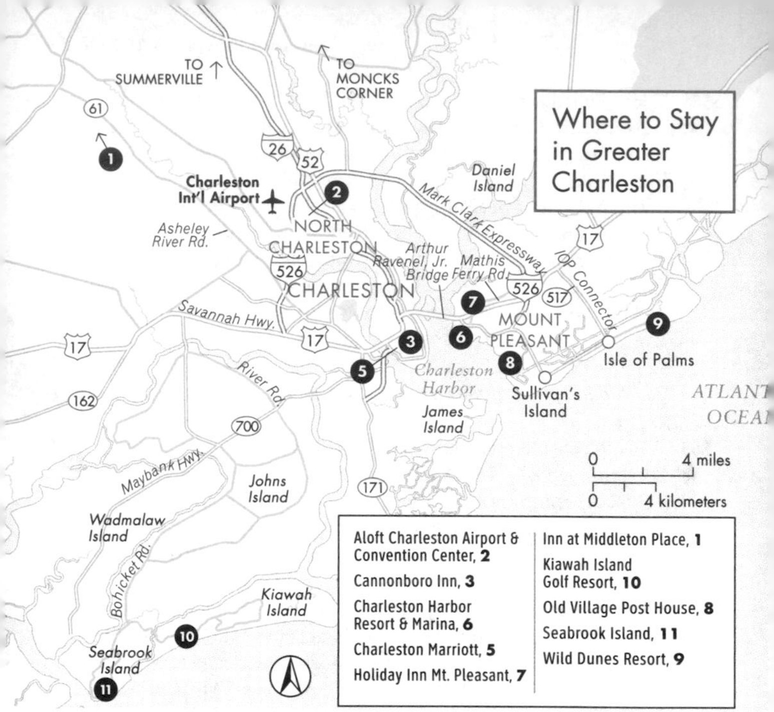
Where to Stay in Greater Charleston
TO SUMMERVILLE
TO MONCKS CORNER
61
26
52
17
526
517
162
700
171
Charleston Int'l Airport
Asheley River Rd.
NORTH CHARLESTON
CHARLESTON
Daniel Island
Mark Clark Expressway
IOP Connector
Arthur Ravenel, Jr. Bridge
Mathis Ferry Rd.
MOUNT PLEASANT
Savannah Hwy.
River Rd.
Charleston Harbor
James Island
Sullivan's Island
Isle of Palms
ATLANT
OCEA
Maybank Hwy.
Johns Island
Wadmalaw Island
Bohicket Rd.
Kiawah Island
Seabrook Island
0
4 miles
0
4 kilometers
Aloft Charleston Airport & Convention Center, 2
Cannonboro Inn, 3
Charleston Harbor Resort & Marina, 6
Charleston Marriott, 5
Holiday Inn Mt. Pleasant, 7
Inn at Middleton Place, 1
Kiawah Island Golf Resort, 10
Old Village Post House, 8
Seabrook Island, 11
Wild Dunes Resort, 9

$ 🏨 **Holiday Inn Mt. Pleasant.** *Hotel.* Just a five-minute drive over the scenic Arthur Ravenel Jr. Bridge to historic downtown Charleston, this is perfect for those who plan to explore the city for hours on end and are simply looking for a high-quality spot to lay their heads.**Pros:** some resort amenities, including a pool; for a small property, it has a good business center; some rooms have microwaves. **Cons:** not downtown; not a place with a historical atmosphere; a condo complex blocks the bridge view. [$] *Rooms from: $129* ✉ *250 Johnnie Dodds Blvd., Mount Pleasant* ☎ *843/884–6000* 🌐 *www.himtpleasant.com* 🔑 *158 rooms* 🍴 *No meals.*

$ 🏨 **Old Village Post House.** *B&B/Inn.* This white wooden building anchoring Mount Pleasant's Historic District on the Cooper River is three-in-one—an excellent restaurant, a neighborly tavern, and a cozy inn, the last of which is set at the top of a high staircase and has rooms with hardwood floors and reproduction furnishings that will remind you of Cape Cod. **Pros:** prices are as affordable as some chain motels on the highway; set on the "Main Street" of the most picturesque and walkable neighborhood in Mount Pleasant; close to Sullivan's Island and Isle of Palms. **Cons:** the inn shares some public spaces with the downstairs restaurant, detracting from privacy; some minor old building woes, including creaky wood floors; not a traditional hotel, so service can be quirky. [$] *Rooms from: $142* ✉ *101 Pitt St., Mount Pleasant* ☎ *843/388–8935* 🌐 *www.oldvillagepost house.com* ⇨ *6 rooms* 🍴 *Breakfast.*

ELSEWHERE IN AND AROUND CHARLESTON

$ 🏨 **Aloft Charleston Airport & Convention Center.** *Hotel.* Designed with the young, hip, and high-tech traveler in mind, this hotel is retro-meets-the-Jetsons. **Pros:** high concept design; convenient for airport and convention center; inexpensive. **Cons:** noise from planes taking off; small, somewhat cramped rooms; far from downtown. [$] *Rooms from: $139* ✉ *4875 Tanger Outlet Blvd., North Charleston* ☎ *843/566–7300* 🌐 *www.starwoodhotels.com/alofthotels* ⇨ *136 rooms.*

$$$ 🏨 **Cannonboro Inn.** *B&B/Inn.* At this B&B on the edge of the Historic District, you can expect a full breakfast served on a wide porch overlooking a garden, tea in the afternoon, and free use of bicycles. **Pros:** free off-street parking for each room; signature fudge, snacks, and wine at the afternoon reception; close to the hospitals (MUSC and Roper). **Cons:** not so convenient to the tourist area (approximately eight blocks away); refrigerator and phone are shared. [$] *Rooms from: $205* ✉ *184 Ashley Ave., Medical University of South Carolina* ☎ *843/723–8572, 800/235–8035* 🌐 *www.charleston-sc-inns.com* ⇨ *7 rooms, 1 suite* 🍴 *Breakfast.*

$$ 🏨 **Charleston Marriott.** *Hotel.* The sunset views from the balconies of this great river-view hotel are better as you go higher and especially good from the rooftop Aqua Terrace, where drinks and tapas are served. **Pros:** $6 shuttle to downtown until 10:30 pm; located near the Citadel, MUSC, hospitals, and marinas; great views of the Ashley River. **Cons:** not in the Historic District; Wi-Fi available, but for a fee; concierge floor does not have breakfast on weekends. [$] *Rooms from: $179* ✉ *170 Lockwood Dr., Medical University of South Carolina* ☎ *843/723–3000* 🌐 *www.marriott.com* ⇨ *333 rooms, 8 suites* 🍴 *No meals.*

$ 🏨 **Inn at Middleton Place.** *B&B/Inn.* Located on the banks of the Ashley River, this country inn offers a peaceful respite from the city—there are even shady hammocks outside for afternoon naps. **Pros:** beautiful setting; unique features; access to all the amenities of Middleton Place. **Cons:** rooms could use a little updating; lodging is separate from reception and breakfast areas, so some walking is required. [$] *Rooms from: $149* ✉ *4290 Ashley River Rd., West Ashley*

☎ *843/556–0500, 800/543–4774* 🌐 *www.theinnatmiddletonplace.com* 🛏 *46 rooms, 9 suites* 🍴 *Breakfast.*

★ $$$ **Fodor's Choice** 🏨 **Kiawah Island Golf Resort.** *Resort.* Choose from one- to four-bedroom villas, three- to eight-bedroom private homes, or the Sanctuary at Kiawah Island, an amazing 255-room luxury waterfront hotel and spa that is one of the most prestigious resorts in the country yet is still kid-friendly. **Pros:** the smaller condo-villas are still fairly affordable; the Ocean Room is an ideal venue for an anniversary or a proposal; the golf courses and tennis programs are ranked among the country's best. **Cons:** not all hotel rooms have a view of the ocean; it is pricey and a substantial drive from town. $ *Rooms from: $225* ✉ *1 Sanctuary Beach Dr., Kiawah Island* ☎ *843/768–2121, 800/654–2924* 🌐 *www.kiawahresort.com* 🛏 *242 rooms, 13 suites, 400 villas, 90 homes* 🍴 *No meals.*

$ 👶 🏨 **Seabrook Island.** *Resort.* About 350 fully equipped one- to six-bedroom villas, cottages, townhomes, and homes are available on Seabrook, one of the most private of the area's island resorts, on a physically beautiful, relatively unspoiled island. **Pros:** great safe haven for kids to play; it's the only place in the area you can ride horses on the beach; nearby Freshfields Village offers upscale shopping and restaurants. **Cons:** accommodations do not include any regular hotel rooms; a good ways (45-minute drive) from Charleston. $ *Rooms from: $140* ✉ *3772 Seabrook Island Rd., Seabrook Island* ☎ *800/247–5050* 🌐 *www.wyndhamvacationrentals.com* 🛏 *350 units* 🍴 *No meals.*

★ $$$$ **Fodor's Choice** 🏨 **Wild Dunes Resort.** *Resort.* Guests, who include many families in the summer, have a long list of recreational options—such as Tom Fazio golf courses and nationally ranked tennis programs—at this 1,600-acre island resort. **Pros:** golf courses and marina are appealing; free shuttle runs from 7 am to 11 pm to wherever you need to go within the complex. **Cons:** in peak summer season, kids dominate the pool areas and the boardwalk, as children's programs run predominantly in summer; a congested, high-density feel exists in all the main facilities. $ *Rooms from: $299* ✉ *4600 Palm Blvd., Isle of Palms* ☎ *843/886–6000, 888/845–8926* 🌐 *www.wilddunes.com* 🛏 *396 units, 93 rooms* 🍴 *No meals.*

Nightlife and the Arts in Charleston

WORD OF MOUTH

"If you want to walk to bars and restaurants you'll want to be in the (Historic District), the area of the peninsula south of Calhoun Street. The exception to that would be Upper King Street—lots of bars and restaurants with lots of young people."

—suewoo

By Rob
Young

For a midsize city, Charleston has a surprisingly varied and sophisticated arts scene, though the city really shines during its major annual arts festival, Spoleto Festival USA. Still, throughout the year, there are other opportunities to explore higher culture. Since Charleston is a college town, the College of Charleston also offers possibilities.

The nightlife scene is similarly comprehensive, with nocturnal venues for all ages and tastes. The town has a large fun quotient. If your image of Charleston is a proper, mannerly, highbred town, with men in seersucker suits and bow ties, think again. That may have been an image of Charlestonians in decades past—and light blue seersucker is still worn on summer nights—but that oldster can probably still out-dance his fraternity son and knock down his share of bourbon along the way. Although some of the nightlife can be rowdy and more youth oriented, there are options from jazz lounges to dance clubs. And here the nightlife begins at happy hour, which can start as early as 4 pm. Several bars and restaurants have incredible happy-hour deals, and a night of barhopping generally includes grazing on small plates. ■TIP→ **If you see long lines outside a place you can usually assume that drinks are inexpensive, and that the crowd is young.** Long lines can also mean that there is a popular band playing, like at the Music Farm.

THE ARTS

ANNUAL FESTIVALS AND EVENTS

Spoleto USA is only the beginning—there are dozens of festivals held throughout the city each year. Some focus on food and wine, whereas others are concerned with gardens and architecture. Charleston is one of the few American cities that can claim a distinctive regional cuisine.

BB&T Charleston Wine + Food Festival. In just a few years, the BB&T Charleston Wine + Food Festival has become a four-day, favored culinary playground for the nation's leading chefs (including several already from Charleston), food writers, and, of course, foodies. Held in late February and early March, events emphasize the Lowcountry's foodways and heritage, as well as restaurant dinners exclusive to the festival that pair Charleston-area chefs with national colleagues. ☎ *843/763–0280, 866/369–3378* ⊕ *charleston wineandfood.com.*

Spoleto Festival USA

Fodor'sChoice★ Spoleto Festival USA. For 17 glorious days in late May and early June, Charleston gets a dose of culture from the Spoleto Festival USA. This internationally acclaimed performing-arts festival features a mix of distinguished artists and emerging talent from around the world. Performances take place in magical settings, such as beneath a canopy of ancient oaks or inside a centuries-old cathedral.

Some 45 events—which cost between $10 (for balcony seats) and $130 (good orchestra seats), with most averaging between $25 and $50—include everything from improv to Shakespeare, from rap to chamber music, from ballet to salsa. A mix of formal concerts and casual performances is what Pulitzer Prize–winning composer Gian Carlo Menotti had in mind when, in 1977, he initiated the festival as a complement to his opera-heavy Italian festival. He chose Charleston because of its European look and because its residents love the arts—not to mention any cause for celebration. He wanted the festival to be a "fertile ground for the young" as well as a "dignified home for the masters." Mayor Joseph Riley has diligently worked to renew that Italian connection with the original mother festival in Spoleto, Italy (⊕ *www.festivaldispoleto.it*). This reaffirmation of sister-city partnership and the sharing of ideas has encouraged and increased tourism between the two cities for both festivals and beyond.

The finale is a must-do, particularly for the younger crowd. Staged outdoors at Middleton Place, the plantation house and lush landscaped gardens provide a dramatic backdrop. The inexpensive seating is unreserved and unlimited. The lawn is covered with blankets and chairs, and many cooks prepare lavish spreads. For decades the Spoleto Festival Orchestra has played a spirited concert of contemporary and classic pieces, followed by spectacular fireworks exploding over the Ashley River. Tradition was broken in 2010 when the Carolina Chocolate Drops, an African-American string band, performed. Because events sell out quickly, insiders say you should buy your Spoleto tickets several weeks in advance. (Tickets to midweek performances are a bit easier to secure.) Hotels definitely fill up quickly, so book a room at the same time and reserve your tables for the trendy downtown restaurants. ☎ *843/722-2764* ⊕ *www.spoletousa.org.*

5

Charleston Fashion Week. Produced by *Charleston Magazine*, the five-night festival in March toasts emerging designer and model talents with several competitions, runway shows, and exhibitions. Held beneath tents in Marion Square at the intersection of King and Calhoun streets, the festival has helped several designers launch their fashion careers. But even more impressive than the festival? Maybe the tony after-parties attended by the designers and models. ⊠ *Marion Square, King and Calhoun Sts., Upper King* ⊕ *www.charlestonmag.com/fashionweek.*

Fall Tours of Homes & Gardens. The Fall Tours of Homes & Gardens, sponsored by the Preservation Society of Charleston in September and October, provides an inside look at Charleston's private buildings and gardens. ⊠ *147 King St.* ☎ *843/722–4630* ⊕ *www.preservationsociety.org.*

Festival of Houses & Gardens. More than 100 private homes, gardens, and historic churches are open to the public for tours during the Festival of Houses & Gardens, held during March and April each year. There are also symphony galas in stately drawing rooms, plantation oyster roasts, and candlelight tours. ⊠ *40 E. Bay St.* ☎ *843/722–3405* ⊕ *www.historiccharleston.org.*

★ **MOJA Arts Festival.** During the last week of September and first week of October, this festival celebrates African heritage and Caribbean influences on African-American culture. It includes theater, dance, and music performances, art shows, films, lectures, and tours of the Historic District. ⊠ *180 Meeting St., Suite 200* ☎ *843/724–7305* ⊕ *www. mojafestival.com.*

Piccolo Spoleto. The spirited companion festival of Spoleto Festival USA showcases the best in local and regional talent from every artistic discipline. There are as many as 700 events—from jazz performances to puppet shows, military band concerts, and expansive art shows in Marion Square—from mid-May through early June. Many of the performances are free or inexpensive, and hundreds of these cultural experiences are kid-friendly. ⊠ *180 Meeting St.* ☎ *843/724–7305* ⊕ *www.piccolospoleto.org.*

Southeastern Wildlife Exposition. One of Charleston's biggest annual events, this celebration of nature takes place in mid-February, offering fine art by renowned wildlife artists, live animals, an oyster roast, and a gala. Across three days, the expo generally attracts more than 40,000 participants and more than 500 artists. ☎ *843/723–1748, 800/221–5273* ⊕ *www.sewe.com.*

CONCERTS

Charleston Symphony Orchestra. The Charleston Symphony Orchestra season runs from October through April, with pops series, chamber series, family-oriented series, and holiday concerts. This symphony is nationally and even internationally renowned, because it is also the Spoleto Festival Orchestra. Look for alternating venues, as the CSO's home court—Gaillard Municipal Auditorium—is undergoing renovations. ☎ *843/723–7528* ⊕ *www.charlestonsymphony.com.*

DANCE

Charleston Ballet Theatre. Performances of everything from classical to contemporary dance take place in a range of venues around town, including the North Charleston Performing Arts Center, the Sottile Theatre, and Charleston Music Hall. ✉ *217 Calhoun St., Upper King* ☎ *843/723–7334* ⊕ *www.charlestonballet.com.*

Robert Ivey Ballet Company. This semiprofessional company, which includes College of Charleston students, puts on a fall and spring program of jazz, classical, and modern dance at the Sottile Theater. ✉ *1910 Savannah Hwy.* ☎ *843/556–1343* ⊕ *www.robertiveyballet.net.*

FILM

Regal Palmetto Grande 16 Cinemas. This grand art-deco-style multiplex makes moviegoing fun in the traditional manner of enjoying popcorn and a soda in a comfortable stadium-style seat. ✉ *1319 Theater Dr., Mount Pleasant* ☎ *843/216–8696.*

THEATER

Footlight Players. With fun plays and musicals, this troupe offers affordable, quality, and original performances to the area. ✉ *20 Queen St., Market area* ☎ *843/722–4487* ⊕ *www.footlightplayers.net.*

VENUES

Charleston Music Hall. Bluegrass, blues, and country musicians step onto the historic stage of the Charleston Music Hall, especially for Piccolo Spoleto performances. It's within walking distance of several popular bars and restaurants. ⊠ *37 John St., Upper King* ☎ *843/853–2252* ⊕ *www.charles tonmusichall.com.*

North Charleston Performing Art Center. Dance, symphony, and theater productions are among those staged at the North Charleston Performing Art Center. In recent years, performers such as Hall & Oates, Edward Sharpe and the Magnetic Zeroes, and Greg Allman have taken the stage. ⊠ *5001 Coliseum Dr., North Charleston* ☎ *843/529–5050* ⊕ *www.northcharlestoncoliseumpac.com.*

Simons Center for the Arts. Performances by the College of Charleston's theater department and musical recitals are presented here during the school year. ⊠ *54 St. Phillips St., College of Charleston Campus* ☎ *843/953–5604* ⊕ *www.cofc.edu.*

NIGHTLIFE

You can find it all here, across the board, for Charleston loves a good party. The more mature crowd goes to the sophisticated spots, and there are many: piano bars, wine bars, lounges featuring jazz groups or a guitarist/vocalist, and cigar lounges. Rooftop bars are a particular Charleston tradition, and the city has several good ones. Many restaurants offer live entertainment on at least one weekend night, and these tend to cater to an older crowd. The Upper King area especially has grown in recent years, overtaking the Market area in terms of popularity and variety. ⚠ **A city ordinance mandates that bars must close by 2 am and that patrons must be out of the establishment and doors locked by that hour. Last call is usually 1:30.**

NORTH OF BROAD

LOWER KING

BARS AND PUBS

Bin 152. Husband-and-wife Patrick and Fanny Panella ply their guests with selections from more than 100 bottles of wine and 35 varieties of cheeses and charcuterie, freshly baked breads, artwork, and antique furniture. All of it is imminently available, too, from the Sauvignon Blanc and

Shiraz to the tables and chairs. Cast in low lighting, the wine bar serves as a comfortable backdrop for a pre- or postdinner drink or an entire evening. ⊠ *152 King St., Lower King* ☎ *843/577–7359* ⊕ *www.bin152.com.*

MARKET AREA

BARS AND PUBS

Club Habana. Located above the Tinder Box tobacco store and cigar shop, Club Habana thrives as a chic martini and cognac bar known for its mixology and classic cocktails. Additionally, it's one of the few establishments in town where you can still smoke inside the club. ⊠ *177 Meeting St., Market area* ☎ *843/853–5900, 843/853–5008* ⊕ *www. tinderboxcharleston.com/habana.*

Gin Joint. The cocktails here—frothy Ramos Fizzes, Sazeracs, slings, smashes, and juleps—are retro, some pre-Prohibition. The bartenders don bow ties and suspenders, but the atmosphere is utterly contemporary, with slick gray walls and subtle lighting. The bar is named after Humphrey Bogart's famous line in *Casablanca*: "Of all the gin joints, in all the towns, in all the world, she walks into mine." The kitchen serves up small plates like foie gras torchon, pheasant potpie, sweets, and cheeses. ⊠ *182 E. Bay St., Market area* ☎ *843/577–6111* ⊕ *www.theginjoint.com.*

The Griffon. Pin a dollar to the wall, or a dart to the board bull's-eye. In the tradition of similar Irish pubs, dollar bills cover just about every inch of real estate at the Griffon, helping the bar achieve institutional status within the city. It's dark, dusty, and well worn, and somehow still seems charming. A rotating draft selection includes beers from local breweries like Westbrook, Coast, and Holy City, providing additional appeal. ⊠ *18 Vendue Range, Market area* ☎ *843/723–1700* ⊕ *www.griffoncharleston.com.*

Henry's House. Henry's House is a Charleston institution. The longest continuously operating restaurant and bar in South Carolina, it has evolved over the decades. On the first floor is a large horseshoe bar with floor-to-ceiling windows looking out to the Market. The second floor has exposed brick, black-and-white photos of jazz musicians, a bar, rugs on hardwood floors, and sofas. A few steps up is the new deck and the enclosed club NV, which is open Thursday through Saturday. ⊠ *54 N. Market, Market area* ☎ *843/723–4363* ⊕ *www.henryshousecharleston.com.*

UP ON THE ROOF. Locals head to the city's rooftop bars on summer evenings where cool breezes offer relief from the heat. Establishments like the Pavilion, Rooftop at Vendue, and Henry's House have made rooftop terraces into bars and lounges. These have become particularly popular for smokers, who are no longer allowed to smoke indoors. At sunset you can watch the horizon change colors and view the boats in the harbor.

★ **Fodor's**Choice **Pavilion Bar.** Atop the Market Pavilion Hotel, the outdoor Pavilion Bar offers panoramic views of the city and harbor. Enjoy appetizers, delicacies created with lobster and duck, with a signature martini, like a pomegranate Paviliontini. This is Charleston's best rooftop bar. The dress code dictates no flip-flops, baseball caps, visors, or tank tops. ⊠ *225 E. Bay St., Market area* ☎ *843/266–4218* ⊕ *www.marketpavilion.com.*

Pearlz Oyster Bar. Visit for the raw or steamed varietal oysters—fat, juicy, and plucked from the Gulf, local waters, and various points in between. But stay for the oyster shooters: one oyster in a shot glass, topped with Absolut Peppar vodka and a few squirts of spicy cocktail sauce. Just stir and shoot. Consider it an opening sortie, providing apt energy for pop-ins at the other East Bay Street–area hot spots in downtown Charleston. ⊠ *153 E. Bay St., Market area* ☎ *843/577–5755* ⊕ *www.pearlzoysterbar.com.*

Rooftop at Vendue. Have a cocktail and appetizer as you watch the colorful sunset behind the church steeples. There are actually two bars at this venue, and the lower Deck Bar has tables and chairs shaded by umbrellas, but the view of the water is partially obscured by condo highrises. The second, higher-level bar, called the Bridge Bar, offers a 360-degree panorama, tables, and chairs, but no umbrellas. You'll find live music by local and regional talent nightly from 6 to 9 pm, and select appetizers are half off during happy hour. ⊠ *23 Vendue Range, Market area* ☎ *843/577–7970* ⊕ *www.vendueinn.com.*

Social Restaurant & Wine Bar. If you need help choosing from among 60 wines by the glass, as well as bottles and flights of everything from Tempranillo to Prosecco, knowledgeable sommelier and owner Brad Ball is your man. The restaurant also features terrific homespun pizzas. ⊠ *188 E. Bay St., Market area* ☎ *843/577–5665* ⊕ *www.socialwinebar.com.*

JAZZ CLUBS

★ **Charleston Grill.** The elegant Charleston Grill has live jazz from 7 to 10 on Friday and 8 to midnight on Saturday. Shows range from the internationally acclaimed, Brazilian-influenced Quentin Baxter Ensemble to the Bob Williams Duo, a father and son who play classical guitar and violin. It draws a mature, upscale clientele, hotel guests, well-known locals, and more recently an urbane thirtysomething crowd. ⊠ *Charleston Place Hotel, 224 King St., Market area* ☎ *843/577–4522* ⊕ *www.charlestongrill.com.*

LIVE MUSIC

Halls Chophouse. This pricey bar and restaurant, which caters to a young to older professional crowd, has contemporary, minimalist interior design. Piano man Anthony serenades the first-floor dinner patrons and the bar crowd, especially those on the front bar stools, five to six nights a week. During Sunday brunch, a throaty gospel singer belts out the spiritual blues. A "must-have" is Halls' signature martini—lavender-infused vodka with rosemary and a trio of berries. ⊠ *434 King St., Market area* ☎ *843/727–0090* ⊕ *www.hallschophouse.com.*

UPPER KING

BARS AND PUBS

The Belmont. The Belmont doesn't seek attention—heck, the place won't even list its phone number. But with a high, tin ceiling, exposed-brick walls, and a penchant for screening black-and-white films, the charisma comes naturally. An inventive cocktail menu helps, too. Try their take on the spicy-sweet Brown Derby, a bourbon drink made with jalapeño-infused honey, or the Bells of Jalisco, featuring *reposado* tequila, more jalapeño honey, and lime juice. ⊠ *511 King St., Upper King* ⊕ *www.thebelmontcharleston.com.*

Burns Alley. You'll do well just to find the place. Attached to La Hacienda Mexican restaurant off King Street (just keep truckin' past the bathrooms at the rear), Burns Alley offers cozy quarters for sports fans in need of cheap beers and a giant projection screen. A small upstairs area also overlooks the action below, offering a premium vantage point during crowded evenings. One warning, though: no underage drinkers. The bar has garnished its walls with more than 1,200 confiscated IDs. ⊠ *354B King St., Upper King* ☎ *843/723–6735* ⊕ *www.burnsalley.com.*

Charleston Beer Works. This beverage-friendly watering hole also offers interesting choices of appetizers, small plates, and buffalo wings. Eighty bottled beers and 20 draft selections make this a popular hangout for the college crowd. ✉ *468 King St., Upper King* ☎ *843/577–5885* ⊕ *www. charlestonbeerworks.com.*

Closed for Business. Closed for Business bills itself as a draught emporium—and we're happy to agree. The downtown bar showcases 42 taps, including several seasonal and local brews. Typified by its light-color woods and unique markings—lightbulbs flickering in a fireplace, for instance— CFB also features a tasty menu containing fresh-ground burgers, Chicago-style hot dogs, and a special fried pork cutlet sandwich called the Pork Slap. ✉ *453 King St., Upper King* ☎ *843/853–8466* ⊕ *www.closed4business.com.*

The Cocktail Club. Perhaps no other Charleston establishment characterizes the craft cocktail movement like the Cocktail Club. The bar showcases exposed-brick walls and wooden beams inside its lounge areas, though warm evenings are best spent outside on the rooftop patio. Inside, some of Charleston's best (and best-looking) bartenders concoct clever mixtures like Safety Word, made from habanero-spiked tequila, muddled kiwi, and lime juice, and the Double Standard, a serrano-pepper-infused gin and cucumber vodka blend. The menu says it best: it's a true farm-to-shaker approach. ✉ *479 King St., #200, Upper King* ☎ *843/724–9411* ⊕ *www. thecocktailclubcharleston.com.*

Dudley's on Ann. Charleston's landmark gay bar has classic, old-timey tavern decor and a poolroom in the back. It can be mellow or hopping and has happy-hour specials from 4 to 9. There is karaoke on Wednesday. ✉ *42 Ann St., Upper King* ☎ *843/577–6779* ⊕ *dudleysonann.com.*

O-Ku. This edgy, black-and-white Japanese bar and restaurant serves exquisite small plates like ceviche with mango, pear, and mint-*yuzu* vinaigrette that pair perfectly with the $10 sake flights. Patrons lounge on the couches during happy hour, which runs from 5 to 7 Monday, Wednesday, and Friday; Saturday nights after 10 a high-energy DJ cranks out tunes. ✉ *463 King St., Upper King* ☎ *843/737–0112* ⊕ *www.o-kusushi.com.*

Proof. The group behind TBonz restaurants (TBonz, Pearlz, Liberty Tap Room, Kaminsky's desserts) introduced Proof in 2012, setting up shop in modern, small quarters on King Street. As another newfangled addition to the upscale cocktail scene, Proof separates its drink menu into two categories: "spirits" and "real good beer." From the spirits side, select from classics like the Dark and Stormy, Sazerac, and Old Fashioned, or try a new concoction like the Charleston Buck with bourbon, citrus, and egg white. ⊠ *437 King St., Upper King* ☎ *843/793–1422.*

DANCE CLUBS

Club Pantheon. Charleston's only gay dance club is a large, unadorned space with a stage where drag shows are performed on Friday and Sunday nights. Male go-go dancers shake their stuff on the bar and there's a DJ every night. The club offers a good dance space with lots of action. Although the crowd is primarily gay, straight folks and bachelorette parties come here, too, and are made welcome. ■ TIP→ **Eighteen- to twenty-year-olds are allowed in but they are given a special bracelet and are not allowed to drink alcohol.** The cover charge is $5. ⊠ *28 Anne St., Upper King* ☎ *843/557–2582* ⊕ *www.clubpantheon.net.*

Trio Club. Funky 1970s and '80s sounds are perennially popular at this dance club, which starts late and runs hard until closing. Listen to the house band downstairs or head upstairs for the dance party. Cover is usually $5. ⊠ *139 Calhoun St., Upper King* ☎ *843/965–5333.*

LIVE MUSIC

Music Farm. Once a train depot and now a live music venue, Music Farm has a warehouse capacity filled to the max when popular bands like Galactic, the North Mississippi Allstars, and Passion Pit play. Tickets typically range from $15 to $25. ⊠ *32 Ann St., Upper King* ☎ *843/577–6969* ⊕ *www.musicfarm.com.*

The Torch Velvet Lounge. This martini and hookah bar offers tobacco in flavors such as mint and passion fruit, and if that's not enough, small bands ranging from bluegrass to rock to beach music play seven nights a week. The back room has semiprivate booths. ⊠ *545 King St., Upper King* ☎ *843/723–9333* ⊕ *www.torch-lounge.com.*

SOUTH OF BROAD

BARS AND PUBS

Salty Mike's. Salty Mike's Deck Bar offers fine service to fishermen, college kids, and locals alike: cheap Natural Light and Pabst Blue Ribbon specials; beefy, half-pound cheeseburgers; and house-made pimiento cheese sandwiches. Situated beneath the Marina Variety Store Restaurant, itself a Charleston landmark dating to 1963, Salty Mike's provides a crusty, no-frills ambience and a dreamy seaside view of the Ashley River and Charleston City Marina. ⊠ *17 Lockwood Dr., South of Broad* ☏ *843/937–0208* ⊕ *www. varietystorerestaurant.com.*

MOUNT PLEASANT AND VICINITY

ISLE OF PALMS

LIVE MUSIC

Windjammer. An oceanfront bar with local and national rock bands playing Thursday through Sunday, Windjammer is mainly a younger, postcollegiate haunt. The cover charge for live music is usually $10. If you sit out on the back deck and bar on a Friday or Saturday night, there's no cover. And don't forget the bikini contests come summer. ⊠ *1000 Ocean Blvd., Isle of Palms* ☏ *843/886–8596* ⊕ *www.jammercam.com.*

NORTH MORRISON

BARS AND PUBS

The Royal American. A relatively new addition to the North Morrison corridor, the Royal American isn't really a dive bar—it's just positioned to look like one. The establishment features dim lighting, decorative top hats, and an expansive front deck. Even better, the bar serves up a gallery of cheap, canned beers and a trio of tasty, 32-ounce signature punches with rum, bourbon, or vodka poured over crushed ice. Hungry? Feast on blue-collar eats like Frito pie, loaded baked potatoes, cheddar cheeseburgers, and house-made beef jerky. ⊠ *970 Morrison Dr., North Morrison* ☏ *843/817–6925* ⊕ *theroyalamerican.com.*

SULLIVAN'S ISLAND

BARS AND PUBS

Dunleavy's Pub. Just a block from the beach, this friendly Irish pub is a local favorite, featuring Irish, folk, and blues music often throughout the week. St. Patrick's Day weekend is a treat, as the main drag on Sullivan's Island is closed, allowing pedestrians to sally forth from bar to bar. ⊠ *2213 Middle St., Sullivan's Island* ☏ *843/883–9646* ⊕ *susanlucas. typepad.com/dunleavys.*

Sports and the Outdoors

WORD OF MOUTH

"Folly Beach is the perfect balance of simple hospitality, salty local character, and untouched, natural beauty. Any sandy spot where you can sip killer margs and enjoy fresh seafood sans shoes & shirt is an obvious winner."

—Erin

By Kinsey
Gidick Charleston is a great place to get outdoors. Called the Lowcountry because it is at sea level—and sometimes even below—the city has an array of tidal creeks, estuaries, and rivers that flow out to the deep blue Atlantic. The region's beaches are taupe sand, and the Carolina sun warms them some nine months out of the year. Many are uncrowded, especially in the spring and fall, and public beaches are kept clean and well maintained, mostly by the staff of the county parks system.

Several barrier islands studded with palm trees and live oaks festooned with Spanish moss thrive. Even though they are fairly extensively developed, some still shelter wildlife that you can frequently see. Charlestonians will tell you (without bragging) that this is one of the most beautiful regions on this planet. Here you can commune with nature, perhaps like you haven't in years.

It can be expensive to take part in some of the region's best outdoor activities, and this may give some pause to families, especially those who might want to charter a boat to do some fishing. But dolphin-watching tours on regularly scheduled group charters are much cheaper on a per-person basis, and crabbing at low tide is free. You'll also find an amazing number of low-cost options, from biking to canoeing and kayaking, and nature walks. Of course, in the warm weather, the beach is the thing. Those looking for more of an adrenaline rush can rent a Jet Ski or surfboard.

Area golf courses are reasonably priced compared with, say, Hilton Head, the public courses being the least expensive. The championship courses on the resort islands are the most beautiful, though they are costly.

Sailing is becoming an increasingly important activity here in this port city. If you already know how to sail, you can rent a small sailboat. You can also take sailing lessons or just go out on crewed charter boats. Among the annual sailing events held here are the Keel Boat Regatta in mid-April; Charleston Race Week, also in April; and the much-televised Charleston-to-Bermuda Race in late May. Charleston's Harbor Fest, traditionally held during the third week in June, has grown in importance and size; its parade of Tall Ships is always a highlight.

SPORTS AND ACTIVITIES

BASEBALL

Fans who like to hear the crack of the bat and the cheers of the crowd can plan on attending a game at "the Joe" (Joseph P. Riley Jr. Stadium).

Charleston Riverdogs. The local minor-league baseball team plays at "the Joe," on the banks of the Ashley River near the Citadel. Kids love their mascot, Charlie T. Riverdog. After games, fireworks often illuminate the summer sky in honor of this all-American pastime. The season runs from April through September. Tickets cost a reasonable $7 to $12. ✉ *Joseph P. Riley Jr. Stadium, 360 Fishburne St., Hampton Park Terrace* ☎ *843/577–3647* ⊕ *www.riverdogs.com.*

BEACHES

There are glorious beaches just outside the Charleston city limits. You and your kids can build sand castles, gather seashells after high tide, or bring a kite and let it loose on a long lead. The Charleston area's mild climate means you can swim from March through October. Public beaches, operated by the Charleston County Parks & Recreation Commission, generally have lifeguards in season, snack bars, restrooms and dressing areas, outdoor showers, umbrella and chair rentals, and large parking lots.

The county park's commission operates three multidimensional family parks, three water parks, and three beach parks. Each offers programming that involves the natural characteristics of each site, but they are careful not to duplicate these leisure services from site to site. There are marinas, fishing piers, dog parks, water parks, campgrounds, cottage rentals, facility and equipment rentals, and boat and kayak landings.

Folly Beach. Folly Beach is the Lowcountry's most iconic summer playground, featuring stronge waves, a narrower beach, and the Folly Beach Pier. However, as of summer 2012, alcohol of any kind is no longer allowed on the beach at any time. To the left of the stairway to the pier is a good seafood restaurant called Blu, with a bar, deck, and incredible ocean views. Street parking is free, but to avoid a ticket, all four wheels have to be on the grass, not the pavement. Small parking lots right next to the beach access cost $1 per hour from 10 to 5. If you are a surfer, keep driving until you reach Folly's Washout. Regulations about littering and parking are strictly enforced. **Amenities:** food and drink; lifeguards; parking (fee). **Best for:** swimming; surfing. ✉ *E. Ashley Ave., off U.S. 17, which becomes Center St.; turn left at the Holiday Inn, Folly Island, Folly Beach* ⊕ *www.cityoffollybeach.com.*

Front Beach. If you want a singles scene and beach bars like the Windjammer, with bands and bikini contests, then the commercial Front Beach section of the Isle of Palms is for you. For generations it has been a big draw for beach lovers. Bicyclists are welcome, as are leashed pets, but no alcohol or beer is allowed. Check out *iop.net/visitors/beachaccessandparking.aspx* for the rules on beach parking outside the Isle of Palms County Park. Parking regulations are strictly enforced. **Amenities:** food and drink; parking (fee). **Best for:** partiers; sunset; sunrise; windsurfing. ✉ *10th Ave.–14th Ave., U.S. 17 north to I–517, the Isle of Palms connector; once on the island look for 10th Ave., Isle of Palms.*

NO SWIMMING. The No Swimming signs by the Isle of Palms Bridge over Breach Inlet are there because the current is treacherous and, sadly, every year people drown.

☻ **Isle of Palms County Park.** Play beach volleyball or quietly sunbathe in a lounge chair at this 600-foot-long beach. This beach is as good as the island's idyllic name. The sands are golden, the water is temperate, and the waves are gentle. It's great for little children, seniors with limited mobility, or those who seek peace. It is also the only lifeguard-protected area on the Isle of Palms. **Amenities:** lifeguards; toilets; food and drink; showers (seasonal). **Best for:** surfing; walking; swimming. ✉ *1 14th Ave., U.S. 17 north to I–517, the Isle of Palms connector; once on the island go through the traffic light and then straight ahead; the parking lot is on the left, Isle of Palms* ☎ *843/886–3863, 843/768–4386* ⊕ *www.ccprc.com* ⌂ *$8 per car* ☉ *Nov.–Feb., daily 10–5; Mar., Apr.,Sept., and Oct., daily 10–6; May–Labor Day, daily 9–7.*

BEACH SAFETY. It may seem inviting to walk out to a sandbar at low tide, but the tide sweeps in fast and the sandbars disappear, leaving people stranded far from shore.

★ **Fodor's Choice Kiawah Beachwalker Park.** The public park about 28 miles southwest of Charleston has an ample 500-foot-wide beach. Kiawah is one of the Southeast's most physically beautiful and largest barrier islands, with 10 miles of

TOP OUTDOOR EXPERIENCES

Beaches: Charleston's palm-studded coastline and the beaches of its barrier islands rival those in the Caribbean—and are often less congested, safer, and cleaner. The shoulder seasons of spring and fall are good for beachcombing, and summer is the time for swimming and water sports.

Biking: Charleston's Historic District is particularly bike-friendly, and riding a bike there is a wonderful way to have the wind in your hair and also avoid automobile and parking hassles. You can ride through the various in-town parks, like Marion Square, Waterfront Park, and Hampton Park, or take the bike path on the colossal Arthur Ravenel Jr. Bridge. On the island resorts, a bike is the ideal way to get around, especially for parents with older kids.

Boating and Sailing: Charleston's waters offer something for both the blue-water sailor and those who just want to take a water-borne tour. Fishing is also a top sport here, and a charter is an excellent way to spend the day.

Kayaking: This relatively low-cost activity is one of the best ways to explore the Lowcountry's many water-ways. Try paddling to keep up with the schools of dolphins you'll encounter while gliding silently in the intracoastal waterway. You can rent kayaks at Middleton Place, offering you the opportunity to push your paddle through former rice fields with views of the famous Butterfly Gardens. In Mount Pleasant, you can kayak in Shem Creek, the center of its shrimping industry, and if you are fit, you can paddle all the way to Sullivan's Island.

Golf: The weather is ideal for golf in the spring and fall, or even during the region's relatively mild winter. Summer's strong rays make morning and late afternoon the most popular tee times. Though some are not quite up to par with the courses of Hilton Head, golf on the nearby island resorts, especially at Kiawah Island Golf Resort, is exceptional.

wide, immaculate ocean beach. Crime is a rarity here, and you can walk safely for miles, shelling and beachcombing. The beach is complemented by the Kiawah River, with lagoons filled with birds and wildlife, and golden marshes that make the sunsets even more glorious. **Amenities:** lifeguards (seasonal); food and drink; toilets; showers. **Best for:** solitude; sunset; swimming; walking. ⊠ *1 Beachwalker Dr.,*

Kiawah Island ☎843/768–2395 ⊕www.ccprc.com ☎$8
per car ⊗*Jan. and Feb., daily 10–5; Mar. and Apr., daily
10–6; May–Labor Day, daily 9–7; Sept., daily 10–6; Oct.,
weekdays 9–5, weekends 10–6; Nov. and Dec., daily 10–5.*

WORD OF MOUTH. "I prefer the flatter, wider beaches with calmer
surf of the southern S.C. coast (Isle of Palms, Hilton Head). The
N.C. beaches tend to be shelly-er, with rougher surf and often
steeper drop offs into the water." —Brian_in_Charlotte

★ **Fodor's Choice Sullivan's Island Beach.** This is one of the most
noncommercialized, pristine beaches in the greater Charleston area. The beachfront lands are owned by the town—
some 190 acres of infant maritime forest with coastal
wildlife, held in a perpetual land easement by the Lowcountry Open Land Trust. The downside is that there are
no amenities that make beach-going easier, like public
toilets and showers. There are, however, a number of good
small restaurants for lunch or drinks on nearby Middle
Street, the island's main drag. There are approximately
30 public-access paths (4 are wheelchair accessible) that
lead to the beach. Alcohol and glass containers are not
allowed. "Sully's" is a delightful island with a rich historic
background that includes a lighthouse and Fort Moultrie
National Monument. The island is home to some 2,000
people, whose numbers swell in summer with vacationers
occupying the many beach houses and rentals. **Amenities:**
none. **Best for:** sunrise; swimming; walking; windsurfing.
✉*Station 9–Station 22 1/2 (stations radiate off Middle St.),
Sullivan's Island* ⊕*www.sullivansisland-sc.com.*

BIKING

The historic district is ideal for bicycling as long as you
stay off the busier roads. Many of the city's green spaces,
including Colonial Lake and Palmetto Islands County Park,
have bike trails. If you want to rent a bike, expect to pay
about $20 for a half day (three hours) and $25 for a full
day. Most of the shops charge the same price, but excep-
tions are noted.

Cycling at your own pace is one of the best ways to see
Charleston. Those staying at the island resorts, particularly
families, almost always rent bikes, especially if they are
there for a week.

Affordabike. This shop sells and rents bikes. Rentals are a mere $20 for a 24-hour day ($45 a week), which includes a helmet, lock, and basket. Conveniently located in the Upper King area, it is also open on Sunday from noon to 5—the best day for riding in downtown Charleston and/or across the Ravenel Bridge. ✉ *534 King St., Upper King* ☎ *843/789–3281* ⊕ *www.affordabike.com.*

Bicycle Shoppe. You can rent bikes at the Bicycle Shoppe seven days a week. The typical rental is a simple beach cruiser for $7 an hour or $28 a day, and includes a helmet. For those wanting to tackle the Ravenel Bridge, the store offers hybrid geared bikes for $10 an hour or $40 a day. ✉ *281 Meeting St., Market area* ☎ *843/722–8168* ⊕ *www.thebicycleshoppecharleston.com* ✉ *1539 Johnnie Dodds Blvd., Mount Pleasant* ☎ *843/884–7433* ⊕ *www. thebicycleshoppe.com.*

Charleston Bicycle Tours. Local tour guides will show you the quiet streets and hidden secrets of Charleston, its historic homes and gardens on the multiday Charleston Bicycle Tours. Groups ride past plantations as well as over the Ravenel Bridge; they explore the islands, and quaint surrounding towns. Tours include quality bikes, four- and five-star hotel accommodations, and dining in the area's best restaurants. There's a van shuttle and support with a licensed guide and mechanic. Custom biking, kayaking, or walking tours can be arranged. Prices range from $995 for a two-day trip to $2,495 for a six-day tour to Savannah. ✉ *1321 Bellview Dr., Mount Pleasant* ☎ *843/881–9878* ⊕ *charlestonbicycletours.com.*

Island Bike and Surf Shop. Rent island cruisers (beach bikes) for a very moderate weekly rate of $34.95, or check out tandem bikes, bicycles built for two, hybrids, mountain bikes, Burley trailers, cargo trailers, adult tricycles with large baskets, joggers' children's strollers, baby strollers, and more. The shop will even deliver to Kiawah and Seabrook islands. If you just want a bike for a day or two ($20 per day), you have to pick it up and return it. Kayak rental costs $40 for a double kayak and $30 for an individual. ✉ *3665 Bohicket Rd., Johns Island* ☎ *843/768–1158, 800/323–0579* ⊕ *www.islandbikeandsurf.com.*

BOATING

★ Kayak through isolated marsh rivers and estuaries to outlying islands, or explore Cape Romain National Wildlife Refuge. Rates vary depending on location and whether you take a guided tour. Typically you can expect to pay $40 a person in a single or double kayak for a two-hour guided tour. Rentals can be $20 a person per hour. Weekly rentals are about $150. The resort islands, especially Kiawah and Wild Dunes, tend to be higher.

The boating options are so varied, from a small johnboat with an outboard motor to a chartered sailboat, that it is best to contact these companies for their litany of pricing. Similarly, small-sailboat lessons can be arranged.

★ **AquaSafaris.** If you want a sailing or motor yacht charter, perhaps a beach barbecue, an ecotour, or just to go offshore fishing, contact AquaSafaris. Captain John takes seaworthy sailors out daily, leaving from Shem Creek and Isle of Palms. A sunset cruise on the *Palmetto Breeze* catamaran offers guests panoramic views of Charleston Harbor serenaded by the sounds of Jimmy Buffett. Enjoy beer and cocktails as you cruise in one of the smoothest sails in the Lowcountry. ⊠ *24 Patriots Point Rd., Mount Pleasant* ☎ *843/886–8133* ⊕ *www.aqua-safaris.com.*

Charleston Kayak Company. Guided kayak tours with Charleston Kayak Company depart from the grounds of the Inn at Middleton Place. Kayakers glide down the Ashley River and through brackish creeks, in an area that is the Lowcountry's only State Scenic River Corridor (22-mile stretch). Naturalist guides interpret the surrounding wetlands and tell of the river's cultural history. It's not uncommon to spot an American alligator but thankfully they take no interest in kayakers. Tours last two hours (reservations essential) and cost $45 per person. Both single and tandem kayaks are available for rent at $40 for a tandem and $30 for a single, including all safety gear. If visiting January through April, inquire about cypress swamp tours. ⊠ *Middleton Place Plantation, 4290 Ashley River Rd., West Ashley* ☎ *843/556–6020, 843/628–2879* ⊕ *www.charlestonkayakcompany.com.*

Coastal Expeditions. Outings for individuals, families, and groups are provided by Coastal Expeditions. They have additional kayak outlets at Crosby's Seafood on Folly Road and at Isle of Palms Marina. A kayak tour with a naturalist guide is $58 per person, and they rent kayaks for $38 (single) or $48 (tandem) for a half day. They provide exclusive access to Cape Romain National Wilderness Area on Bull Island via the Bull Island Ferry. The ferry departs from Garris Landing and runs Tuesday and Thursday–Saturday from April through November. It costs $30 round-trip. Bull Island has rare natural beauty, a "boneyard beach," shells galore, and 277 species of migrating birds. ⊠ *Shem Creek Maritime Center, 514B Mill St., Mount Pleasant* ☎ *843/884–7684* ⊕ *www.coastalexpeditions.com.*

Island Bike & Surf Shop. Island Bike & Surf Shop rents surfboards and bicycles and will deliver to the resort islands. Boards cost $20 a day, $15 after four days. Bikes are $34.95 plus tax for a weeklong rental including delivery and pickup. ⊠ *3665 Bohicket Rd., Johns Island* ☎ *843/768–1158* ⊕ *www.islandbikeandsurf.com.*

Ondeck Charleston. Take your family sailing, take the helm, and learn how to command your own 26-foot sailboat on Charleston's beautiful harbor with the guidance of an instructor at Ondeck Charleston. This academy can teach you how to sail comfortably on any size sailboat, and can take you from coastal navigation to ocean proficiency. Instructors are fun and experienced, and are US Sailing–certified professionals. Skippered charters are also available: three-hour sails are an affordable $150 for a Colgate 26-footer; $200 for a full day. ⊠ *24 Patriots Point Rd., Mount Pleasant* ☎ *843/971–0700* ⊕ *www.ondecksailing.us.*

St. John's Kayaks. Based on a historic plantation just minutes from the entrance to Kiawah and Seabrook islands, St. John's Kayaks offers guided ecotours by kayak and fishing and ecological powerboat excursions. Safe and stable, easy-boarding kayaks are ideal for active seniors and kids. Local owners share their love and passion for the barrier sea islands. They welcome groups and offer them discounted rates; call for group rates. ⊠ *4460 Betsy Kerrison Pkwy., Johns Island* ☎ *843/330–9777* ⊕ *www.stjohnskayaks.com.*

Thriller. Thriller is a high-powered, adrenaline-spiking tour for Charleston. This brightly painted catamaran is propelled by two turbo-diesel engines and it can clock 25 miles an hour. It runs from Charleston harbor to the Morris Lighthouse and back, passing another lighthouse and five forts. The live narration is broken up by rock music. Tours cost $35 per adult. ⊠ *1529 Strathmore La., Mount Pleasant* ☎ *843/276–4203* ⊕ *www.thrillercharleston.com.*

FISHING

★ **Fodor's**Choice Fishing can be a real adventure here, and if you go offshore with an experienced fishing guide, you can have enough fish stories to tell until the next trip. This is a pricey adventure best shared with as many of your fishing buddies as possible; expect to pay about $120 an hour, including bait and tackle but not your lunch. For inshore (saltwater) fly-fishing, guides generally charge $350 (for two people) for a half day. Deep-sea fishing charters cost about $1,400 for 12 hours for a boatload of anglers.

Bohicket Marina. Bohicket Marina has half- and full-day charters on 24- to 48-foot boats. Small-boat rentals are also available, as well as sunset dolphin-watching cruises. This marina is the closest to Kiawah and Seabrook, and this charter company has a long-standing reputation. For inshore fishing, expect to pay about $375 for three hours minimum for one to three people and $400–$600 for four or more people, including bait, tackle, and licenses. ⊠ *1880 Andell Bluff Blvd., Johns Island* ☎ *843/768–1280* ⊕ *www.bohicket.com.*

Captain Richard Stuhr. Saltwater fly-fishers looking for an Orvis-endorsed guide do best by calling Captain Richard Stuhr, who has been fishing the waters of Charleston, Kiawah, and Isle of Palms since 1991. He'll haul his 19-foot Action Craft to you and take you on a half-day tour through Charleston's harbor and tributaries for $375. ⊠ *547 Sanders Farm La.* ☎ *843/881–3179* ⊕ *www.captstuhr.com.*

GOLF

With fewer golfers than in Hilton Head, the courses around Charleston have more prime starting times available. Nonguests can play at private island resorts, such as Kiawah Island, Seabrook Island, and Wild Dunes. There you will find breathtaking ocean views within a pristine setting. They offer enchantment and escape from the stresses of the workaday world. Don't be surprised if a white-tailed deer is grazing a green or a gator is drinking from the water holes. For top courses like Kiawah's Ocean Course, nonguests can expect to pay $222 to $338 (peak season spring and early fall). Municipal golf courses are a golfing bargain, from $27 to $39 for 18 holes. Somewhere in between are the Shadowmoss Plantation Golf Club, west of the Ashley River, for $30 to $52, and the Links at Stono Ferry in Hollywood for $39 to $80.

Charleston Area Golf Guide. From green fees to course statistics and golf vacation packages in the area, contact the Charleston Area Golf Guide. ☎ *800/774–4444* ⊕ *www. charlestongolfguide.com.*

Charleston Municipal Golf Course. This walker-friendly public course isn't gorgeous like some of the resort courses—a highway bisects it—but it does have a lot of shade trees and the price is right. About 20 miles from the resort islands of Kiawah and Seabrook and about 6 miles from downtown, the course has a simple snack bar serving breakfast, lunch, and beer and wine. ✉ *2110 Maybank Hwy., James Island* ☎ *843/795–6517* ⊕ *www.charleston-sc.gov* ⅃ *18 holes. 6450 yds. Par 72. Green Fee: $27/$39* ↪ *Facilities: Driving range, putting green, pitching area, golf carts, pull carts, rental clubs, lessons, restaurant, bar.*

Charleston National Golf Club. The best nonresort golf course in Charleston is well maintained and tends to be quiet on weekdays, which translates to lower prices. The setting is captivating, with the course carved along the intracoastal waterway, traversing wetlands, lagoons, and pine and oak forests. Finishing holes are set along golden marshland. Diminutive wooden bridges and a handsome, salmon-color clubhouse that looks like an antebellum mirage add to the natural beauty. ✉ *1360 National Dr., Mount Pleasant* ☎ *843/884–7799, 843/884–4653* ⊕ *www.charlestonnationalgolf.com* ⅃ *18 holes. 6412 yds. Par 72. Green Fee: $48/$58* ↪ *Facilities: Driving range, putting green, pitching area, golf carts, pull carts, rental clubs, pro shop, golf academy/lessons, restaurant, bar.*

6

WORD OF MOUTH. "Downtown Charleston, obviously, will not have golf courses, but my husband loves to play golf and there is plenty of golf within an easy drive of town.... We usually have Fall Break the second week of October and there is nothing I love better than renting a house on Isle of Palms or Sullivan's Island, spending my days on the very pleasant beaches and then spending the afternoons and/or evenings downtown.... I would rent a house on IOP or Sullivan's Island, let my husband play golf in the mornings while I was at the beach, go shop myself silly in the afternoons, and then save the evenings for those romantic dinners!" —BetsyinKY

Dunes West Golf & River Club. This semiprivate, championship golf course was designed by Arthur Hill. It has great marshland and river views and lots of modulation on the Bermuda-covered greens shaded by centuries-old oaks. The generous fairways with greens that may be considered small by today's standards make approach shots very important to scoring low. Located about 15 miles from downtown Charleston, it is in a gated residential community with an attractive antebellum-style clubhouse. ⊠ *3535 Wando Plantation Way, Mount Pleasant* ☏ *843/856–9000* ⊕ *www.duneswestgolfclub.com* ⅃ *18 holes. 6871 yds. Par 72. Green Fee: $46/$95* ⌑ *Facilities: Driving range, putting green, pitching area, golf carts, rental clubs, pro shop, golf academy/lessons, restaurant, bar.*

Links at Stono Ferry. A popular semiprivate course with reasonable rates, this is the closest golf course to Kiawah and Seabrook islands and is 30 minutes from downtown Charleston. In past years, it has ranked as one of the top 100 courses in the Carolinas. Set in a rural area, Stono Ferry is an upscale residential community with a focus on golf and horses. Its clubhouse has Southern style. ⊠ *4812 Stono Links Dr., Hollywood* ☏ *843/763–1817* ⊕ *www.stonoferrygolf.com* ⅃ *18 holes. 6814 yds. Par 72. Green Fee: $41/$87* ⌑ *Facilities: Driving range, putting green, pitching area, golf carts, rental clubs, pro shop, golf academy/lessons, restaurant, bar.*

Patriots Point Links. A partly covered driving range and spectacular harbor and bridge views make this golf experience special. It is just across the spectacular Ravenel Bridge, with free public parking. You could also take the water taxi from downtown to the nearby Hilton and arrange for a Links staffer to pick you up. Four pros instruct, and there are lessons and clinics, as well as a junior camp during the summer. ⊠ *1 Patriots Point Rd., Mount Pleasant* ☏ *843/881–0042* ⊕ *www.patriotspointlinks.com* ⅃ *18 holes. 6900 yds. Par 72. Green Fee: $60/$85* ⌑ *Facilities: Driving range, putting green, pitching area, golf carts, rental clubs, pro shop, golf academy/lessons, restaurant, bar.*

Seabrook Island Resort. There are two championship courses here: Crooked Oaks, by Robert Trent Jones Sr., and Ocean Winds, by Willard Byrd. Seabrook Island has acres of untamed maritime forest and natural coastline. Crooked Oaks, an interior course, is the more player friendly of the two. Ocean Winds is aptly named for three holes that run along the Atlantic; when the wind is up, those ocean breezes make it challenging. Both courses are run out of the same pro shop and have the same green fee. Seabrook is, however, a private island, although guest privileges are extended to anyone who has a membership in a golf club. To play here, your hometown golf pro must call Seabrook's pro for a reservation. ⊠ *Seabrook Island Rd., 3772 Seabrook Island Rd., Seabrook Island* ☎ *843/768–2529* ⊕ *www.discoverseabrook.com* ⚐ *36 holes. 6800 yds. Par 72. Green Fee: $105/$165* ⚐ *Facilities: Driving range, putting green, pitching area, golf carts, pull carts, rental clubs, pro shop, golf academy/lessons, restaurant, bar.*

Shadowmoss Plantation Golf Club. This is a well-marked, forgiving course with one of the best finishing holes in the area. It is just off Highway 61, close to Middleton and Magnolia plantations, and is about 20 miles from the resort islands of Kiawah and Seabrook. A seasoned, well-conditioned course, it was designed in the 1970s and a residential enclave grew up around it. It's a good value for the money. ⊠ *20 Dunvegan Dr.* ☎ *843/556–8251* ⊕ *www.shadowmossgolf.com* ⚐ *18 holes. 6701 yds. Par 72. Green Fee: $36/$42* ⚐ *Facilities: Driving range, putting green, pitching area, golf carts, pull carts, rental clubs, pro shop, golf academy/lessons, restaurant, bar.*

KIAWAH ISLAND GOLF RESORT GOLF COURSES

Kiawah Island Golf Resort is home to five championship courses: the world-famous **Ocean Course,** designed by Pete Dye; the Jack Nicklaus–designed **Turtle Point;** **Osprey Point,** designed by Tom Fazio; **Cougar Point,** designed by Gary Player; and **Oak Point,** redesigned by Clyde Johnston, just outside the Kiawah gate.

Cougar Point. This is Kiawah's Gary Player design, which features holes playing along tidal marshes and offering panoramic views of the Kiawah River and golden spans of spartina grass. Reservations essential. ⊠ *Kiawah Island Golf Resort, 1 Sanctuary Beach Dr., Kiawah Island* ☎ *843/266–4020* ⊕ *www.kiawahresort.com* ⚐ *18 holes. 6503 yds. Par 72. Green Fee: $215 nonguests/$183 resort guests* ⚐ *Facilities: Driving range, putting green, pitching area, golf carts, caddies, rental clubs, pro shop, golf academy/lessons, restaurant, bar.*

★ **Fodor's**Choice **Ocean Course.** Golf fans and media from around the world flocked to the Ocean Course in 2012 for the PGA Championship, where Rory McIlroy grabbed the win.

Considered one of Pete Dye's most superb designs, this sea-side course received worldwide attention as the host of the dramatic 1991 Ryder Cup. The course starred in Robert Redford's *The Legend of Bagger Vance* in 2000. In 2007, it hosted the Senior PGA Championship. Named by *Golf Digest* as America's Toughest Course, it offers spectacular views along 2½ miles of Atlantic Ocean. The superbly manicured fairways and greens challenge amateurs and professionals alike. Caddies are included in the green fee (but not their gratuity), as are carts. However, know that in the morning, it is a walking course only. The stellar clubhouse with its seafood restaurant and full-service bar are exceptional. Reservations essential. ⊠ *Kiawah Island Golf Resort, 1000 Ocean Course Dr., Kiawah Island* ☎ 843/266–4670 ⊕ *www.kiawahresort.com* ⚑ *18 holes. 7873 yds. Par 72. Green Fee: $222–$338* ⚐ *Facilities: Driving range, putting green, pitching area, golf carts, caddies, rental clubs, pro shop, golf academy, restaurant, bar.*

Oak Point. Outside the Kiawah gate, in the center of Hope Plantation, a residential enclave that was an indigo plantation, lies this Scottish-American-style course and its $1 million clubhouse. Reservations essential. ⊠ *Kiawah Island Golf Resort, 4394 Hope Plantation Dr., Kiawah Island* ☎ 843/266–4100 ⊕ *www.kiawahresort.com* ⚑ *18 holes. 6450 yds. Par 72. Green Fee: $66–$215 depending on season* ⚐ *Facilities: Driving range, putting green, pitching area, golf carts, caddies, rental clubs, pro shop, golf academy/lessons, restaurant, bar.*

Osprey Point. This Tom Fazio course offers the utmost in views that the Lowcountry has to offer: maritime forests, pristine lagoons, natural lakes, and saltwater marshes. Every hole has picturesque vistas. It's a favorite of residents and resort guests. The impressive clubhouse with 14,000 square feet of pro shop selling attractive, high-quality apparel; attended locker rooms; and a semiprivate dining room certainly add points. ⊠ *Kiawah Island Golf Resort, 1000 Governors Dr., Kiawah Island* ☎ 843/266–4640 ⊕ *www.kiawahresort.com* ⚑ *18 holes. 6932 yds. Par 72. Green Fee: $114/$212* ⚐ *Facilities: Driving range, putting green, pitching area, golf carts, caddies, rental clubs, pro shop, golf academy/lessons, restaurant, bar.*

Turtle Point. This famed Jack Nicklaus course has hosted many amateur and professional tournaments, including the 1990 PGA Cup Matches and the Carolinas Amateur

Championship. It features three spectacular oceanfront holes. The undulating course flows seamlessly through interior forests of hardwoods and palmettos and along backwater lagoons, and boasts a $7.5 million clubhouse built in a classic Lowcountry style. Reservations essential. ⊠ *Kiawah Island Golf Resort, 1 Turtle Point Dr., Kiawah Island* ☎ *843/266–4050* ⊕ *www.kiawahresort.com* ⅄ *18 holes. 7061 yds. Par 72. Green Fee: $99–$215* ☞ *Facilities: Driving range, putting green, pitching area, golf carts, caddies (on request), rental clubs, pro shop, golf academy/ lessons, restaurant, bar.*

WILD DUNES RESORT GOLF COURSES

Wild Dunes Resort is a 1,600-acre oceanfront resort on the tip of the Isle of Palms some 30 minutes from downtown Charleston. It has two nationally renowned, Tom Fazio–designed courses, the **Links** and the **Harbor** courses. Groups frequent this family-friendly resort because of its meeting facilities, and many resort guests opt for the golf package.

Harbor Course. Tom Fazio designed this course, a thing of beauty, with a million dollars' worth of dirt and named his sculpture "Wild Dunes." The dunes are adorned with greens, and severe hazards can be found around every bend. Of the 18 holes, 17 incorporate water, marsh, or both, as well as bunkering. Nine holes are situated along the Intracoastal Waterway and require shots from one island to the other across the water. ⊠ *Wild Dunes Resort, 5757 Palm Blvd., Isle of Palms* ☎ *843/886–2004* ⊕ *www.wilddunes.com* ⅄ *18 holes. 6446 yds. Par 70. Green Fee: $65/$110* ☞ *Facilities: Driving range, putting green, pitching area, golf carts, rental clubs, pro shop, golf academy/lessons, restaurant, bar.*

Links Course. With prevailing ocean breezes, undulating dunes, and natural water hazards, it's been called a sea-side masterpiece. Considered one of architect Tom Fazio's best Lowcountry layouts, the Links Course is challenging enough for the most avid golfer. Links has been ranked as one of the top 100 courses in the United States and in the world by both *Golf Magazine* and *Golf Digest.* Players are permitted to walk the length of the course, regardless of time or day. ⊠ *Wild Dunes Resort, 10001 Back Bay Dr., Isle of Palms* ☎ *843/886–2002* ⊕ *www.wilddunes. com* ⅄ *18 holes. 6396 yds. Par 70. Green Fee: $115/$165* ☞ *Facilities: Driving range, putting green, pitching area, golf carts, caddies, rental clubs, pro shop, golf academy/ lessons, restaurant, bar.*

HORSEBACK RIDING

★ Put your foot in the stirrup and get a leg up! You can tour the beaches, maritime forests, marshlands, and former rice fields all from horseback. Several good stables in the area offer trail rides, and there are also equestrian centers, lessons, and jumping rings. Trail rides average from $40 for wooded terrain to $85 for an advanced beach ride; they go out for about an hour.

Middleton Equestrian Center. This long-established stable specializes in English riding lessons. It offers trail rides through wooded and open terrain and former rice fields. All experience levels are welcome, and headgear is provided. The price is $45 for the trail that is taken at a walk, but only children 10 and older can ride. ⊠ *Middleton Place, 4280 Ashley River Rd., West Ashley* ☎ *843/556–8137* ⊕ *www. middletonplace.org.*

Seabrook Island Equestrian Center. Open to the public, this center 24 miles south of Charleston has walking trail rides for $65 (children must be eight years old and up) and $70 for advanced riders. Beach rides are only for advanced riders and are $95 for an hour. "Advanced" here means that you can handle a horse competently at a walk, trot, and canter. Parent-led pony rides are $40 for a half hour and as many as three kids can take a turn. The boarding stable will board short-term for $45 a day. Private instructions by the director are $55 for a half hour, and there are several lesson options. This is a classy operation that hosts annual equestrian events and notable hunter and jumper shows. ⊠ *3772 Seabrook Island Rd., Seabrook Island* ☎ *843/768–7541* ⊕ *www.discoverseabrook.com.*

Stono River Riding Academy. About 7 miles south of Charleston, Stono River Riding Academy is a well-established and caring school and stable that offers trail rides through 300 acres of maritime forests, with excellent instructors and guides. Rides must be arranged in advance and cost $65 an hour; only English saddles are used. The trail rides are generally done at a walk, with a guide giving commentary on riding techniques and on the Lowcountry. ⊠ *2962 Hut Rd., Johns Island* ☎ *843/559–0773* ⊕ *stono.thechartgroup.com.*

SCUBA DIVING

Experienced divers can explore the Cooper River Underwater Heritage Diving Trail, upriver from Charleston. The 2-mile-long trail has six submerged sites, including ships that date to the Revolutionary War. Charters will run you out to the starting point. Expect to pay $95 to $145 a trip. Equipment rentals average $10 for a tank.

Charleston Scuba. This outfitter has maps, equipment rentals, and charter trips to the Cooper River Trail and off-shore starting in September, weather permitting. They frequent a total of eight sites, and prices range from $120 to $170 for two tank dives. ⌧ *335 Savannah Hwy., West Ashley* ☎ *843/763–3483* ⊕ *www.charlestonscuba.com.*

SOCCER

Charleston Battery. Charleston's soccer team plays at Blackbaud Stadium, the first privately funded soccer-specific facility in the United States. Games are played from April through September and feature fun-filled giveaways and promotions. The faithful team supporters of the Charleston Battery are referred to as "The Regiment," and after the games, fans retreat to the clubby English pub. The stadium seats 5,100, and tickets range from $10 to $18. ⌧ *Blackbaud Stadium, 1990 Daniel Island Dr., Daniel Island* ☎ *843/971–4625* ⊕ *www.charlestonbattery.com.*

TENNIS

Whether your interest in tennis is casual or serious, the Charleston area, especially its resort islands, offers tennis options for every skill level. Spring and fall are simply ideal for play. You can play for free at neighborhood courts, including several near Colonial Lake and at the Isle of Palms Recreation Center. Others owned by the city charge a mere $4 to $9 an hour for nonresidents. The resort islands are the most costly, depending on whether or not you are a guest.

Not only is the Lowcountry home to a pair of top-ranked tennis resorts, but it has a thriving year-round tennis community and is the home of the Family Circle Cup, a world-class professional women's tournament. Undoubtedly, this is a great place for avid players to enjoy a getaway vacation immersed in the sport they love.

6

The annual Family Circle Cup, held over nine days every April at the Family Circle Tennis Center, attracts some 90,000 fans from around the globe and boasts a roster of former champions, including Chris Evert, Martina Navratilova, Jennifer Capriati, and Venus and Serena Williams.

Charleston Tennis Center. Appropriate clothes and tennis shoes are required on the center's 15 hard courts, which at $8 an hour are inexpensive even for nonresidents. The courts are lighted at night, and there are restrooms on the premises. Tennis balls and racquets are also for sale. ⊠ *19 Farmfield Ave., West Ashley* ☎ *843/769–8258* ⊕ *www.charleston-sc.gov.*

★ **Fodor's Choice Family Circle Tennis Center.** World class, the Family Circle Tennis Center is, without question, one of the top facilities in the Southeast. The 17 courts (13 clay, 4 hard) are all lighted for night play and open to the public. Rates are $10 for the hard courts, $15 for clay. Four Quick Starts, miniature courts for children four to eight years old, have been added. The Instinctive Tennis Academy has private lessons (prices vary) and clinics for adults and children as young as four years old. It has one of the best-qualified teaching staffs in the country. The women's tennis Family Circle Cup is hosted here each April. A signature event for women's tennis, this tourney has brought in the sport's top names. Not incidentally, it is the city's top year-round outdoor arena and a venue for music concerts under the stars. ⊠ *161 Seven Farms Dr., Daniel Island* ☎ *843/856–7900* ⊕ *www.familycirclecup.com.*

Maybank Tennis Center. Maybank Tennis Center is public and has lights on its eight hard courts ($4 an hour for nonresidents). Its three clay courts are $9 an hour. Tennis balls and racquets are available for purchase; restrooms are on the premises. ⊠ *1880 Houghton Dr., James Island* ☎ *843/406–8814* ⊕ *www.charleston-sc.gov.*

KIAWAH ISLAND GOLF RESORT TENNIS COMPLEXES

Kiawah Island Golf Resort is also known for its high-quality tennis, instruction, special events, and nationally recognized tournaments. It has two tennis complexes, the **Roy Barth Tennis Center** and the **West Beach Tennis Club.** Both centers have pro shops, rentals, and even matchmaking services.

Roy Barth Tennis Center. The Roy Barth Tennis Center is in Kiawah Island Golf Resort's East Beach Village, a short walk from the Sanctuary, the resort's luxurious oceanfront hotel and spa. Open year-round, it has nine Har-Tru courts (one lighted), three hard courts (one lighted), and a practice court with a ball machine and automated ball retrieval system. Court time is $34 an hour for guests renting accommodations through Kiawah Resort and the Sanctuary, $43 for all others. ⊠ *Kiawah Island Golf Resort, East Beach Village, 1 Sanctuary Dr., Kiawah Island* ☎ *843/768–2838* ⊕ *www.kiawahresort.com.*

West Beach Tennis Club. Adjacent to the Straw Market's shops, this seasonal club (open March 2–September 7) features 10 Har-Tru courts and two lighted hard courts. Private instruction ranges from $80 an hour with a center's director to $30 per person per hour for three or more people with a teaching pro. ⊠ *Kiawah Island Golf Resort, West Beach Village, 1000 Kiawah Beach Dr., Kiawah Island* ☎ *843/768–2820* ⊕ *www.kiawahresort.com.*

WILD DUNES RESORT TENNIS CENTER

The Wild Dunes Tennis Center. This tennis center started out as a small, local tennis club, and it has never lost its love for the game. The tennis complex lies in the center of the Wild Dunes resort, where 17 Har-Tru courts include 1 stadium-style court and 5 lighted for night play. The pros in the ranked teaching program gear their lessons to each player, from novice to expert. Wild Dunes offers adult, junior, and Tiny Tot programs, professional instruction, and matchmaking for all levels. The full-service pro shop sells, rents, and repairs racquets. All Wild Dunes Resort guests can have one hour of complimentary court time per room, per day from noon to 6. For additional hours or court times reserved before noon, the cost is $15 per hour for guests renting accommodations. ⊠ *Wild Dunes Resort, 5757 Palm Blvd., Isle of Palms* ☎ *843/886–2113, 843/886–6000* ⊕ *www.wilddunes.com.*

6

WATER SPORTS

Although the ocean waters are warm and inviting, you'll also find surf and waves at some beaches, notably at Folly and Kiawah Island. Surfboards can be rented from McKelvin's for as little as $5 per hour to $25 for 24 hours (or $75 for a week); an hour of instruction is an additional $40 and includes board use. Out on John's Island, near Kiawah and Seabrook islands, instruction is $15 a day. Jet Skis are available at Folly Beach for $50 a half hour and $85 an hour, and a second rider pays just $10.

Island Bike and Surf Shop. Island Bike and Surf Shop rents surfboards and kayaks and will deliver to the resort islands. Boards cost $20 a day, $15 after four days. ⊠ *3665 Bohicket Rd., Johns Island* ☎ *843/768–1158* ⊕ *www.kiawahisland-bikerental.com.*

McKevlin's Surf Shop. The pros at McKevlin's Surf Shop can teach you what you need to know about surfing at Folly Beach. Surfboards can be rented for as little as $7 per hour to $30 for 24 hours (or $75 for a week); an hour of instruction is an additional $40 and includes board use. ⊠ *8 Center St., Folly Beach* ☎ *843/588–2247* ⊕ *www.mckevlins.com.*

Sun & Ski. Rents Jet Skis at this shop off the beach, just to the right of the fishing pier. You can also rent a double-chair setup and an umbrella for the day for $23. ⊠ *1 Center St., Folly Beach* ☎ *843/588–0033.*

SPAS

Unlock your senses, breathe in the aromatherapy, indulge your body, and let the pampering begin. You will be rejuvenated, relaxed, and refreshed in one of Charleston's top spas with some therapeutic and enjoyable treatments. Prices vary, depending on whether you choose a facial or a salt scrub or some other exotic treatment. As a rule of thumb, prices here are lower than in a major metropolis, with pedicures at these spas starting at $35, facials at $88, scrubs at $75–$100, and a 60-minute deep-tissue massage from $88 to $108. The beauty of Charleston-area spas is the benefit of small-town Southern hospitality combined with high-end service.

Charleston Place Spa. This truly deluxe day spa has nine treatment rooms and a wet room where exotic body wraps like their signature Magnolia Moments treatment and other treatments, like the Moroccan oil scalp, neck, and shoulder massage with hot stones, are administered. Four-handed massages for couples are a popular option. Locker rooms for men and women have showers and saunas; men also have a steam room. Adjacent is a fitness room, an indoor/outdoor pool with retractable roof, and a spacious hot tub available for hotel guests or clients who purchase a spa package. Also any purchase of their signature bracelets funds the spa's I Will Reflect campaign to help melanoma research. ⊠ *130 Market St., Market area* ☎ *843/722–4900* ⊕ *www.charlestonplacespa.com.*

Earthling Day Spa. Charleston's first global spa continues to grow. Decorated in a soothing, Southeast Asian design, the spa has an extensive menu that includes two-hour treatments from $200 to $250: Javanese beauty rituals, a Thai detox ritual (in which you're wrapped in banana leaves), and the hammam Turkish cleansing with a red-flower scrub. The latter is based on Turkish bath rituals with exotic spices like cardamom and olive stones to invigorate the circulation and lymph systems. Facials are Earthling's specialty, and the Alpha Effect with algae mineral mask will leave you glowing. There is also a Pilates studio, and a well-being boutique offers spa products, jewelry, and gifts. ⊠ *245 E. Bay St., Market area* ☎ *843/722–4737* ⊕ *www. earthlingdayspa.com.*

★ **Fodor's Choice** **Seeking Indigo.** This spa is 6,000 square feet of delightful, positive sensory overload. Behind the carved wooden Indonesian doors, a tranquil day spa, a Pilates studio, and a holistic wellness center await. Here, ancient healing meets modern technology with everything from detox footbaths to ayurvedic treatments and Thai massage. Stressed professionals stop by for a 20-minute ($30) thermal massage on the Migun bed, donning meditative headphones. Ladies book ahead for the ayurvedic session ($275) complete with Reiki, ginger compress, and pichu treatment. A holistic naturopath conducts metabolic assessments, and there is detoxing and a state-of-the-art hyperbaric oxygen chamber. ⊠ *445 King St., Upper King* ☎ *843/725–0217* ⊕ *www.seekingindigo.com.*

DOWNWARD DOG IN DOWNTOWN. If you'd like to boost your relaxation and get in a little yoga on your trip, Seeking Indigo also offers yoga classes. For $12 you can stretch and chant in a candlelit room while world music plays. (Mats are free.)

Stella Nova. In an historic Charleston "single house," Stella Nova is just off King Street. It's serious about all of its treatments, from waxing to salt scrubs. If antiaging is a priority, the collagen masque and massage can erase years. For couples, there are aromatherapy massages and men's services, too. Enjoy refreshments on the breezy verandas. Stella Nova has a top-of-the-line salon, with specially trained haircutters and makeup artists. It offers eyebrow threading as an alternative for waxing. The VIP Spa Suite, with butler service, is a good bet for bridal parties and girlfriend getaways. Known for its excellent service, the spa is open daily, even on Sunday, when street parking is easier to find. Check their website for their other locations in the Charleston area. ⊠ *78 Society St., Lower King* ☎ *843/723–0909* ⊕ *www.stella-nova.com.*

Shopping

WORD OF MOUTH

"Charleston is one of my favorite destinations because it literally has something for everyone.... Shopping on King with its array of name brands, boutiques, antiques is like strolling back into a time when main street offered everything for the family."

—Melissa

By Kinsey
Gidick

The shopping scene that exists today is a far cry—more like a shout for joy—from what existed here in the 1980s. In the not-so-distant past, King Street was still lined with retail shops with 1950s' facades, which sold merchandise that was not much more current. When Charleston Place (then the Omni) first opened its gallery of upscale shops in 1986, a spark was ignited that has continued to fire up a whole new generation of shops.

One-of-a-kind, locally owned boutiques, where the hottest trends in fashion hang on the racks, make up an important part of the contemporary Charleston shopping experience. Long-established, Christian Michi anchors the corner of Market and King across from the former Saks Fifth Avenue; its window displays are like artworks, and its innovative and European designs are treasured by well-heeled, sophisticated clients. Forever 21 has replaced Saks, which is indicative of Charleston's demographics. More mature shoppers are pleased to find such high-end shops that sell either their own designer fashions or carry names that are found in Paris, New York, and South Beach, like Kate Spade in the Shops at Charleston Place.

High-end shoe stores make up a category that tends to draw repeat visitors. The number and quality of shoe stores on King Street is surprising for the city's size. Family-owned shops like Berlin's are city institutions. Newer is Farushga, which is turning heads with its emphasis on handmade, cutting-edge Italian leather shoes; you'll often see boots and accessories there that are usually found only in Europe.

The Upper King District has furniture shops interspersed between the clothing boutiques and restaurants. These locally owned shops give the personal service that has always been a hallmark of existing King Street merchants in this area. The revival of this neighborhood has sparked a new wave of home-fashion stores; long-term antiques hunters, accustomed to buying on Lower King, have been lured uptown as well. Haute Design is one of the most tasteful of these shops, offering a wide selection of antiques, particularly lighting, imported from France and Italy. Charleston has more than 25 fine-art galleries, making it one of the top art towns in America. Local Lowcountry art, which includes both traditional landscapes of the region as well as more contemporary takes, is among the most prevalent styles here. Such innovative artists as Betty Smith and Fred Jamar, a Belgian known for his whimsical cityscapes, can give you a piece of Charleston to keep close until your next visit. Collectors will find high-end nationally and internationally renowned work in such exquisite galleries as Ann Long Fine Art and the more contemporary Martin Gallery.

SHOPPING REGIONS

City Market. The Market area is a cluster of shops and restaurants centered around the City Market. Sweetgrass basket weavers work here, and you can buy the resulting wares, although these artisan-crafts have become expensive. There are T-shirts and souvenir stores here as well as upscale boutiques. In the covered, open-air market, shops are open daily and vendors have stalls with everything from jewelry to dresses and purses. And, thanks to a beautiful 2011 remodel, you can peruse the middle section of the market in enclosed, air-conditioned comfort. ⊠ *E. Bay and Market Sts., Market area* ⊕ *www.thecharlestoncitymarket.com.*

Freshfields Village. At the crossroads of Kiawah and Seabrook islands, this shopping area includes a variety of homegrown stores. In addition to the gourmet Freshfields market (a supermarket with prepared food), there are French and Italian restaurants, an ice-cream shop, a sports outfitter, and stores selling upscale merchandise and apparel. It was a welcome addition to the area since the islands were distant from all shopping options for decades. More than a shopping destination, Freshfields has become a major social center for everything from wine and beer tastings to movies and music concerts on the village green. ⊠ *Kiawah Island Pkwy., Johns Island* ☎ *843/768–6491* ⊕ *www.freshfieldsvillage.com* ☉ *Mon.–Sat. 10–6, Sun. 1–6.*

★ **Fodor's**Choice **King Street.** King Street is Charleston's main street and the major shopping corridor downtown. The latest lines of demarcation divide the street into districts: Lower King (from Broad Street to Market Street) is the Antiques District, lined with high-end antiques dealers; Middle King (from Market Street to Calhoun Street) is now called the Fashion District and is a mix of national chains like Banana Republic and Pottery Barn, alternative shops, and locally owned landmark stores and boutiques; and Upper King (from Calhoun Street to Spring Street) has been dubbed the Design District, an up-and-coming area becoming known for its furniture and interior-design stores selling home fashion. Check out Second Sundays on King, when the street closes for pedestrian use from

7

CLOSE UP

Sweetgrass Baskets

The purchase of a handwoven Charleston sweetgrass basket is proof to your friends that you've been here. For centuries, African-American (Gullah) artisans have been weaving and selling these baskets in the City Market, where they sit busily in their chairs and place their wares on the sidewalk around them. Other places where they are known to set up are beside the downtown post office on Meeting and Broad streets, and on the right side of Highway 17 North, past Mount Pleasant (where you'll find the best prices). Prices range from about $60 for a small basket up into the hundreds for the larger sizes. Many buyers display these treasures in their homes like artwork or sculptures. Please be respectful of the renowned presence of the "basket ladies" in this city. Before taking their photograph, ask permission and offer a tip to show your appreciation.

Calhoun Street to Queen Street, and visit the Farmers' Market in Marion Square throughout the summer months. ⊕ *www.kingstreetantiquedistrict.com, www.kingstreet-fashiondistrict.com,* or *littleworksofheart.typepad.com/upperkingcharleston.*

Mount Pleasant Towne Centre. Across the Ravenel Bridge from Charleston, this mall has 60 stores, including Old Navy, White Market/Black Market, Loft, Barnes & Noble, and more. The mall has the area's best movie theater, the wide-screen Palmetto Grande. ⊠ *Hwy. 17 N at the Isle of Palms Connector, Mount Pleasant* ☎ *843/216–9900* ⊕ *www.mtpleasanttownecentre.com* ☺ *Daily 10–6.*

Tanger Outlet. If you are a dedicated outlet shopper, head to Tanger Outlet in North Charleston. This spiffy, contemporary mall is not far from the airport. It houses 80 name-brand outlets, like Loft, Kenneth Cole, J.Crew, Timberland, and Saks Fifth Avenue OFF 5TH. ⊠ *I–26 eastbound Exit 213A, or westbound Exit 213; left on Montague Ave., right on International Dr., North Charleston* ☎ *843/529–3095* ⊕ *www.tangeroutlet.com* ☺ *Mon.–Sat. 10–9, Sun. 11–6.*

SHOPPING REVIEWS

NORTH OF BROAD

LOWER KING

ANTIQUES

George C. Birlant & Co. You'll find mostly 18th- and 19th-century English antiques here, but keep your eye out for a Charleston Battery bench (which you can spot at White Point Garden), for which they are famous. Founded in 1922, Birlant's is fourth-generation family-owned. ⊠ *191 King St., Lower King* ☏ *843/722–3842* ⊕ *www.birlant.com* ⊙ *Mon.–Sat. 9–5:30.*

Jacques' Antiques. As the name suggests, most of the antiques here are imported from France, but all are either European or English, from the 17th to the 20th century. Decorative arts include ceramics, porcelains, and crystal. From the candlesticks to the armoires, all are in exquisite taste. ⊠ *160 King St., Lower King* ☏ *843/577–0104* ⊕ *www.jacantiques. com* ⊙ *Mon.–Sat. 10–5.*

CLOTHING

Ben Silver. Charleston's own Ben Silver, premier purveyor of blazer buttons, has more than 800 designs, including college and British regimental motifs. They also sell British neckties, embroidered polo shirts, blazers, and eyewear, both sunglasses and frames. This Charleston institution was founded in the 1960s. ⊠ *149 King St., Lower King* ☏ *843/577–4556* ⊕ *www.bensilver.com* ⊙ *Weekdays 9–6, Sat. 10–6.*

Berlin's Clothing Store. Family-owned for four generations since 1883, this Charleston landmark has clothing and sporting goods for men and is known as a destination for special-occasion clothing. The store, which for generations sold the preppy, Charlestonian look, has now added European designer styles. There is a complimentary parking lot across the street for customers. ⊠ *114–116 King St., Lower King* ☏ *843/722–1665 men's shop, 843/723–5591 ladies' shop* ⊕ *www.berlinsclothing.com* ⊙ *Mon.–Sat. 9:30–6.*

Billy Reid. The darling of Southern tailors offers fashion-forward shoppers the best in men's and women's rustic, aristocratic-chic clothing. Be sure to check out the basement sale racks, where prices are slashed as much as 50%. ⊠ *150 King St., Lower King* ☏ *843/577–3004* ⊕ *www.billyreid. com* ⊙ *Mon.–Sat. 10–6, Sun. noon–6.*

7

Christian Michi. This shop carries tony women's clothing and accessories. Designers from Italy, such as Piazza Sempione, are represented, as is Hoss Intropia from Spain. Known for its evening wear, it has pricey but gorgeous gowns and a fine selection of cocktail dresses. High-end fragrances add to the luxurious air. ✉ *220 King St., Lower King* ☎ *843/723–0575* ⊕ *www.christianmichi.com* ⊙ *Mon.–Sat. 10–6, Sun. noon–6.*

CLOTHING: CHILDREN
Sugar Snap Pea. This sweet shop stocks the ultimate in totwear, from Petit Bateau to Jellycat and Tea brand. Owner Zhenya Kuhne keeps the clothing options fresh and new. Also check out their baby shower registry. ✉ *161½ King St., Lower King* ☎ *843/793–2621* ⊕ *www.sugarsnappea. com* ⊙ *Mon.–Sat. 10–6.*

FOOD AND DRINK
Robot Candy Co. Willy Wonka ain't got nothing on Charleston. This divine confectionery is a child's dream, chockfull of tasty treats and toys. ✉ *322 King St., Lower King* ☎ *843/608–8090* ⊕ *www.robotcandyco.com* ⊙ *Mon.–Thurs. 11–6, Fri. and Sat. 11–8, Sun. noon–6.*

JEWELRY
Buckar Jewelry Architects. This shop has been crafting custom-design jewelry in Charleston for decades. Their friendly staff will take the time to visit as well as find the perfect gem for you. ✉ *239½ King St., Lower King* ☎ *843/937–8400* ⊕ *www.buckar.com.*

Croghan's Jewel Box. Ring the doorbell (literally) for fine new and estate jewelry as well as antiques at this Charleston institution with more than 100 years of service to the community. ✉ *308 King St., Lower King* ☎ *843/723–3594* ⊕ *www.croghansjewelbox.com* ⊙ *Weekdays 9:30–5:30, Sat. 10–5.*

Dixie Dunbar Studio. Dealing in artistic, unique jewelry, this contemporary jewelry shop has been here for decades. The handmade pieces can be delightfully unpredictable. ✉ *192 King St., Lower King* ☎ *843/722–0006* ⊕ *www.dixiedunbar. com* ⊙ *Mon.–Sat. 10–5:30.*

SHOES AND ACCESSORIES
Bob Ellis. In business for more than 60 years, this Charleston landmark sells some gorgeous shoes from Prada, Manolo Blahnik, YSL, Jimmy Choo, and Christian Louboutin,

among other high-end designers. ✉ *332 King St., King St.–Fashion District* ☎ *843/722–2515* ⊕ *www.bobellisshoes. com* ⊗ *Mon.–Sat.10–6; some Sun.*

Farushga. Farushga sells high-quality, cutting-edge Italian shoes for both men and women, from chic daytime looks to pulling-out-all-the-stops evening glamour. But the real beauty of Farushga is that you will not find the same fine brands sold at every other upscale Italian shoe store. Be warned, this boutique carries only one pair per size for every style, so if you see something you like, you may want to buy it on the spot. ✉ *377-A King St., Lower King* ☎ *843/722–3131* ⊗ *Mon.–Sat. 10:30–6:30, Sun. noon–5.*

MARKET AREA

ART GALLERIES

City Gallery on Waterfront Park. This city-owned art gallery, with handsome contemporary architecture and a delightful location within Waterfront Park, rotates paintings and sculpture shows and showcases predominately Charleston and South Carolina artists. Young and emerging talents exhibit, and residents and visitors alike love the many opening receptions and artist lectures. From the second floor, particularly, one has a privileged riverfront view. ✉ *34 Prioleau St. A, Market area* ☎ *843/958–6484* ⊕ *www. charlestonarts.sc* ⊗ *Tues.–Fri. 11–6, weekends noon–5.*

Corrigan Gallery. Owner Lese Corrigan displays her own paintings and rotates shows from some 16 other painters and photographers, as many as 12 shows a year. Most pieces fit the genre of contemporary Southern art. Prices range from $50 to $18,000. ✉ *62 Queen St., Market area* ☎ *843/722–9868* ⊕ *www.corrigangallery.com* ⊗ *Mon.–Sat. 10–5; by appointment.*

Horton Hayes Fine Art. This gallery carries the sought-after Lowcountry paintings depicting coastal life by Mark Kelvin Horton, who also paints architectural and figurative works. Shannon Rundquist is among the other Lowcountry artists shown; she has a fun, whimsical way of painting local life and is known for her blue-crab art. ✉ *30 State St., Market area* ☎ *843/958–0014* ⊕ *www.hortonhayes.com* ⊗ *Mon.–Sat. 10–5:30, Sun. 12:30–5.*

Robert Lange Studio. The most *avant* of the contemporary galleries, this striking, minimalist space is a working studio for Robert Lange and the other exceptionally talented young artists who are on exhibit and who come by to paint. Most of the work has a hyper-realistic style with surreal over-tones. Belgian Fred Jamar is the senior anchorman here, and his "bubble tree" Charleston cityscapes are whimsical, even cartoonlike. ⊠ *2 Queen St., Market area* ☎ *843/805–8052* ⊕ *www.robertlangestudios.com* ⊙ *Daily 11–5.*

Smith-Killian Fine Art. This gallery exhibits contemporary paintings and Lowcountry-scapes by Betty Smith and her talented triplets, Jennifer, Shannon, and Tripp. Her son, Tripp, is a nature photographer specializing in black-and-white images. The bronze wildlife sculpture is by nationally recognized Darrell Davis; the acclaimed oil paintings by Kim English are attention-getters. ⊠ *9 Queen St., Market area* ☎ *843/853–0708* ⊕ *www.smithkillian.com* ⊙ *Mon.–Sat. 10–6, Sun. by appointment.*

★ **Fodor'sChoice Wells Gallery.** Showcasing the talents of many fine artists, Wells Gallery shows Lowcountry-scapes, still lifes, black-and-white photographs, bronze sculpture, and hand-blown glass sculpture. Everything here is done in excellent taste, from the contemporary decor to its meet-the-artist receptions. Felice Designs, one-of-a-kind jewelry art, mainly of Italian Murano glass beads, is on exhibit, too. ⊠ *125 Meeting St., Market area* ☎ *843/853–3233* ⊕ *www.wellsgallery.com* ⊙ *Mon.–Sat. 10–5* ⊠ *1 Sanctuary Beach Dr., Kiawah Island* ☎ *843/576–1290.*

CLOTHING

The Trunk Show. This upscale consignment shop sells designer dresses, handbags and shoes, and vintage apparel. The back room has been converted into a men's department, with mostly new clothes but some vintage items as well. The shop has become known for its estate jewelry and also custom-made jewelry from semiprecious stones. It has an excellent selection of gowns and evening wear. Many items now come in new from other shops. ⊠ *281 Meeting St., Market area* ☎ *843/722–0442* ⊕ *www.charlestontrunkshow.com* ⊙ *Mon.–Sat. 11–6.*

FOOD AND DRINK

Charleston Candy Kitchen. This sweets shop sells freshly made fudge, Charleston chews, and benne-seed (sesame-seed) wafers. It has a bigger sister in Savannah. ⊠ *32A N. Market St., Market area* ☎ *843/723–4626* ⊕ *www.savannahcandy.com* ⊙ *Daily 9:30 am–10 pm.*

Charleston's Sweet Tooth

CLOSE UP

Pralines, glazed pecans, bear claws, and benne wafers—Charlestonians have a sweet tooth.

Stroll the sidewalks of the Market area and breathe in the come-hither aroma of pralines. Employees of candy shops like **Market Street Sweets** (⊠ 100 N. Market St.) stand outside offering samples of their wares, including pralines and cinnamon-and-sugar-glazed pecans.

Benne wafers, which are sweet cookies rather than sesame crackers as the name might suggest, are a Charleston original. Benne is the African word for sesame seeds, which were brought over on slave ships. Once in Charleston, all it took was a little brown sugar, and a confection was born. A traditional recipe for benne wafers can be found in the classic cookbook *Charleston Receipts*. These diminutive cookies, the size of a quarter, can be sampled at Charleston's Farmers' Market, downtown on Marion Square on Saturday. They are also found at **Harris Teeter** (⊠ 290 E. Bay St.), packaged appropriately for gift giving by Charleston Favorites.

If you develop an addiction to them, they can be ordered online at *www.foodforthesouthernsoul.com*, along with benne candy, praline pecans, and more.

And, so y'all don't think we're behind the sweet times, the cupcake invasion made it down to Charleston a while back. **Cupcake** (⊠ 433 King St.) sells the latest flavors popularized in Manhattan, like dark chocolate with caramel frosting sprinkled with sea salt. The adorably quaint **Sugar Bake Shop** (⊠ 59½ Cannon St.) specializes in cupcakes such as grapefruit and chocolate raspberry, homemade ice cream, and cookies. And on a final sweet note, we have been invaded once again, this time by macaroons. The French-influenced confection can be bought at **The Macaroon Boutique** (⊠ 45 John St. ⊕ www.macaroonboutique.com). Raspberry is proving to be the flavor of choice, but then, it is one of Charleston's favorite colors—pink.

7

Market Street Sweets. Make time to stop at Market Street Sweets for the melt-in-your-mouth pralines, bear claws, fudge, and their famous glazed pecans—cinnamon and sugar is the favorite. Its mother store is in Savannah. ⊠ 100 N. Market St., Market area ☎ 843/722–1397 ⊕ www.riverstreetsweets.com ☉ Tues.–Sun. 9 am–11 pm.

O'Hara & Flynn. One of Charleston's best-known wineshops also has a wine bar, open Monday through Saturday until 10 pm. If you buy a bottle of wine at retail price, you can drink it at the tables or right at the wine bar for just a $10 corkage fee. Cheeses, meats (including imported sausage and salami), and fresh olive oil are sold here, and you can order some as small appetizer plates. French bonbons are a new delicacy. There's live jazz and acoustic music on Friday and Saturday evenings. ✉ *225 Meeting St., Market area* ☎ *843/534–1916* ☉ *Mon.–Thurs. 11–11, Fri. and Sat. 11 am–midnight.*

Ted's Butcherblock. In addition to gourmet meals to go, you can buy wines, cheeses, cold meats, and olive oil, attend one of the frequent wine tastings, or stop by to see what's cooking on Ted's Big Green Egg grill. ✉ *334 E. Bay St., Ansonborough* ☎ *843/577–0094* ⊕ *www.tedsbutcherblock. com* ☉ *Tues.–Sat. 11–7.*

GIFTS

Charleston Cooks/Maverick Kitchen Store. You'll find just about every gourmet kitchen tool and accessory you can think of here. Regional food and cookbooks, as well as culinary gifts, abound. And you can also enjoy cooking classes and demonstrations. ✉ *194 E. Bay St., Market area* ☎ *843/722–1212* ⊕ *www.charlestoncooks.com* ☉ *Mon.–Sat. 10–9, Sun. noon–6.*

Indigo. Indigo stocks funky home and garden accessories. In addition, there are both locally made and handmade products that come from unique vendors, from quirky clothes to artisan jewelry. ✉ *4 Vendue Range, Market area* ☎ *843/723–2983* ⊕ *www.indigohome.com* ☉ *Mon.–Sat 10–9, Sun. 10–7.*

The Smoking Lamp. Charleston's oldest smoke shop sells cigars, pipes, and accessories. ✉ *401 B King St., Market area* ☎ *843/577–7339* ⊕ *www.smokinglamp.com* ☉ *Mon.–Thurs. 10–10, Fri. and Sat. 10–midnight, Sun. 10–6.*

HOME DECOR AND FURNITURE

Historic Charleston Foundation. Bring home superb replicas of Charleston furniture, china, and decorative accessories. The variety and quality of these Charleston mementos, from the high-end pieces to the bags of Carolina Rice, make treasured gifts. Royalties from sales contribute to restoration projects. ✉ *108 Meeting St., Market area* ☎ *843/723–1623* ⊕ *www. historiccharleston.org* ☉ *Mon.–Sat. 9–6, Sun. noon–5.*

MIDDLE KING

BOOKS

Heirloom Book Co. Thanks to Charleston's booming culinary scene, Heirloom Book Co. is a thriving cookbook shop. From hard-to-find vintage cookbooks to the latest best sellers, chef Sean Brock's favorite bookstore keeps acclaimed toques and wannabe Julia Childs up-to-date. Check their website for frequent events. ✉ *123 King St., Middle King* ☎ *843/722–6377* ⊕ *www.heirloombookcompany.com.*

CLOTHING

Copper Penny. Shop Copper Penny for trendy dresses and names like Trina Turk, Millie, Tibi, and Diane Von Furstenberg. ✉ *311 King St., Middle King* ☎ *843/723–2999* ⊕ *www. shopcopperpenny.com* ☺ *Mon.–Sat. 10–7, Sun. noon–6.*

Everything But Water. In the Shops at Charleston Place, this store has one of the town's largest and finest collections of swimwear for all ages. ✉ *130 Market St., Shops at Charleston Place, Middle King* ☎ *843/722–5884* ⊕ *www. everythingbutwater.com* ☺ *Mon.–Wed. 10–6, Thurs.–Sat. 10–8, Sun. noon–5.*

Finicky Filly. Boutique favorite Finicky Filly carries exceptional women's apparel and accessories by such designers as Lela Rose, Schumacher, All Dressed Up, and Etro. The Filly appeals to women from college age to seniors. ✉ *303 King St., Middle King* ☎ *843/534–0203* ⊕ *thefinickyfilly. com* ☺ *Mon.–Sat. 10–5:30, Sun. 1–5.*

Hampden Clothing. One of the city's trendiest boutiques attracts the young and well heeled, who come here for an edgier style. The shop's sophisticated sensitivity and hot new designers such as Yigal Azrouël, Vena Cava, Alexander Wang, and Jenni Kayne help make it a premier destination for the latest in fashion. ✉ *314 King St., Middle King* ☎ *843/724–6373* ⊕ *www.hampdenclothing.com* ☺ *Mon.– Sat. 10–6, Sun. noon–5.*

CLOTHING: LINGERIE

Bits of Lace. When this exclusive lingerie shop opened in 1977 with its sexy French imports, no one thought it would make it in such a conservative town. It's still here and now stocks beautiful maternity sleepwear and Eres swimsuits. It has become known for its bra-fitting service, especially for bigger cup sizes—up to K. ✉ *302 King St., Middle King* ☎ *843/266–6985* ⊕ *www.bitsoflace.com* ☺ *Mon.–Sat. 10–6.*

FOOD AND DRINK

Caviar and Bananas. This upscale specialty market and café features not-so-ordinary supermarket items like epicurean prepared foods and artisanal cheeses. Note the locally made items such as Callie's Pimento Cheese. ⊠ *51 George St., Middle King* ☎ *843/577–7757* ⊕ *www.caviarandbananas. com* ☯ *Weekdays 7 am–8:30 pm, Sat. 8:30–8:30, Sun. 8–8.*

GIFTS

Vieuxtemps. This is where Charlestonians go to pick out wedding china. The only Charleston store to offer Herend, Royal Crown Derby, Haviland, and Spode, the store is a discerning bride's dream. Gifts, linens, and antiques are also a great reason to pop by. ⊠ *180 King St., Middle King* ☎ *843/723–7309* ⊕ *www.vieuxtemps.net* ☯ *Mon.–Sat. 10–5:30.*

Worthwhile. Artsy and hip baby gear, women's clothes and shoes, housewarming gifts, jewelry, books, and even office supplies make the mundane fun at Worthwhile. ⊠ *268 King St., Middle King* ☎ *843/723–4418* ⊕ *www.shopworthwhile. com* ☯ *Mon.–Sat. 10–6, Sun. noon–5.*

SHOES AND ACCESSORIES

Gucci of Charleston. In the Shops at Charleston Place, this Gucci location carries a full line of handbags, luggage, beautiful designer jewelry, and even a dress or two. ⊠ *132 Market St., Middle King* ☎ *843/722–3788* ⊕ *www.gucci. com* ☯ *Mon.–Wed. 10–6, Thurs.–Sat. 10–7, Sun. noon–5.*

UPPER KING

ANTIQUES

Haute Design. This shop sells antiques, chandeliers, and French and Italian furniture, as well as custom-designed pieces like tables and mirrors. Belgian linen and hand-screen-printed fabrics are a specialty, and available accessories include Vinnini blown glass and "antique" pillows. Interior-design services are available. ⊠ *489 King St., Upper King* ☎ *843/577–9886* ⊕ *www.hautedesign.com.*

ART GALLERIES

Gallery Chuma. This gallery showcases Gullah (Lowcountry African-American) art from inexpensive mini-prints to the work of its primary artist, Jonathan Green. The popularity of Gullah art and its growth as a genre is attributed to this highly successful South Carolina artist. ⊠ *188 Meeting St., Upper King* ☎ *843/722–1702* ⊕ *www.gallerychuma.com* ☯ *Daily 9:30–6.*

BOOKS

Blue Bicycle Books. Look for out-of-print and rare books, including hardcover classics, at Blue Bicycle Books. It has a large selection of everything from fiction to military history and cookbooks. Check their website for frequent book signings by the likes of Pat Conroy and Dorothea Benton Frank. ✉ *420 King St., Upper King* ☎ *843/722–2666* ⊕ *www.blue bicyclebooks.com* ⊙ *Mon.–Sat. 10–7:30, Sun. 1–6.*

CLOTHING

Ellington. Chic and classy, this shop is known for its washable, packable travel pieces, its flowing tops, its feel-good fabrics like silk, linen, and cashmere. Its fashions have classic styles, but with new arrangements. ✉ *473 King St., Upper King* ☎ *843/722–7999* ⊙ *Mon.–Sat. 10:30–5:30.*

CLOTHING: CHILDREN

Kids on King. Having traveled the world and countless fashion centers, the owners of Kids on King bring you the finest in children's apparel and accessories from everywhere. Be transported to other lands with handcrafted unique designs just for your kids. ✉ *195 King St., Upper King* ☎ *843/720–8647* ⊕ *www.kidsonking.com* ⊙ *Mon.–Sat. 10–6, Sun. noon–5.*

HOME DECOR AND FURNITURE

Old Charleston Joggling Board Co. As the name suggests, this shop sells joggling boards, historic Lowcountry oddities on which young, courting couples once bounced toward each other. Nowadays, they are simply used for sitting, usually on front verandas. ✉ *652 King St., Upper King* ☎ *843/723–4331* ⊕ *www.oldcharlestonjogglingboard.com* ⊙ *Mon.–Thurs. 8:30–4, Fri. 8:30–noon.*

JEWELRY

Felice Designs. Owner Felice Killian forms Italian Murano glass into beads to create her mesmerizing jewelry collection. She also pairs the beads with crystals and pearls. Many designs mirror sea life such as sea anemones and jellyfish. ✉ *424 King St., Upper King* ☎ *843/853–3354* ⊕ *www.felice designs.com* ⊙ *Weekdays 10–5:30, Sat. 10–5.*

SHOES AND ACCESSORIES

Magar Hatworks. Selling handcrafted headgear, young milliner Leigh Magar has stood the test of some time now and has introduced her love of hats to the young and fashionable. Her wholesale business includes sales to Barneys New York, and she has received national attention and media cover-

7

age, with celebs from Eartha Kitt to Sean Lennon buying her wares. ⊠ *57 Cannon St., Upper King* ☎ *843/345–4483* ⊕ *www.magarhatworks.com* ⊗ *By appointment.*

SOUTH OF BROAD

ART GALLERIES

Ann Long Fine Art. Serious art collectors head to Ann Long Fine Art for neoclassical and modern works. This elite, world-class gallery has some outstanding, albeit pricey work, by both gifted American and European artists. Many are painted with old master techniques. In addition, the gallery manages the estate of Otto Neumann. ⊠ *54 Broad St., South of Broad* ☎ *843/577–0447* ⊕ *www.annlongfineart. com* ⊗ *Weekdays 10–5; summer hrs vary.*

Charleston Renaissance Gallery. This gallery carries museum-quality Southern art framed in a period manner. In fact, 60% of their sales are to museums; the average cost is $35,000–$38,000. Visit, nonetheless—these are paintings of rare beauty. ⊠ *103 Church St., South of Broad* ☎ *843/723–0025* ⊕ *www.charlestonrenaissancegallery.com* ⊗ *Weekdays 9:30–5:30.*

Ellis-Nicholson Gallery. Showcasing artists and sculptors who span many levels, from emerging artists to those with international recognition, this gallery has a premier selection of oils, acrylics, mixed media, bronze, clay, glass, wood, and handcrafted jewelry. ⊠ *1½ Broad St., South of Broad* ☎ *843/722–5353* ⊕ *www.ellis-nicholsongallery.com* ⊗ *Mon.–Sat. 10–6, Sun. by appointment.*

★ **Fodor's Choice Martin Gallery.** In a former bank building, this is the city's most impressive gallery, selling art by nationally and internationally acclaimed artists, sculptors, and photographers. The gallery is known especially for its bronzes and large wooden sculptures, as well as glass sculpture and custom-designed jewelry. ⊠ *18 Broad St., South of Broad* ☎ *843/723–7378* ⊕ *www.martingallerycharleston. com* ⊗ *Mon.– Sat. 10–6, Sun. 11–5.*

JEWELRY

Paulo Geiss Jewelers. Paulo Geiss Jewelers has been a family tradition for more than 90 years and is a member of the American Gem Society. The shop features the work of couture jewelry designers as well as high-end timepieces by Rolex and some custom designs. ⊠ *116 E. Bay St., South of Broad* ☎ *843/577–4497* ⊕ *www.geissjewelers.com* ⊗ *Mon.–Sat. 9:30–5:30.*

MOUNT PLEASANT AND VICINITY

ANTIQUES

Page's Thieves Market. Specializing in furniture, especially medium- to large-scale pieces such as tables, desks, and chests, this market frequently hosts auctions on the weekends. Stop on your way to the beach at Sullivan's Island or Isle of Palms. ✉ *1460 Ben Sawyer Blvd., Mount Pleasant* ☎ *843/884–9672* ⊕ *www.pagesthievesmarket.com* ⊘ *Weekdays 9–5, Sat. 9–4.*

HOME DECOR AND FURNITURE

Carolina Lanterns. Stop in for copper gas and electric lanterns based on designs from downtown's Historic District, among a host of other lights and accessories. ✉ *1362 Chuck Dawley Blvd., Mount Pleasant* ☎ *843/881–4170, 877/881–4173* ⊕ *www.carolinalanterns.com* ⊘ *Mon.–Thurs. 9–5:30, Fri. 9–5, Sat. 11–3.*

GREATER CHARLESTON

CANNONBOROUGH

CLOTHING

Indigo & Cotton. This Cannonborough men's store is the go-to boutique for the latest in gentlemen's tailoring featuring brands such as Gitman Vintage, Filson Red Label bags, and Raleigh Denim, along with bow ties, handkerchiefs, and other accessories. ✉ *79 Cannon St., Cannonborough* ☎ *843/718–2980* ⊕ *www.indigoandcotton.com* ⊘ *Weekdays 11–6, Sat. 11–5.*

GIFTS

Mac & Murphy. This Cannonborough hole-in-the-wall is for the lover of traditional snail-mail letters, with the trendiest in notepads, pens, note cards, wrapping paper, and stationery, including Cheree Berry, Crane & Co., Dude and Chick. ✉ *74 Cannon St., Cannonborough* ☎ *843/576–4394* ⊕ *www. macandmurphy.com* ⊘ *Weekdays 10:30–6, Sat. 10:30–5.*

WEST ASHLEY

ANTIQUES

Livingston Antiques. This shop deals in 18th- and 19th-century English and Continental furnishings, clocks, and bric-a-brac. Moderate pricing can be found here, as it is in a suburb. ✉ *2137 Savannah Hwy., West Ashley* ☎ *843/556–6162* ⊕ *www.livingstonantiques.com* ⊘ *Tues.–Sat. 10–4.*

Hilton Head and the Lowcountry

WORD OF MOUTH

"Hilton Head is a nice family vacation place for those who want lots of variety . . . There's great golf, biking, horseback riding, restaurants, and outlet shopping."

—willowjane

Updated
by Sally
Mahan

Hilton Head Island is a unique and incredibly beautiful resort town that anchors the southern tip of South Carolina's coastline. What makes this semitropical island so unique? At the top of the list is the fact that visitors won't see large, splashy billboards or neon signs. What they will see is an island where the environment takes center stage, a place where development is strictly regulated.

There are 12 miles of sparkling white sand beaches, amazing world-class restaurants, top-rated golf courses—Harbour Town Golf Links annually hosts the Heritage Golf Tournament, a PGA Tour event—and a thriving tennis community. There are also many animals, including loggerhead sea turtles, alligators, snowy egrets, wood storks, great blue heron, and, in the waters, dolphins, manatees, and various species of fish. There are lots of activities offered on the island, including parasailing, charter fishing, kayaking, and many other water sports.

The island has several large, private, gated communities. They include Sea Pines, Hilton Head Plantation, Shipyard, Wexford, Long Cove, Port Royal, Indigo Run, Palmetto Hall, and Palmetto Dunes. Within most of the plantations are vacation rentals, upscale housing, golf courses, shopping, and restaurants. For instance, Sea Pines has a shopping center, restaurants, three golf courses, and the iconic candy-cane-striped Hilton Head Lighthouse. There are also many housing and shopping areas on the island that are not behind security gates.

ORIENTATION AND PLANNING

GETTING ORIENTED

Hilton Head is just north of South Carolina's border with Georgia. This part of South Carolina is best explored by car, as its points of interest spread over a flat coastal plain that is a mix of wooded areas, marshes, and sea islands, the latter of which are sometimes accessible only by boat or ferry. The 42-square-mile island is shaped like a foot, hence the reason locals often describe places as being at the "toe" or "heel" of Hilton Head.

Hilton Head's neighbor, Bluffton, is a quirky, artsy town rich with history. In the last several years it has grown from 1 square mile to about 50 square miles. South of Hilton Head is the city of Savannah, which is about a 45-minute

TOP REASONS TO GO

Beachcombing: Hilton Head Island has 12 miles of beaches. You can swim, soak up the sun, or walk along the sand.

Challenging Golf: Hilton Head's nickname is "Golf Island," and its many challenging courses have an international reputation.

Serving Up Tennis: Home to hundreds of tennis courts, Hilton Head is one of the nation's top tennis destinations.

Staying Put: This semitropical island has been a resort destination for decades, and it has all the desired amenities for visitors: a vast array of lodgings, an endless supply of restaurants, and excellent shopping.

Beaufort: This small antebellum town offers large doses of heritage and culture; nearly everything you might want to see is within its downtown historic district.

drive from the island. North of Hilton Head is Beaufort, a cultural treasure and a graceful antebellum town. Beaufort is also about 45 minutes from Hilton Head.

Hilton Head Island. One of the Southeast coast's most popular tourist destinations, Hilton Head is known for its golf courses and tennis courts. It's a magnet for time-share owners and retirees. Bluffton is Hilton Head's neighbor to the west. The old-town area is laden with history and charm.

Beaufort. This charming town just inland from Hilton Head is a destination in its own right, with a lively dining scene and cute bed-and-breakfasts.

Daufuskie Island. A scenic ferry ride from Hilton Head, Daufuskie is now much more developed than it was during the days when Pat Conroy wrote *The Water Is Wide,* but it's still a beautiful island to explore, even on a day trip. You can stay for a few days at a variety of fine rental properties, tool down shady dirt roads in a golf cart, and delight in the glorious, nearly deserted beaches.

PLANNING

WHEN TO GO

The high season follows typical beach-town cycles, with June through August and holidays year-round being the busiest and most costly. Mid-April, during the annual Heritage Golf Tournament, is when rates tend to be highest. Thanks to the Lowcountry's mostly moderate year-round temperatures, tourists are ever-present. Spring is the best time to visit, when the weather is ideal for tennis and golf. Autumn is almost as active for the same reason.

WILL IT RAIN? Don't be discouraged when you see a weather forecast during the summer months saying there's a 30% chance of rain for Hilton Head. It can be an absolutely gorgeous day and suddenly a storm will "pop up" late in the afternoon. That's because on hot sunny days, the hot air rises up into the atmosphere and mixes with the cool air, causing the atmosphere to become unstable, thereby creating thunderstorms. Not to worry, though: these storms move in and out fairly quickly.

To get a good deal, it's imperative that you plan ahead. The choicest locations can be booked six months to a year in advance, but booking agencies can help you make room reservations and get good deals during the winter season, when the crowds fall off. Villa-rental companies often offer snowbird rates for monthly stays during the winter season. Parking is always free at the major hotels, but valet parking can cost from $15 to $20; the smaller properties have free parking, too, but no valet service.

PLANNING YOUR TIME

No matter where you stay, spend your first day relaxing on the beach or hitting the links. After that, you'll have time to visit some of the area's attractions, including the Coastal Discovery Museum or the Sea Pines Resort. You can also visit the Tanger outlet malls on U.S. 278 in Bluffton. Old-town Bluffton is a quaint area with many quirky, locally owned shops and art galleries. If you have a few more days, visit Beaufort or even spend the night there. This historic antebellum town is rich with history. Savannah is also a short day trip away.

GETTING HERE AND AROUND

AIR TRAVEL

Most travelers use the Savannah/Hilton Head International Airport, less than an hour from Hilton Head, which is served by American Eagle, Delta, United, and US Airways. Hilton Head Island Airport is served by US Airways.

Air Contacts Hilton Head Island Airport ⊠ *120 Beach City Rd., North end, Hilton Head* ☎ *843/255–2950* ⊕ *www.hiltonheadairport.com.* **Savannah/Hilton Head International Airport** ⊠ *400 Airways Ave., Northwest, Savannah, Georgia* ☎ *912/964–0514* ⊕ *www.savannahairport.com.*

BOAT AND FERRY TRAVEL

Hilton Head is accessible via boat, with docking available at Harbour Town Yacht Basin, Skull Creek Marina, and Shelter Cove Harbor.

Boat Docking Information Harbour Town Yacht Basin ✉ *Sea Pines, 149 Lighthouse Rd., South end, Hilton Head* ☎ *843/671–4534* ⊕ *harbourtownyachtbasin.com.* **Shelter Cove Marina** ✉ *Shelter Cove, 1 Shelter Cove La., Mid-Island, Hilton Head* ☎ *843/842–7001, 866/400–7894* ⊕ *www.palmettodunes.com.* **Skull Creek Marina** ✉ *1 Waterway La., North end, Hilton Head* ☎ *843/681–8436* ⊕ *www.theskullcreekmarina.com.*

BUS TRAVEL

The Lowcountry Regional Transportation Authority, known as the Palmetto Breeze, has a transportation-on-demand service that ranges from $6 to $10 one way. The service also has buses that leave Bluffton in the morning for Hilton Head, Beaufort, and some of the Sea Islands. The fare is $2. Exact change is required.

Bus Contacts The Lowcountry Regional Transportation Authority ✉ *25 Benton Field Rd., Bluffton* ☎ *843/757–5782* ⊕ *www.palmettobreezetransit.com.*

CAR TRAVEL

Driving is the best way to get onto Hilton Head Island. Off Interstate 95, take Exit 8 onto U.S. 278 East, which leads you through Bluffton and then onto Hilton Head proper. Once on Hilton Head, U.S. 278 forks. On the right is William Hilton Parkway and on the left is the Cross Island Parkway, which is a toll road ($1.25 each way). If you take the Cross Island (as the locals call it) to the south side where Sea Pines and many other resorts are, it will take about 10 to 15 minutes to get to Sea Pines Circle, depending on traffic. If you take William Hilton Parkway (business U.S. 278), it will take about 30 minutes, again depending on traffic. Be aware that at check-in and checkout times on Friday, Saturday, and Sunday, U.S. 278 can slow to a crawl. ■TIP➜ **Be careful of putting the pedal to the metal, particularly on the Cross Island Parkway. The speed limits change dramatically, and it is patrolled regularly.**

Once on Hilton Head Island, signs are small and blend in with the trees and landscaping, and nighttime lighting is kept to a minimum. The lack of streetlights makes it difficult to find your way at night, so be sure to get good directions.

TAXI TRAVEL

There are several taxi services available on Hilton Head, including Hilton Head Taxi and Limousine, Yellow Cab HHI, and Diamond Transportation of Hilton Head, which has SUVs and passenger vans available for pickup to and from Savannah/Hilton Head International Airport and Hilton Head Airport. Prices range from $20 to $110.

Taxi Contacts Diamond Transportation ⊠ *5 Gumtree Rd., Mid-Island, Hilton Head* ☎ *843/247-2156* ⊕ *hiltonheadrides.com.* **Hilton Head Taxi and Limousine** ⊠ *374 Spanish Wells Rd., Mid-Island, Hilton Head* ☎ *843/785-8294.* **Yellow Cab HHI** ☎ *843/686-6666* ⊕ *www.yellowcabhhi.com.*

TRAIN TRAVEL

Amtrak gets you as close as Savannah or Yemassee.

Train Contacts Savannah Amtrak Station ⊠ *2611 Seaboard Coastline Dr., Savannah, Georgia* ☎ *800/872-7245* ⊕ *www.amtrak.com.*

TOURS

Hilton Head's Adventure Cruises hosts dolphin-watching cruises, sport crabbing, and more. Several companies, including H2O Sports, Live Oac, Outside Hilton Head, and Low Country Nature Tours in Hilton Head, run dolphin-watching, shark-fishing, kayak, sunset, and delightful environmental trips. Low Country Nature Tours offers a family-friendly fireworks tour during the summer, as well as educational and fun bird-watching tours that children are sure to enjoy.

Gullah Heritage Trail Tours gives a wealth of history about slavery and the Union takeover of the island during the Civil War; tours leave from the Coastal Discovery Museum at Honey Horn Plantation and cost $32.

There's a wide variety of tours available at Harbour Town Yacht Basin, including sunset cruises, fireworks, and dolphin tours. Pau Hana & Flying Circus Sailing Charters offers tours on a catamaran sailboat, and fireworks and sunset cruises. The captains provide an interactive, educational adventure, and the catamaran makes for smooth sailing.

Tour Contacts Adventure Cruises ⊠ *Shelter Cove Marina, 9 Harbourside La., Mid-Island, Hilton Head Island* ☎ *843/785-4558* ⊕ *www.hiltonheadisland.com/adventure.* **Gullah Heritage Trail Tours** ⊠ *Coastal Discovery Museum, 70 Honey Horn Dr., North end, Hilton Head* ☎ *843/681-7066* ⊕ *www.gullaheritage.com.* **H2O Sports** ⊠ *Harbour Town Marina, 149 Lighthouse Rd., South End, Hilton Head Island* ☎ *843/671-4386, 877/290-4386* ⊕ *www.*

h2osportsonline.com. **Harbour Town Yacht Basin** ⊠ *Sea Pines, 149 Lighthouse Rd., South End, Hilton Head Island* ☎ *843/363–2628* ⊕ *harbourtownyachtbasin.com.* **Live Oac** ⊠ *Hilton Head Harbor, 43A Jenkins Rd., North End, Hilton Head Island* ☎ *888/254–8362* ⊕ *www. liveoac.com.* ⟐ **Low Country Nature Tours** ⊠ *Shelter Cove Marina, 1 Shelter Cove La., Mid-Island, Hilton Head Island* ☎ *843/683–0187* ⊕ *www.lowcountrynaturetours.com.* **Outside Hilton Head** ⊠ *Shelter Cove Marina, 1 Shelter Cove La., Mid-Island, Hilton Head Island* ☎ *843/686–6996* ⊕ *www.outsidehiltonhead.com.* ⟐ **Pau Hana & Flying Circus Sailing Charters** ⊠ *Palmetto Bay Marina, 86 Helmsman Way, South End, Hilton Head Island* ☎ *843/686–2582* ⊕ *www. hiltonheadislandsailing.com.*

RESTAURANTS

The number of fine-dining restaurants on Hilton Head Island is extraordinary, given the size of the island. Because of the proximity to the Atlantic and small farms on the mainland, most locally owned restaurants are still heavily influenced by the catch of the day and seasonal field harvests. Most of the fine-dining restaurants open at 11 and don't close until 9 or 10, but some take a break between 2 and 4. Most of the more expensive restaurants have an early dining menu, and this is a popular time to dine. During the height of the summer season, reservations are a good idea, though in the off-season you may need them only on weekends. There are plenty of great delis where you can pick up lunch, several locally owned breakfast joints, and plenty of sports bars. There are also numerous national chain and fast-food restaurants, including Panera Bread, Olive Garden, IHOP, Applebee's, Burger King, Wendy's, McDonald's, and Subway. Smoking is prohibited in restaurants and bars in Bluffton, Beaufort, and on Hilton Head Island. Beaufort's restaurant scene has certainly evolved, with more trendy restaurants serving contemporary cuisine moving into the immediate downtown area.

HOTELS

Hilton Head is known as one of the best vacation spots on the East Coast, and its hotels are a testimony to its reputation. The island is awash in regular hotels and resorts, not to mention beachfront or golf-course-view villas, cottages, and luxury private homes. You can expect the most modern conveniences and world-class service at the priciest places. Clean, updated rooms and friendly staff are everywhere, even at lower-cost hotels—this is the South, after all. Staying in cooler months, for extended periods of time, or commuting from nearby Bluffton can save money.

HILTON HEAD ISLAND

Hilton Head Island is known far and wide as a vacation destination that prides itself on its top-notch golf courses and tennis programs, world-class resorts, and beautiful beaches. But the island is also part of the storied American South, steeped in a rich, colorful history. It has seen Native Americans and explorers, battles from the Revolutionary War to the Civil War, plantations and slaves, and development and environmentally focused growth.

More than 10,000 years ago, the island was inhabited by Paleo-Indians. From 8000 to 2000 BC, Woodland Indians lived on the island. A shell ring made from their discarded oyster shells and animal bones from that period can be found in the Sea Pines Nature Preserve.

The recorded history of the island goes back to the early 1500s, when Spanish explorers sailing coastal waters came upon the island and found Native American settlements. Over the next 200 years, the island was claimed at various times by the Spanish, the French, and the British. In 1663, Captain William Hilton claimed the island for the British crown (and named it for himself), and the island became home to indigo, rice, and cotton plantations.

During the Revolutionary War, the British harassed islanders and burned plantations. During the War of 1812, British troops again burned plantations, but the island recovered from both wars. During the Civil War, Union troops took Hilton Head in 1861 and freed the more than 1,000 slaves on the island. Mitchelville, one of the first settlements for freed blacks, was created. There was no bridge to the island, so its freed slaves, called "Gullah," subsisted on agriculture and the seafood-laden waters.

Over the years, much of the plantation land was sold at auction. Then, in 1949, General Joseph Fraser purchased 17,000 acres, much of which would eventually become various communities, including Hilton Head Plantation, Palmetto Dunes, and Spanish Wells. The general bought another 1,200 acres, which his son, Charles, used to develop Sea Pines. The first bridge to the island was built in 1956, and modern-day Hilton Head was born.

What makes Hilton Head so special now? Charles Fraser and his business associates focused on development while preserving the environment. And that is what tourists will see today: an island that values its history and its natural beauty.

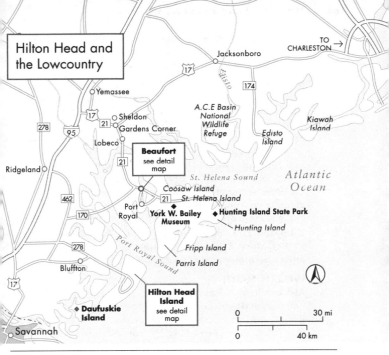

Hilton Head and the Lowcountry

TO CHARLESTON →

Jacksonboro

Yemassee

A.C.E Basin National Wildlife Refuge

Kiawah Island

Sheldon
Gardens Corner
Lobeco

Edisto Island

Ridgeland

Beaufort see detail map

St. Helena Sound

Atlantic Ocean

Coosaw Island
St. Helena Island

Port Royal

York W. Bailey Museum

◆ Hunting Island State Park

Hunting Island

Port Royal Sound

Fripp Island

Bluffton

Parris Island

◆ Daufuskie Island

Hilton Head Island see detail map

Savannah

0   30 mi
0   40 km

EXPLORING

GETTING HERE AND AROUND

Hilton Head Island is 19 miles east of Interstate 95. Take Exit 8 off Interstate 95 and then U.S. 278 east, directly to the bridges. If you're heading to the southern end of the island, your best bet to save time and avoid traffic is the Cross Island Parkway toll road. The cost is $1.25 each way.

TOP ATTRACTIONS

★ Fodor'sChoice **Coastal Discovery Museum.** This wonderful museum has a variety of art and historical exhibits that tell the story of the Lowcountry and Hilton Head Island's history. For instance, visitors will learn about the early development of Hilton Head as an island resort from the Civil War to the 1930s. There is also a new butterfly enclosure, various hands-on programs for children, guided walks, and much more. Admission is free; lectures and tours on subjects both historical and natural cost $7 and up. Although the museum is just off the Cross Island Parkway, the peaceful grounds make it feel a century away. ■TIP➔ **Take a walk around the grounds to see marshes, open fields, old live-oak trees dripping with Spanish moss, and South**

Carolina's largest southern red cedar tree, which dates to 1595. ⊠ *Hwy. 278 at Gumtree Rd., 70 Honey Horn Dr., North End* ☎ *843/689–6767* ⊕ *www.coastaldiscovery.org* ⊠ *Free.*

Sea Pines Forest Preserve. Walking trails take you past a stocked fishing pond, a waterfowl pond, and a 3,400-year-old Native American shell ring at this 605-acre public wilderness tract. Pick up the extensive activity guide at the Sea Pines Welcome Center to take advantage of goings-on—moonlight hayrides, storytelling around campfires, and alligator- and bird-watching boat tours. The preserve is part of the grounds at Sea Pines Resort. ■TIP→ **Head to the preserve's outdoor chapel for some quiet meditation.** The chapel overlooks a small lake and has five wooden pews and a lectern, all with the Prayer of St. Francis engraved in the wood. You can get directions at the Sea Pines Welcome Center. ⊠ *Sea Pines Resort, South End* ☎ *843/363–4530* ⊕ *www.seapines.com* ⊠ *$5 per car* ☉ *Daily dawn–dusk.*

WORTH NOTING

Audubon-Newhall Preserve. There are trails, a self-guided tour, and seasonal walks on this 50-acre preserve. Native plant life is tagged and identified in this pristine forest. ⊠ *Palmetto Bay Rd. near southern base of Cross Island Pkwy., South End* ⊕ *www.hiltonheadaudubon.org.*

Bluffton. Tucked away from the resorts, charming Old Town Bluffton has several historic homes and churches, an active artists' colony in the Calhoun Street area, good restaurants (including the fun-named Squat 'n' Gobble, Sippin' Cow, and Pepper's Porch), and oak-lined streets dripping with Spanish moss. At the end of Wharf Street in Old Town Bluffton is the Bluffton Oyster Company, a place to buy fresh raw local shrimp, fish, and oysters. Grab some picnic fixings from the Downtown Deli (27 Dr. Mellichamp Dr.) and head to the boat dock at the end of Pritchard Street for a meal with a view. ■TIP→ **Another incredibly beautiful spot for a picnic is the grounds of the Church of the Cross on the May River at 60 Calhoun Street.** Bluffton's chain hotels—including Candlewood Suites, Holiday Inn Express, and the Comfort Inn—a few miles from the Old Town district provide a nearby alternative to Hilton Head's higher prices. ⊠ *S.C. 46 and May River Rd., Old Town, Bluffton.*

Palmetto Dunes Resort. The renowned Rod Laver Tennis Center, a good stretch of beach, three golf courses, a golf academy, and oceanfront villas can be found at this complex. The oceanfront Hilton Head Marriott Resort & Spa

Hilton Head Island

Port Royal Sound

HILTON HEAD PLANTATION

Seabrook Landing

Country Club of Hilton Head

PALMETTO HALL PLANTATION

Pickney Island

Old South Golf Links

Arthur Hills and Robert Cupp at Palmetto Hall

Hilton Head Island Airport

Welcome Center of Hilton Head

Seabrook Drive

Beach City Rd.

← TO SAVANNAH, GEORGIA

NORTH END

May River Golf Club

Main Street

Port Royal Plantation

Matthews Dr.

Coastal Discovery Museum

MID-ISLAND

Cross Island Pkwy.

Golden Bear at Indigo Run

Folly Field Rd.

Bull Island

Marshland Rd.

Shelter Cove Lane

Broad Creek

Shelter Cove Marina

Palmetto Dunes Resort

Shelter Cove

Harbourside Lane

Palmetto Bay Rd.

Intracoastal

Audubon-Newhall Preserve

SOUTH END

Robert Trent Jones at Palmetto Dunes

Sea Pines Forest Preserve

Shipyard Racquet Club

Lighthouse Road

Sea Pines Resort

North Forest Beach Drive

Harbour Town

Pope Ave.

Greenwood Dr.

Cordillo Pkwy.

South Forest Beach Drive

Cooper River Landing

Plantation Dr.

Harbour Town Golf Links

Sea Pines Dr.

OCEANSIDE

Daufuskie Island

SOUTH BEACH

South Beach Marina

South Beach Marina

Atlantic Ocean

0   1/2 mi

0   1/2 km

KEY	
🏖	Beach
⛴	Ferry

and the Omni Oceanfront Resort are also within this plantation, as are villa-condo complexes with large inventories of rental units. ✉ *4 Queens Folly Rd., Mid-Island, Hilton Head* ☎ *866/380–1778* 🌐 *www.palmettodunesresort.com.*

Port Royal Plantation. The main draws here are the posh Westin Resort, which is on the beach. It boasts three PGA-championship golf courses, and the Port Royal racquet club, with 16 tennis courts. The drive into the plantation toward the Westin is beautiful and lush. ✉ *S. Port Royal Dr., 10 Coggins Point Rd., Mid-Island* ☎ *843/681–1700* 🌐 *www.portroyalplantation.net.*

Sea Pines Resort. The oldest and best known of Hilton Head's developments, this resort occupies 4,500 thickly wooded acres with three golf courses, tennis clubs, stables, a fine beach, and shopping plazas. The focus of Sea Pines is **Harbour Town,** a charming marina with a luxury hotel, shops, restaurants, condominiums and vacation rental homes, and the landmark candy-cane-stripe Hilton Head Lighthouse. A free trolley shuttles visitors around the resort. ■ **TIP→ Check out the Stoney-Baynard Ruins, the remnants of a plantation home and slave quarters built in the 1700s by Captain John "Saucy Jack" Stoney.** On the National Register of Historic Sites, they're not easy to find, so ask for directions at the Sea Pines Welcome Center at the Greenwood Drive gate. ✉ *32 Greenwood Dr., South End* ☎ *866/561–8802* 🌐 *www.seapines.com* 🎟 *$5 per car for nonguests.*

WHERE TO EAT

$$ 🍴 **Captain Woody's.** *Seafood.* If you're looking for a fun, casual, kid-friendly restaurant with terrific seafood and reasonable prices, Captain Woody's is the place to go. The restaurant has two locations, one in Hilton Head and one in Bluffton. The Hilton Head location overlooks Palmetto Bay Marina and has a beach-y feel with ceiling fans, aquariums, and outdoor seating. Start with a dozen oysters on the half shell or the sampler platter, which includes crab legs, shrimp, and oysters. The grouper sandwiches are a staple of Captain Woody's, and include the buffalo grouper, grouper melt, and grouper Reuben. Also available are salads, burgers, and homemade soups—the crab bisque is creamy and delicious. [$] *Average main: $19* ✉ *Palmetto Bay Marina, 86 Helmsman Way, South End* ☎ *843/785–2400* 🌐 *www.captainwoodys.com* ✍ *Reservations not accepted.*

Where to Eat on Hilton Head Island

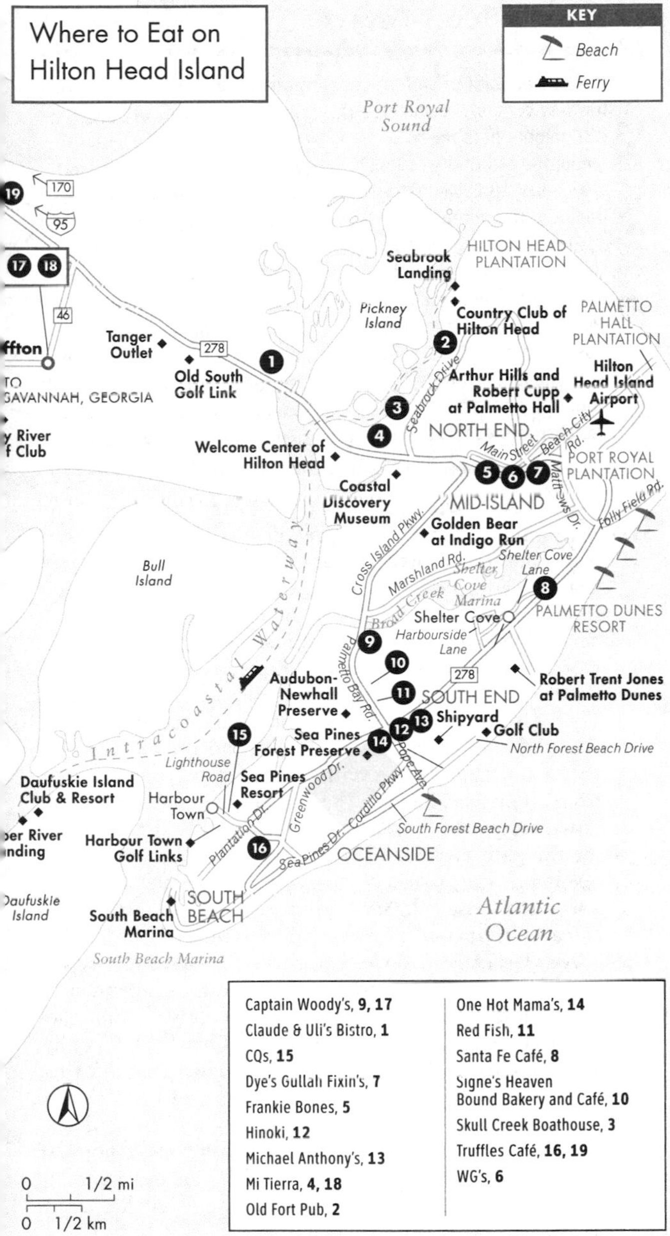
KEY
Beach
Ferry
Port Royal Sound
170
95
19
17 18
46
278
Tanger Outlet
Old South Golf Link
TO SAVANNAH, GEORGIA
Seabrook Landing
HILTON HEAD PLANTATION
Pickney Island
Country Club of Hilton Head
PALMETTO HALL PLANTATION
Seabrook Drive
Arthur Hills and Robert Cupp at Palmetto Hall
Hilton Head Island Airport
NORTH END
Main Street
Beach City Rd.
PORT ROYAL PLANTATION
Welcome Center of Hilton Head
Coastal Discovery Museum
MID-ISLAND
Matthews Dr.
Folly Field Rd.
Golden Bear at Indigo Run
Cross Island Pkwy.
Marshland Rd.
Shelter Cove Lane
Shelter Cove Marina
Broad Creek
Bull Island
Intracoastal Waterway
Shelter Cove
Harbourside Lane
PALMETTO DUNES RESORT
Palmetto Bay Rd.
Audubon-Newhall Preserve
SOUTH END
Robert Trent Jones at Palmetto Dunes
Shipyard
Golf Club
Sea Pines Forest Preserve
North Forest Beach Drive
Pope Ave.
Lighthouse Road
Sea Pines Resort
Greenwood Dr.
Daufuskie Island Club & Resort
Harbour Town
Cordillo Pkwy.
South Forest Beach Drive
Harbour Town Golf Links
Plantation Dr.
Sea Pines Dr.
OCEANSIDE
SOUTH BEACH
South Beach Marina
Atlantic Ocean
0 1/2 mi
0 1/2 km

- Captain Woody's, **9, 17**
- Claude & Uli's Bistro, **1**
- CQs, **15**
- Dye's Gullah Fixin's, **7**
- Frankie Bones, **5**
- Hinoki, **12**
- Michael Anthony's, **13**
- Mi Tierra, **4, 18**
- Old Fort Pub, **2**
- One Hot Mama's, **14**
- Red Fish, **11**
- Santa Fe Café, **8**
- Signe's Heaven Bound Bakery and Café, **10**
- Skull Creek Boathouse, **3**
- Truffles Café, **16, 19**
- WG's, **6**

CLOSE UP

Shrimp Boats Forever

The sunset sight of shrimp trawlers coming into homeport, with mighty nets raised and an entourage of hungry seagulls, is a cherished Lowcountry tradition. The shrimping industry has been an integral staple of the South Carolina economy for nearly a century. (Remember Bubba Gump?) It was booming in the 1980s. But alas, cheap, farm-raised shrimp from foreign markets and now the cost of diesel fuel are decimating the shrimpers' numbers.

The season for fresh-caught shrimp is May to December. Lowcountry residents support the freelance fishermen by buying only certified, local wild shrimp in restaurants and in area fish markets and supermarkets. Visitors can follow suit by patronizing local restaurants and markets that display the logo that reads "Certified Wild American Shrimp." Or you can simply ask before you eat.

★ Fodor'sChoice 🍴 **CQs.** *Eclectic.* If you heard that all island
$$$$ restaurants are in shopping centers and lack atmosphere, then you need to experience CQs. Its rustic ambience—heart-pine floors, sepia-tone island photos, and a lovely second-story dining room—coupled with stellar cuisine, a personable staff, live piano music, and a feel-good spirit put most of the island's other restaurants to shame. Start with the mussels with lemon butter broth, herbs, and crostini. Try the oven-roasted beets with pecan-crusted goat cheese, arugula, and strawberry balsamic, and the ahi tuna for your main course. The staff can pair your wine perfectly from an impeccable list. The restaurant is in the Harbour Town section of Sea Pines resort and will reimburse you for the gate pass fee ($5) with the purchase of at least one main course. [$] *Average main: $29* ✉ *Harbour Town, 140 Lighthouse Rd., South End* ☎ *843/671–2779* 🌐 *www.cqsrestaurant.com* ✍ *Reservations essential* ⏲ *No lunch.*

$$ 🍴 **Dye's Gullah Fixin's.** *Southern.* It's often hard to find the real thing, but this is true Gullah food: decadent, delicious, and comforting. Owner Dye Scott-Rhodan uses recipes handed down by generations of her Gullah family. Those recipes include dishes like fried chicken, pork ribs, macaroni and cheese, collard greens, and Lowcountry boil (shrimp, smoked sausage, potatoes, corn, and seasonings). Wash it down with the South's most popular beverage, sweet tea. There is also a full bar, and a Sunday buffet from noon to 3. The small restaurant has occa-

sional entertainment, including karaoke. It is located in the Pineland Station shopping center. [$] *Average main: $18* ✉ *Pineland Station, 430 William Hilton Pkwy., Mid-Island* ☎ *843/681–8106* 🌐 *www.dyesgullahfixins.com* ✍ *Reservations essential* ⏲ *No lunch Sat.*

$$$ ✕ **Frankie Bones.** *Italian.* Since this restaurant is dedicated to the loving memory of Frank Sinatra, you might assume that its name is also one of the handles of "ole blue eyes." But you'd be wrong. "Bones" was a Chicago gangster before Prohibition. This place appeals to an older set of regulars who like the traditional parmesagnas and marsalas on the early dining menu. But during happy hour, the bar and tall cocktail tables are populated with younger patrons who order flat-bread pizzas and small portions of pasta. It's especially popular with guys who prefer the substantial and familiar, but some dishes have more innovative twists, including a 16-ounce rib eye with a sweetened coffee rub. Be an honorary Italian and just drink your dessert, something Amaretto-based such as a Godfather or a Burnt Almond. [$] *Average main: $22* ✉ *1301 Main St., North end, Hilton Head* ☎ *843/682–4455* 🌐 *www.frankiebonesbhi.com* ✍ *Reservations essential* ⏲ *Closed Sun. No lunch.*

QUICK BITES. **Harold's Country Club & Grill. "Not the 'country club' you might expect, Harold's Country Club & Grill is a sprawling, remodeled gas station in the little town of Yemassee, a short way east of Interstate 95, south of Charleston. Cheerful ladies slap a steak (or whatever the featured entrée is that evening) on your plate, then you proceed past an array of sides and find a place in one of the large, kitschy dining rooms. Karaoke begins in the bar 6:30 and at 8 pm on weekends; good-natured local people throng in to sing or watch." —John Jakes. Reservations are required on steak night, which is Saturday.** ✉ ***97 Hwy. 17A, at U.S. 21, Yemassee*** ☎ ***843/589–4360*** 🌐 ***www.haroldscountryclub.com*** ⏲ ***Closed Sun.–Tues.***

★ $$$ Fodor's Choice ✕ **Hinoki.** *Japanese.* A peaceful oasis awaits you at Hinoki, which has repeatedly been voted best sushi on Hilton Head Island. As you make your way into the restaurant, fishponds and Japanese flora flank the boardwalk. The interior has an intimate feel, and includes a bar, regular seating, a sushi bar, and a few sunken tables, with bamboo touches throughout. Try the Hilton Head roll, which is white fish tempura and avocado, or the Hinoki roll of asparagus and spicy *masago* (Capelin roe), topped

8

with tuna and avocado. The sushi chef will also make specialty rolls as requested. One of the specialties of the house is a to-die-for tuna sashimi salad with spicy mayo, cucumbers, onions, salmon roe, and crabmeat. There are more than 50 sushi and sashimi choices, along with udon noodle dishes and bento boxes. There's also an extensive sake menu. $ *Average main: $22* ⊠ *Orleans Plaza, 37 New Orleans Rd., South End* ☎ *843/785–9800* ⊕ *hinokihhi.com* ⊘ *Closed Sun.*

MODERN TAKEOUT. When you just don't feel like going out for a bite, a local delivery service is here to help. Hiltonheaddelivers.com delivers restaurant food to homes, condos, and hotels from 5 to 10 pm seven days a week for a $5.50 delivery charge. A variety of restaurants take part, including One Hot Mama's, WG's, and more. Visit ⊕ *hiltonheaddelivers.com* for more details.

★ **Fodor's**Choice ✕ **Michael Anthony's.** *Italian.* A throwback to $$$$ the days when the most exotic ethnic restaurant in town was a family-owned Italian spot, Michael Anthony's is more upscale, with fresh, top-quality ingredients, simple yet elegant sauces, and waiters who know and care about the food they serve. Owned by a talented, charismatic Philadelphia family, the restaurant has a convivial spirit, and its innovative pairings and plate presentations are au courant. Added bonus: The restaurant offers cooking demonstrations/classes and wine tastings in their upstairs dining room, which has a Tuscan farmhouse feel. $ *Average main: $30* ⊠ *Orleans Plaza, 37 New Orleans Rd., Suite L, South End* ☎ *843/785–6272* ⊕ *www.michael-anthonys.com* ⌂ *Reservations essential* ⊘ *Closed Sun. No lunch.*

COOKING CLASS. Learn to prepare Italian cuisine in a hands-on cooking class at Michael Anthony's. Classes include samples of the dishes and wine. Demonstration classes, wine tastings, and programs for visiting corporate groups are also available. There is a high demand for these classes, so reserve your place as far in advance as possible on Michael Anthony's website (⊕ *www.michael-anthonys.com*).

$ ✕ **Mi Tierra.** *Mexican.* There's nothing fancy here, just really good Mexican food. The decor has a Southwest, rustic feel with tiled floors, colorful paintings of chili peppers, and sombreros. Start with a margarita and the chips and salsa (don't forget to order the guacamole and bean dip to accompany the chips). For the main course, try the *enchi-*

CLOSE UP

The Food Network Triumvirate

Locals and tourists alike are getting on the Food Network bus and visiting the triumvirate of stars from the channel's popular shows. The first stop is eat!, a Robert Irvine restaurant on Hilton Head Island. Irvine is the star of Dinner Impossible and Restaurant Impossible. Then it's on to One Hot Mama's on Hilton Head Island, where chef Orchid Paulmeier was one of the contestants on Food Network Star. From there, head about 45 minutes to Savannah to eat at Lady and Sons, the hugely popular restaurant of Paula's Dishes star Paula Deen.

ladas suiza, tortillas filled with chicken and topped with cheese and green tomatillo sauce, sour cream, and avocado. Another local favorite is the *arroz con camarones*, butterfly shrimp sautéed with garlic butter and vegetables on a bed of rice. The menu is extensive and includes a kid's menu. There are three Mi Tierra locations, one in Bluffton and the other two on Hilton Head Island. All have the same menu. [$] *Average main: $12* ✉ *160 Fairfield Sq., North End* ☎ *843/342–3409* 🌐 *www.hiltonheadweb.com/mitierra1old.htm* 🕓 *No lunch weekends* [$] *Average main: $12* ✉ *160 William Hilton Pkwy., North End* ☎ *843/342–3409* 🌐 *www.hiltonheadweb.com/mitierra1old.htm.*

$$$$ 🍴 **Old Fort Pub.** *European.* Overlooking the sweeping marshlands of Skull Creek, this romantic restaurant has almost panoramic views. It offers one of the island's best overall dining experiences: the building is old enough to have some personality, and the professional waiters do their duty. More important, the kitchen serves flavorful food, including a great appetizer of roasted calamari with sun-dried tomatoes and olives. Entrées like the bouillabaisse and filet mignon with chanterelles hit the spot. The wine list is extensive, and there's outdoor seating plus a third-floor porch for toasting the sunset. Sunday brunch is celebratory and includes a mimosa. [$] *Average main: $30* ✉ *Hilton Head Plantation, 65 Skull Creek Dr., North End* ☎ *843/681–2386* 🌐 *www.oldfortpub.com* 🕓 *No lunch.*

$ 🍴 **One Hot Mama's.** *Barbecue.* In the South, heaven is barbecue, and at One Hot Mama's, the barbecue makes the angels sing. This Hilton Head institution, with its graffiti-strewn walls and upbeat atmosphere, is known for its melt-in-the-mouth pulled pork and fall-off-the-bone ribs. But it also offers some unusual choices. The wings, which have won multiple awards at Hilton Head's Rib Burnoff and Wing Fest, come in tasty sauces ranging from strawberry-jalapeño to sriracha to "Devil Caution." The winning rib sampler includes hot Asian, chocolate barbecue, and "Mama's Perfect 10." In addition to food that will wake up your taste buds, there are also 15 beers on tap, about a dozen flat-screen TVs, and an outdoor patio with a big brick fireplace for the cooler months. [$] *Average main: $14* ✉ *7A Greenwood Dr., South End* ☎ *843/682–6262* 🌐 *onehotmamas.com.*

★ Fodor's Choice 🍴 **Red Fish.** *American.* The "naked" catch of the
**$$$$** day—seafood grilled with olive oil, lime, and garlic—is a low-cal, heart-healthy specialty that many diners opt for. Caribbean and Cuban flavors permeate the rest of the menu in dishes such as Latin ribs and a Cajun shrimp-and-lobster burger. The restaurant's wine cellar is filled with some 1,000 bottles, and there's also a retail wine shop on-site. Although the location in a commercial strip isn't inspired, the lively crowd sitting amid candlelight, subdued artwork, dark furniture, and white linens more than makes up for it. [$] *Average main: $28* ✉ *8 Archer Rd., South End* ☎ *843/686–3388* 🌐 *www.redfishofhiltonhead.com* ⏲ *No lunch Sun.*

$$$$ 🍴 **Santa Fe Cafe.** *Southwestern.* The Southwest has been convincingly re-created here in South Carolina. Guests are greeted by the sights, sounds, and aromas of New Mexico: Native American rugs, Mexican ballads, steer skulls and horns, and the pungent smells of chilies and mesquite on the grill. The restaurant is perhaps best experienced on a rainy, chilly night when the adobe fireplaces are cranked up. Go for the rush of spicy food chased with an icy Mexican *cerveza* (beer) or one of the island's best margaritas (order one up, with top-shelf tequila, and let the fiesta begin). It's a party for the senses: after the fiery and artistic Painted Desert soup (a thick puree of red pepper and chilies in chicken stock), you can chill with the tortilla-crusted salmon. Forgo Tex-Mex standards like burritos or the appetizer sampler and experience instead the better Southwestern dishes like mesquite lamb with cranberry-chipotle sauce. Plan on listening to *guitarra* music in the rooftop cantina on Wednesday through Saturday nights. [$] *Average main: $28* ✉ *807 William Hilton Pkwy., Mid-Island* ☎ *843/785–3838* 🌐 *santafecafehiltonhead.com* ✍ *Reservations essential* ⏲ *No lunch weekends.*

★ $ **Fodor'sChoice** 🍴 **Signe's Heaven Bound Bakery & Café.** *American.* Every morning locals roll in for the deep-dish French toast, crispy polenta, and whole-wheat waffles. Since 1972, European-born Signe has been feeding islanders her delicious soups, curried chicken salad, quiches, and loaded hot and cold sandwiches. The beach bag ($12 for a cold sandwich, pasta or fresh fruit, chips, a beverage, and cookie) is a great deal. The melt-in-your-mouth cakes and the rave-worthy breads are amazing. [$] *Average main: $8* ✉ *93 Arrow Rd., South End* ☎ *843/785–9118* 🌐 *www.signesbakery.com* ⏲ *Closed Sun. Dec.–Feb. No dinner.*

★ $$ **Fodor'sChoice** 🍴 **Skull Creek Boathouse.** *American.* The Skull Creek Boathouse invites patrons to soak up the salty, casual atmosphere. In the two indoor dining areas, almost every table has a view of the water. Outside is a dining area and a bar called the Buoy Bar at Marker 13. Adirondack chairs invite you to sit back, relax, and catch the sunset. The Dive Bar features seafood raw, in sushi, and as carpaccio. A wide variety of other options include chilled seafood, salads, sandwiches, po'boys, burgers, and hot dogs. The dinner offerings include salmon, mahimahi, tuna, steaks, chicken, ribs, and more. Patrons can also bring in their freshly caught fish and the chef will prepare it to order. The problem with the Skull Creek Boathouse is deciding what to order, but you can take your time and enjoy the beautiful view. [$] *Average main: $16* ✉ *397 Squire Pope Rd., North End* ☎ *843/681–3663* 🌐 *www.skullcreekboathouse.com.*

$$ 🍴 **Truffles Cafe.** *American.* When a restaurant survives here for more than 20 years, there's a reason. And when they add two more locations, you know it's a success. There are three Truffles Cafes, one in Bluffton and the other two on Hilton Head. The same menu can be found at each location. You won't find any of the namesake truffles, but instead there's grilled salmon with a mango-barbecue glaze and pineapple chutney, and barbecued baby-back ribs. The Oriental Napa salad with tuna is big enough to be a main course. If you're on a budget, choose a specialty like the Kobe burger with pimento cheese. Or, for a splurge, choose the juicy, center-cut steaks. You will need to order sides, too. As always with Price Beall's restaurants, the ingredients are super-fresh and the preparations are wholesome. The Bluffton location has a lovely outdoor seating area. [$] *Average main: $17* ✉ *Sea Pines Center, 71 Lighthouse Rd., South End* ☎ *843/671–6136* 🌐 *www.trufflescafe.com* ✍ *Reservations essential* ⏲ *Closed Sun. No lunch .*

$$$$ 🍴 **WG's.** *Steakhouse.* There's a whole new feel at this sophisticated, urban restaurant, renovated and reopened in 2012. The red-and-black decor is modern, but with a Sinatra throwback feel: it's a little art deco, a little contemporary. The food is a spin on the classics with unique fusions, like traditional Southern grits, but with Gouda, and the plating is minimalist, clean, and beautiful. Choose from small plates, including fun items like seared tuna sliders and an incredible beef tenderloin carpaccio topped with baby arugula and horseradish cream. The go-to entrée is definitely the charred rib-eye steak, which comes with a choice of butters that include brandied mushroom, fois gras, and truffle. The attentive waitstaff is well trained and can recommend what to sip from the extensive wine list. To-die-for desserts include the delightful crème brûlée flight and deep-fried bread pudding so good you may feel like you just died and went to heaven. [$] *Average main: $25* ✉ *1513 Main St., North End* ☎ *843/842–8866* 🌐 *wiseguyshhi.com* 🕒 *No lunch.*

BLUFFTON

$$ 🍴 **Captain Woody's.** *Seafood.* The Bluffton location of this casual seafood joint opened in 2009 and instantly became a hit. There is outdoor seating and live music on select nights, in addition to oyster roasts, end-of-summer parties, and more. [$] *Average main: $19* ✉ *17 State of Mind St., Bluffton* ☎ *843/757–6222* 🌐 *www.captainwoodys.com* ✍ *Reservations not accepted.*

$$$ ★ 🍴 **Claude & Uli's Bistro.** *European.* It's hard to go wrong with a chef who has cooked at Maxim's in Paris, the Connaught Hotel in London, and Ernie's in San Francisco. Chef Claude Melchiorri, who grew up in Normandy, France, and his wife, Uli, offer divine food at this atmospheric restaurant tucked away in a strip mall right before the bridges to Hilton Head Island. Candles and fresh flowers top the white linen–covered tables. Parisian art lines the walls; a large painting of dogs at a French bar adds a touch of humor. The French-European cuisine is simply irresistible. Before ordering appetizers and dinner, order the Soufflé Grand Marnier with chocolate sauce ahead for dessert, then start with the seafood crepe with white-wine sauce. For the entrée, try the veal Normandy with brandied mushroom cream sauce. All the seafood is fresh, and all the sauces are handmade. [$] *Average main: $22* ✉ *Moss Creek Village, 1533 Fording Island Rd., Suite 302, Bluffton* ☎ *843/837–3336* 🌐 *claudebistro.com* 🕒 *No lunch in summer.*

$ 🍴 **Mi Tierra.** *Mexican.* Like its sister restaurant on Hilton Head Island, Mi Tierra has an extensive menu that features fresh Mexican fare. There are the standard burritos and tacos, but this restaurant goes a step further with delectable shrimp fajitas, shrimp enchiladas, and crab chimichangas. This casual restaurant is a local favorite. [$] *Average main: $12* ✉ *Old Town, 27 Mellinchamp Center, Bluffton* ☎ *843/757–7200* 🌐 *www.hiltonheadweb.com/mitierra1old.htm* ⏰ *No lunch weekends.*

$$ 🍴 **Truffles Cafe.** *American.* The third Truffles Café (the original is on Hilton Head) offers the same menu of mouthwatering American standards and an extensive wine list. A lovely outdoor seating area overlooks a small plaza that features a flower garden and brick sidewalks. [$] *Average main: $17* ✉ *91 Towne Dr., Bluffton* ☎ *843/815–5551* 🌐 *www.trufflescafe.com.*

WHERE TO STAY

$$$ 🏨 **The Beach House Holiday Inn Resort.** *Resort.* This high-rise on one of the island's most popular beaches and within walking distance of major South End shops and restaurants underwent $5 million in renovations in 2012 and has a very upscale yet beach-y feel. **Pros:** the location cannot be beat; the renovations have made this once-tired property a very desirable vacation destination; strong professional management and corporate standards. **Cons:** in summer the number of kids raises the noise volume; small front desk can back up. [$] *Rooms from: $249* ✉ *1 S. Forest Beach Dr., South End* ☎ *843/785–5126* 🌐 *www.hihiltonhead.com* 🛏 *202 rooms* 🍽 *No meals.*

$$$$ 👋 🏨 **Disney's Hilton Head Island Resort.** *Resort.* The typical cheery colors and whimsical designs of Disney create a look that's part Southern beach resort, part Adirondack hideaway, and the villas here have fully furnished dining, living, and sleeping areas, as well as porches with rocking chairs and picnic tables.**Pros:** it is all about kids; young and friendly staffers. **Cons:** many guests actually think that there is a theme park here and are disappointed; it is a time-share property; not inexpensive. [$] *Rooms from: $325* ✉ *22 Harbourside La., Mid-Island* ☎ *843/341–4100* 🌐 *www.disneybeachresorts.com/hilton-head-resort/* 🛏 *102 villas, 21 deluxe studios* 🍽 *No meals.*

$ 👋 🏨 **Hampton Inn on Hilton Head Island.** *Hotel.* Although it's not on the beach, this recently renovated and attractive hotel is a good choice for those traveling on a budget. **Pros:** good

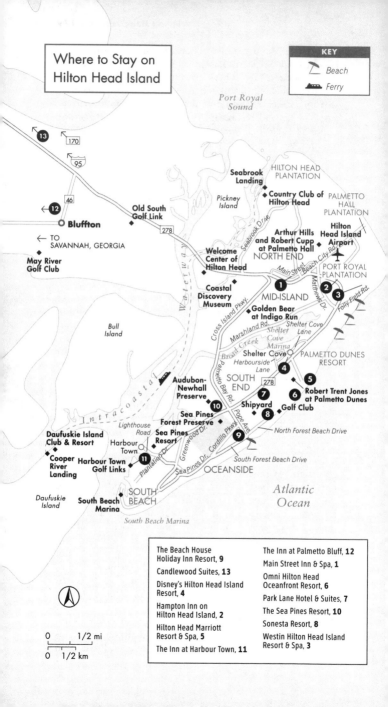

customer service; clean; moderate prices. **Cons:** not on a beach; view is often the parking lot. [$] *Rooms from: $149* ✉ *1 Dillon Rd., Mid-Island* ☎ *843/681–7900* 🌐 *www.hamptoninn.com* 🛏 *95 rooms, 8 suites, 12 studios* 🍴 *Breakfast.*

$$$$ 🏨 **Hilton Head Marriott Resort & Spa.** *Hotel.* The Marriott's standard rooms get a tropical twist at this palm-enveloped resort: sunny yellow-and-green floral fabrics and cheery furnishings are part of the peppy decor. **Pros:** steps from the beach; three superb golf courses; 25 tennis courts; one of the best-run operations on the island. **Cons:** rooms could be larger; in summer kids are everywhere; in-room Wi-Fi costs $9.95 a day. [$] *Rooms from: $299* ✉ *1 Hotel Circle, Palmetto Dunes, Mid-Island* ☎ *843/686–8400* 🌐 *www.hiltonheadmarriott.com* 🛏 *476 rooms, 36 suites* 🍴 *No meals.*

★ $$$ **Fodor's Choice** 🏨 **The Inn at Harbour Town.** *Hotel.* At the most buzz-worthy of Hilton Head's properties, this European-style boutique hotel has a proper staff, clad in kilts, to pamper you with British service and a dose of Southern charm; butlers are on hand any time of the day or night, and the kitchen delivers around the clock. **Pros:** a service-oriented property; central Sea Pines address; unique, it is one of the finest hotel operations on island; complimentary parking. **Cons:** no water views; two-day minimum on most weekends in season. [$] *Rooms from: $249* ✉ *Sea Pines, 32 Greenwood Dr., South End* ☎ *843/785–3333* 🌐 *www.seapines.com* 🛏 *60 rooms* 🍴 *No meals.*

★ $$$$ **Fodor's Choice** 🏨 **The Inn at Palmetto Bluff.** *B&B/Inn.* Fifteen minutes from Hilton Head and a member of the Leading Small Hotels of the World, the Lowcountry's most luxurious resort sits on 20,000 acres that have been transformed into a perfect replica of a small island town, complete with its own clapboard church. **Pros:** the tennis/bocce/croquet complex has an atmospheric, impressive retail shop; the river adds both ambience and boat excursions; pillared ruins dotting the grounds are like sculpture. **Cons:** the mock Southern town is not the real thing; not that close geographically to the amenities of Hilton Head. [$] *Rooms from: $556* ✉ *1 Village Park Sq., Bluffton* ☎ *843/706–6500, 866/706–6565* 🌐 *www.palmettobluffresort.com* 🛏 *50 cottages* 🍴 *No meals.*

8

★ $$ **Fodor's Choice** 🏨 **Main Street Inn & Spa.** *B&B/Inn.* This Italianate inn has stucco facades ornamented with lions' heads, elaborate ironwork, and shuttered doors: staying here is like being a guest at a rich friend's estate. **Pros:** pampering and indulgence is the order of the day; the service, the atmosphere and the rooms are all excellent. **Cons:** weddings can overwhelm the resort, especially on weekends and throughout June; regular rooms are small. Ⓢ *Rooms from: $159* ✉ *2200 Main St., North End* ☎ *843/681–3001, 800/471–3001* ⊕ *www.mainstreetinn.com* ☞ *29 rooms, 4 suites* ❘❂❘ *Breakfast.*

$$$ 🖳 **Omni Hilton Head Oceanfront Resort.** *Resort.* At this five-story beachfront hotel with a Caribbean sensibility, the smallest accommodations are large, commodious studios with a kitchenette and the largest are two-bedroom suites; many rooms face the ocean, and all are decorated with elegant wood furnishings, such as hand-carved armoires. **Pros:** competes more with condos than hotels because of the size of its accommodations; lots of outdoor dining options. **Cons:** wedding parties can be noisy; cell phone service is spotty. Ⓢ *Rooms from: $229* ✉ *Palmetto Dunes, 23 Ocean La., Palmetto Dunes, Mid-Island* ☎ *843/842–8000* ⊕ *www. omnihilton.com* ☞ *303 studios, 20 suites* ❘❂❘ *No meals.*

$ 🖳 **Park Lane Hotel & Suites.** *Hotel.* The island's only all-suites property has a friendly feel, since many guests settle in for weeks, enjoying the private balcony and full kitchen in every suite; most suites have a fireplace. **Pros:** this is one of the island's most reasonably priced lodgings; the bigger the unit, the nicer the condition and decor; flat-screen TVs; playground. **Cons:** not high-end; more kids mean more noise, especially around the pool area. Ⓢ *Rooms from: $99* ✉ *12 Park La., South End* ☎ *843/686–5700* ⊕ *www. hiltonheadparklanehotel.com* ☞ *156 suites.*

$$ 🖳 **Sea Pines Resort.** *Rental.* The vast majority of the overnight guests at Sea Pines Resort rent one of the 500 suites, villas, and beach houses. Ⓢ *Rooms from: $200* ✉ *Sea Pines, 32 Greenwood Dr., South End* ☎ *843/785–3333, 866/561–8802* ⊕ *www.seapines.com/vacation-rentals* ☞ *Approximately 500 houses, villas, and condos.*

$$$$ 🖳 **Sonesta Resort.** *Resort.* Decorated in a classy nautical theme and set in a luxuriant garden, the Sonesta is the centerpiece of Shipyard Plantation, which means guests have access to all its amenities, including golf and tennis. **Pros:** close to all the restaurants and nightlife in Coligny Plaza; parking is free, although valet parking costs $10. **Cons:** Wi-Fi and cell service problematic because of low-rise, older concrete structures; large and sometimes impersonal. Ⓢ *Rooms from: $289* ✉ *Shipyard Plantation, 130 Shipyard Dr., South End* ☎ *843/842–2400, 800/334–1881* ⊕ *www.sonesta.com/hiltonheadisland* ☞ *331 rooms, 9 suites* ❘❂❘ *No meals.*

$$$$ ⓉWestin Hilton Head Island Resort & Spa. *Resort.* A circular drive winds around a metal sculpture of long-legged marsh birds as you approach this beachfront resort, whose lush landscape lies on the island's quietest, least inhabited stretch of sand. **Pros:** a great destination wedding hotel, ceremonies can be performed on the beach and other outdoor or indoor venues; the beach here is absolutely gorgeous. **Cons:** in the off-season, the majority of its clientele are large groups; hotel's phone service can bog down. Ⓢ*Rooms from: $279* ⊠*Port Royal Plantation, 2 Grass Lawn Ave., North End* ☎*800/933–3102, 843/681–4000* ⊕*www.westinhiltonhead-island.com* ↘*412 rooms, 29 suites* ��|*No meals.*

BLUFFTON

$ ⓉCandlewood Suites. *Hotel.* At this suites-only hotel, opened in 2010, every room has a dishwasher, full-size refrigerator, microwave, and two-burner stove, as well as big, cozy leather recliners and flat-screen TVs. **Pros:** location makes it convenient to Hilton Head, Beaufort, and Savannah. **Cons:** cell phone service inside the hotel is hit-or-miss; set back from road and difficult to find (it's just past Sun City Hilton Head on U.S. 278). Ⓢ*Rooms from: $109* ⊠*5 Young Clyde Court, Bluffton* ☎*843/705–9600, 877/226–3539* ⊕*www.ichotelsgroup.com* ↘*124 suites.*

PRIVATE VILLA RENTALS

Hilton Head has some 6,000 villas, condos, and private homes for rent, almost double the number of the island's available hotel rooms. Villas and condos seem to work particularly well for families with children, especially if they want to avoid the extra costs of staying in a resort. Often these vacation homes cost less per diem than hotels of the same quality. Guests on a budget can further economize by cooking some meals at the vacation rental. There are several grocery stores on the island, including Fresh Market, Publix, Food Lion, Piggly Wiggly, and BiLo. ■TIP→ **There are also some small markets to get fresh, local seafood on the island, including Barnacle Bill's Seafood & Produce Market (614 William Hilton Pkwy., 843/785–9007) and Benny Hudson Seafood (175 Squire Pope Rd., 843/682–3474).**

Villas and condos are primarily rented by the week, Saturday to Saturday. It pays to make sure you understand exactly what you're getting before making a deposit or signing a contract. For example, a property owner in the Hilton Head Beach & Tennis Club advertised that his villa sleeps six. That villa had one small bedroom, a foldout

How to Talk to Locals

Hilton Head is known as a place where people come to start a new life, or to happily live out their golden years. It is politically incorrect to immediately ask someone you just met, "Where did you come from?" or "What brought you here?" or "What did you do in your former life?" Residents are asked these questions all the time, and it gets old, especially if they moved here decades ago. Their reluctance to tell all does not mean that they necessarily have skeletons in their closets. Now, conversely, they are allowed to ask *you* where you are from—not to mention how long you are staying—or they may be considered unwelcoming. But do let them tell you about themselves in time, or over a cocktail. You may learn that your golfing partner was the CEO of a big national corporation, or the guy next to you at the bar is a best-selling author, or the friendly fellow in line at the store is a billionaire entrepreneur who might even be a household name.

couch, and a hall closet with two very narrow bunk beds. That's a far cry from the three-bedroom villa you might have expected. ■TIP➜ **Before surfing the web or calling a vacation rental company, make a list of the amenities you want.** Ask for pictures of each room and ask when the photos were taken. If you're looking for a beachfront property, ask exactly how far it is to the beach. Make sure to ask for a list of all fees, including those for parking, cleaning, pets, security deposits, and utility costs. Finally, get a written contract and a copy of the refund policy.

RENTAL AGENTS

Hilton Head Rentals and Golf. With more than 250 vacation rentals on Hilton Head ranging in size from one to seven bedrooms, Hilton Head Rentals and Golf offers a wide variety of options. Many of its villas, condos, and homes for rent have oceanfront views. It also offers various packages that include golf and other activities. Rentals are generally for three to seven days. ✉ *578 William Hilton Pkwy.* ☎ *843/785–8687* ⊕ *www.hiltonheadvacation.com* .

Resort Rentals of Hilton Head Island. This company represents some 275 homes and villas island-wide, from the gated communities of Sea Pines, Palmetto Dunes, and Shipyard to some of the older nongated areas that have the newest homes such as North and South Forest Beach and the Folly

Field, Singleton Beach area. Stays are generally Saturday to Saturday during the peak summer season; three- or four-night stays may be possible off-season. Most of the properties are privately owned, so decor and amenities can vary. In addition to the rental fee, you'll pay 10% tax, an $85 reservation fee, and a 7% resort fee. Linens and departure cleaning are included in the quoted rates, but daily maid service or additional cleaning is not. ⊠ *32 Palmetto Bay Rd., Suite 1B, Mid-Island* ☎ *843/686–6008, 800/845–7017* ⊕ *www.hhivacations.com.*

NIGHTLIFE AND THE ARTS

THE ARTS

Hilton Head Island Gullah Celebration. This showcase of Gullah life through arts, music, and theater is held at a variety of sites throughout the Lowcountry in February. ⊠ *Hilton Head* ☎ *843/255–7304* ⊕ *www.gullahcelebration.com.*

Hilton Head Symphony Orchestra. A selection of summer concerts—including "Picnic and Pops"—in addition to a wide variety of performances year-round, are held by the symphony. John Morris Russell, formerly the conductor of the Cincinnati Pops, was named music director and principal conductor in 2012. The symphony also hosts the International Piano Competition. ⊠ *Performs at First Presbyterian Church, 540 William Hilton Pkwy., and other sites in Hilton Head and Bluffton, Mid-Island* ☎ *843/842–2055* ⊕ *www.hhso.org.*

🜁 **Main Street Youth Theatre.** A variety of performances showcasing young local talent are presented by Main Street Youth Theatre. ⊠ *25 New Orleans Rd., Mid-Island* ☎ *843/689–6246* ⊕ *www.msyt.org.*

NIGHTLIFE

Bars, like everything else on Hilton Head, are often in plantations or shopping centers. A fair number of clubs (often restaurants that crank up the music after dinner) cater to younger visitors, others to an older crowd, and still others are "ageless" and are patronized by all generations. Some places are hangouts frequented by locals, and others get a good mix of both locals and visitors.

Big Bamboo. Decked out like a World War II–era South Pacific officers' club, this bar and restaurant features live music most nights of the week. ⊠ *Coligny Plaza, 1 N. Forest Beach Dr., South End* ☎ *843/686–3443* ⊕ *www.bigbamboocafe.com.*

Hilton Head Comedy Club. This lounge brings top-flight comedic talent to Hilton Head Island Wednesday through Sunday. The red-and-black candlelit room is dark and intimate, and there are fantastic waterfront views. Start off with dinner and drinks downstairs at the Kingfisher, which serves some of the best crab in town. Stick around for music and dancing, and then head up to the "Top of the Kingfisher" for the comedy. Tickets are $12 per person. ■TIP→**Make reservations, because the shows sell out fairly quickly.** ⊠ *Shelter Cove, 18 Harbourside La., South End* ☎ *843/681–7757* ⊕ *www.hiltonheadcomedyclub.com.*

Hilton Head Plaza. Dubbed "the Barmuda Triangle" by locals, the bars at this plaza include One Hot Mama's, Reilley's, the Hilton Head Brew Pub, the Lodge Martini, and Jump & Phil's Bar & Grill. The plaza is near the Sea Pines Circle and it's where the kids go. It's the closest thing Hilton Head Island has to a raging club scene. ⊠ *Hilton Head Plaza, Greenwood Dr. right before gate to Sea Pines, South End.*

★ **Fodor's Choice The Jazz Corner.** The intimate, elegant supperclub atmosphere at this popular spot is a wonderful setting in which to enjoy an evening of world-class entertainment and great food. The Jazz Corner is known for its jazz, swing, blues, and Motown performances. Owner, jazz historian, and horn player Bob Masteller sometimes takes the stage, too. The Jazz Corner offers a signature martini menu, extensive wine list, full bar, and late-night menu. It fills up quickly, so make reservations. ⊠ *The Village at Wexford, 1000 William Hilton Pkwy., Suite C-1, South End* ☎ *843/842–8620* ⊕ *www.thejazzcorner.com.*

Remy's Bar & Grill. Off-duty food and beverage workers love this spot, which is an island institution. Plus, it serves food until the sun comes up. Bonus: Shag lessons are on Friday night. ⊠ *Arrow Center, 130 Arrow Rd., Suite 104, South End* ☎ *843/842–3800* ⊕ *remysbarandgrill.com* ☉ *Closed Sun.*

☾ **The Salty Dog Cafe.** If there's one thing you shouldn't miss on Hilton Head Island, it's the iconic Salty Dog Cafe. It's the ideal place to escape, sit back, and enjoy the warm nights and ocean breezes in a tropical setting at the outdoor bar. There's music à la Jimmy Buffett seven nights a week during the summer and five nights a week in the off-season. Bring the family along for kids' entertainment, including music, magic, and face painting at 7 pm throughout the summer. ⊠ *South Beach Marina, 224 S. Sea Pines Dr., South End* ☎ *843/671–5199* ⊕ *www.saltydog.com.*

Santa Fe Cafe. A sophisticated spot to grab some cocktails in the early evening, it's also a great place to lounge in front of the fireplace or sip top-shelf margaritas on the rooftop cantina. ✉ *807 William Hilton Pkwy., Mid-Island* ☎ *843/785–3838* ⊕ *www.santafecafeofhiltonhead.com.*

SPORTS AND THE OUTDOORS

Hilton Head Island is a mecca for the sports enthusiast and for those who just want a relaxing walk or bike ride on the beach. There are 12 miles of beaches, more than 50 miles of public bike paths, 24 public golf courses, and more than 300 tennis courts. There's also tons of water sports, including kayaking and canoeing, parasailing, fishing, sailing, and much more.

BEACHES

A delightful stroll on the beach can end with an unpleasant surprise if you don't put your towels, shoes, and other earthly possessions way up on the sand. Tides here can fluctuate as much as 7 feet. Check the tide chart at your hotel.

Alder Lane Beach Park. A great place for solitude during the summer season and especially during the off-season, the beach has hard-packed sand at low tide, making it great for walking. Accessible from the Marriott Grand Ocean Resort. **Amenities:** lifeguards; showers; toilets. **Best for:** solitude; walking; swimming. ✉ *South Forest Beach Rd. at Alder La., 2 Woodward Ave., South End.*

8

BEACH RULES. Animals are not permitted on Hilton Head beaches between 10 and 5 from Memorial Day through Labor Day. Animals must be on leash. No alcohol, glass, littering, indecent exposure, unauthorized vehicles, fires and fireworks, shark fishing, removal of any live beach fauna, sleeping between midnight and 6 am, and kites not under manual control.

Burkes Beach. This beach is usually not crowded, mostly because it is a bit hard to find and there are no lifeguards on duty. **Amenities:** none. **Best for:** solitude; sunrise; swimming; windsurfing. ✉ *60 Burkes Beach Rd., at William Hilton Pkwy. (U.S. 278), Mid-Island.*

★ Fodor'sChoice **Coligny Beach.** The most popular beach on the ☺ island is a lot of fun, but can get very crowded. Accessible from the Holiday Inn Oceanfront, Comfort Inn, Hilton Head Metropolitan Hotel, and Players Club Hotel, it has

CLOSE UP

Island Gators

The most famous photo of Hilton Head's brilliant developer, Charles Fraser, ran in the *Saturday Evening Post* in the late 1950s. It shows him dressed as a dandy, outfitted with a cane and straw hat, with an alligator on a leash.

These prehistoric creatures are indeed indigenous to this subtropical island. What you will learn if you visit the Coastal Discovery Museum, where the old photograph is blown up for an interpretive board on the island's early history, is that

someone else had the gator by the tail (not shown) so that it would not harm Fraser or the photographer.

Nowadays, in Sea Pines Center, there is a life-size, metal sculpture of an alligator that all the tourists, and especially their kids, climb on to have their pictures taken. And should you happen to see a live gator while exploring the island or playing a round of golf, please don't feed it. Although, if you have the courage, you might want to take a snapshot.

---

choreographed fountains for children to play under, Wi-Fi, bench swings, and beach umbrellas and chaise longues for rent. **Amenities:** lifeguards; food and drink; parking; showers; toilets. **Best for:** windsurfing; swimming. ⊠ *1 Coligny Circle, at Pope Ave. and South Forest Beach Dr., South End.*

☾ **Driessen Beach.** A good beach for families, Driessen is peppered with people flying kites, making it colorful and fun. There is a long boardwalk to the beach. **Amenities:** parking; lifeguards; toilets; showers. **Best for:** walking; sunrise; swimming. ⊠ *43 Bradley Beach Rd., at William Hilton Pkwy., Mid-Island.*

SAND DOLLARS. Hilton Head Island's beaches hold many treasures, including starfish, sea sponges, and sand dollars. Note that it is strictly forbidden to pick up any live creatures on the beach, especially live sand dollars. How can you tell if they are alive? Live sand dollars are brown and fuzzy and will turn your fingers yellow and brown. You can take sand dollars home only if they're white. Soak them in a mixture of bleach and water to remove the scent once you get home.

Folly Field Beach Park. Next to Driessen Beach, Folly Field is also very nice for families. It can get crowded in season, but it's a wonderful spot for a day of sunbathing and swimming. The first beach cottages on Hilton Head Island were built here in the mid-1950s. **Amenities:** lifeguards; parking; toilets; outdoor showers. **Best for:** swimming; sunrise; walking. ⊠ *55 Starfish Dr., off Folly Field Rd., North End.*

Mitchelville Beach Park. Not good for swimming due to the many sharp shells and rocks on the beach and in the water, but this is a terrific spot for a walk or shelling. It is not on the Atlantic Ocean, but rather on Port Royal Sound. **Amenities:** parking; toilets. **Best for:** solitude; walking. ⊠ *Hilton Head Plantation, 124 Mitchelville Rd., North End.*

MAY RIVER SANDBAR. Known as the "Redneck Riviera," the May River Sandbar is pure party. Basically, the sandbar is just that: a small island of sand on the May River in Bluffton, which is the town that vacationers must go through on U.S. 278 to get to Hilton Head. The sandbar is accessible only by boat and only at low tide. Locals will plan their weekends around the time of low tide to head out to the sandbar. Boaters drop anchor and the party begins. Horseshoe and cornhole games are set up, picnic baskets unpacked, and cold drinks poured. To get there, go north by boat on Calibogue Sound and turn left (west) at the May River. The sandbar is at Red Marker 6.

8

BIKING

Bikes with wide tires are a must if you want to ride on the beach. They can save you a spill should you hit loose sand on the trails. More than 50 miles of public paths crisscross Hilton Head Island, and pedaling is popular along the firmly packed beach. The island keeps adding more to the boardwalk network as visitors are using it and because it's such a safe alternative for kids. Keep in mind when crossing streets that, in South Carolina, vehicles have the right-of-way. ■TIP→ For a map of trails, visit ⊕ www.hiltonheadislandsc. gov and click on "Our Island."

Bicycles from beach cruisers to mountain bikes to tandem bikes can be rented either at bike stores or at most hotels and resorts. Many bikes can be delivered to your hotel, along with helmets, baskets, locks, child carriers, and whatever else you might need.

Hilton Head Bicycle Company. You can rent bicycles, helmets and adult tricycles from the Hilton Head Bicycle Company. ⊠ *112 Arrow Rd., South End* ☎ *843/686–6888, 800/995–4319* ⊕ *www.hiltonheadbicycle.com.*

Pedals Bicycles. Rent beach bikes for adults and children, kiddy karts, jogging strollers, and mountain bikes at Pedals. ⊠ *71A Pope Ave., South End* ☎ *843/842–5522, 888/699–1039* ⊕ *www.pedalsbicycles.com.*

South Beach Cycles. Rent bikes, helmets, tandems, and adult tricycles at this spot in Sea Pines. ⊠ *Sea Pines, 230 S. Sea Pines Dr., South End* ☎ *843/671–2453* ⊕ *www.south-beach-cycles.com.*

CANOEING AND KAYAKING

This is one of the most delightful ways to commune with nature on this commercial but physically beautiful island. Paddle through the creeks and estuaries and try to keep up with the dolphins.

Outside Hilton Head. Boats, canoes, kayaks, and paddleboards are available for rent. The company also runs nature tours and dolphin-watching excursions. ⊠ *Shelter Cove Marina, 1 Shelter Cove La., Mid-Island* ☎ *843/686–6996, 800/686–6996* ⊕ *www.outsidehiltonhead.com.*

FISHING

Anglers can fish year-round in island waters, with April starting to crank up the season and May heavily booked. May is the season for cobia, especially in Port Royal Sound. In the Gulf Stream you can hook king mackerel, tuna, wahoo, and mahimahi. ■ TIP→ **A fishing license is necessary if you are fishing from a beach, dock, or pier. For nonresidents, they are $11 for seven days.** Licenses aren't necessary on charter fishing boats because they already have their licenses. For more information, visit ⊕ *www.dnr.sc.gov.*

Bulldog Fishing Charters. Captain Christian offers his guests 4-, 6-, 8-, and 10-hour fishing tours on his 32-foot boat. ⊠ *Departs from docks at the Chart House, 2 Hudson Rd., Mid-Island* ☎ *843/422–0887* ⊕ *bulldogfishingcharters.com.*

☾ **Capt. Hook Party Boat.** Shark and deep-sea fishing tours are available on this large party boat, which sells concessions as well. The friendly crew helps teach children how to bait and reel in fish. ⊠ *Shelter Cove Marina, 1 Shelter Cove La., Mid-Island* ☎ *843/785–1700.*

Fishin' Coach. Captain Dan Utley offers a variety of fishing tours on his 22-foot boat to catch redfish and other species year-round, and cobia, shark, and other species by season. ⊠ *1640 Fording Island Rd., Mid-Island* ☎ *843/368–2126* ⊕ *www.fishincoach.com.*

Integrity. The 38-foot charter boat *Integrity* offers offshore and near-shore fishing. ⊠ *Harbour Town Yacht Basin, Sea Pines, 32 Greenwood Dr., South End* ☎ *843/671–2704* ⊕ *www.integritycharterfishing.com.*

Palmetto Bay Charters. Palmetto Bay Charters offers a wide variety of charters on various size boats. ⊠ *Palmetto Bay Marina, 86 Helmsman Way, South End* ☎ *843/785–7131* ⊕ *www.palmettobaymarinahhi.com.*

Palmetto Dunes. Fishing trips are available on the 34-foot *Gullah Gal* (six people), the 34-foot *True Grits* (six people), the 24-foot *Bayrunner* (four people), and at Palmetto Lagoon Charters in Shelter Cove. ⊠ *Departs from Shelter Cove Marina, 4 Queens Folly Rd., Mid-Island* ☎ *866/380–1778* ⊕ *www.palmettodunes.com/south-carolina-fishing-charters.php.*

GOLF

Hilton Head is nicknamed "Golf Island" for good reason: the island itself has 24 championship courses (public, semiprivate, and private), and the outlying area has 16 more. Each offers its own packages, some of which are great deals. Almost all charge the highest green fees in the morning and lower fees as the day goes on. Lower rates can also be found in the hot summer months. It's essential to book tee times in advance, especially in the busy spring and fall months; resort guests and club members get first choices. Most courses can be described as casual-classy, so you will have to adhere to certain rules of the greens.

■TIP→ **The dress code on island golf courses does not permit blue jeans, gym shorts, or jogging shorts. Men's shirts must have collars.**

The Heritage PGA Tour Golf Tournament. The most internationally famed golf event in Hilton Head is the annual Heritage PGA Tour Golf Tournament, which is held mid-April. ⊠ *Sea Pines Resort, 2 Lighthouse La., South End* ☎ *843/671–2448* ⊕ *www.theheritagegolfsc.com.*

TEE OFF ON A BUDGET. Golfing on Hilton Head can be very expensive after you tally up the green fee, cart fee, rental clubs, gratuities, and so on. But there are ways to save money. There are several courses in Bluffton that are very popular with the locals, and some are cheaper to play than the courses on Hilton Head Island. Another way to save money is to play late in the day. At some courses, a round in the morning is more expensive than 18 holes in the late afternoon.

GOLF SCHOOLS

Golf Academy at Sea Pines Resort. The academy offers one- to three-day schools, hourly private lessons by PGA-trained professionals, and comprehensive analysis. ⊠ *Sea Pines, 100 North Sea Pines Dr., South End* ☎ *843/785–4540* ⊕ *www. golfacademy.net.*

Palmetto Dunes Golf Academy. There's something for golf-lovers of all ages at the academy. Lessons are offered for ages three and up, and there are ladies' programs, instructional videos, daily clinics, and multiday schools. Free demonstrations are held at 4 pm each Monday with Doug Weaver, former PGA Tour pro and director of instruction for the academy. Free club-fittings are also available. ⊠ *Palmetto Dunes Oceanfront Resort, 7 Trent Jones La., Mid-Island* ☎ *843/785–1138* ⊕ *www.palmettodunes.com.*

The PGA Tour Academy of Palmetto Hall Plantation. Affiliated with the PGA, the academy is one of only six in the country. It is known for its teaching technologies that include video analysis, which compares one's swing on a split-screen with the best golfers in the world. Students can choose from a one-hour private lesson to up to five days of golf instruction. ⊠ *Palmetto Hall Plantation, 108 Fort Hollow Dr., North End* ☎ *843/342–2582* ⊕ *www.palmettohallgolf.com.*

GOLF COURSES

Arthur Hills and Robert Cupp at Palmetto Hall. There are two prestigious courses at Palmetto Hall Plantation: Arthur Hills and Robert Cupp. Arthur Hills is a player favorite, with trademark undulating fairways punctuated with lagoons, and winding around moss-draped oaks and towering pines. Robert Cupp is a very challenging course, but is great for the higher handicappers as well. ⊠ *Palmetto Hall, 108 Fort Howell Dr., North End* ☎ *843/689–9205* ⊕ *www. palmettohallgolf.com* ⌖ *Reservations essential* ⚑ *Arthur Hills: 18 holes. 6257 yds. Par 72. Green Fee: $145. Rob-*

ert Cupp: 18 holes. 6025 yds. Par 72. Green Fee: $145 ☞ Facilities: Driving range, 2 putting greens, pitching area, golf carts, rental clubs, pro shop, lessons, restaurant, bar.

Country Club of Hilton Head. Although it's part of a country club, the course is open for public play. A well-kept secret, it's rarely overcrowded. This 18-hole Rees Jones–designed course is a more casual environment than many of the other golf courses on Hilton Head. ✉ Hilton Head Plantation, 70 Skull Creek Dr., North End ☎ 843/681–4653, 866/835–0093 ⊕ www.clubcorp.com/Clubs/Country-Club-of-Hilton-Head ⚲ 18 holes. 6162 yds. Par 72. Green Fee: $85–$105 ☞ Facilities: Driving range, putting green, pitching area, golf carts, rental clubs, pro shop, golf academy/ lessons, restaurant (for members), snack bar for guests.

Golden Bear Golf Club at Indigo Run. On an island renowned for its exceptional golf, Jack Nicklaus, the golf legend and course designer, created another must-play course for Hilton Head. Located in the upscale Indigo Run community, its natural woodlands setting offers easygoing rounds. It is a course that requires more thought than muscle, yet you will have to earn every par you make. Though fairways are generous, you may end up with a lagoon looming smack ahead of the green on the approach shot. And there are the fine points—the color GPS monitor on every cart and women-friendly tees. After an honest, traditional test of golf, most golfers finish up at the plush clubhouse with some food and drink at Just Jack's Grille. ✉ Indigo Run, 100 Indigo Run Dr., North End ☎ 843/689–2200 ⊕ www.goldenbear-indigorun.com ⚲ 18 holes. 6184 yds. Par 72. Green Fee: $79–$99 ☞ Facilities: Driving range, putting green, pitching area, golf carts, rental clubs, pro shop, golf academy/lessons, restaurant, bar.

★ **Fodor's Choice Harbour Town Golf Links.** This is considered by many golfers to be one of those must-play-before-you-die courses. It's extremely well known because it has hosted the Heritage Golf Tournament every spring for the last four decades. Designed by Pete Dye, the layout is reminiscent of Scottish courses of old. The Golf Academy at the Sea Pines Resort is ranked among the top 10 in the country. ✉ Sea Pines Resort, 11 Lighthouse La., South End ☎ 843/842–8484, 800/732–7463 ⊕ www.seapines.com/ golf ⚲ Reservations essential ⚲ 18 holes. 6603 yds. Par 71. Green Fee: $200–$250 ☞ Facilities: Driving range, putting green, pitching area, golf carts, pull carts, caddies, rental clubs, pro shop, golf academy/lessons, restaurant, bar.

Robert Trent Jones at Palmetto Dunes. One of the island's most popular layouts, this course's beauty and character are accentuated by the par-5, 10th hole, which offers a panoramic view of the ocean. ⊠ *Palmetto Dunes, 7 Robert Trent Jones La., North End* ☎ *843/785–1138* ⊕ *www.palmetto-dunes.com* ⚓ *Reservations essential* ⚑ *18 holes. 6122 yds. Par 72. Green Fee: $55–$155* ⚑ *Facilities: Driving range, putting green, pitching area, golf carts, pull carts, rental clubs, pro shop, golf academy/lessons, restaurant, bar.*

BLUFFTON GOLF COURSES

There are several beautiful golf courses in Bluffton, which is just on the other side of the bridges to Hilton Head Island. These courses are very popular with locals and can often be cheaper to play than the courses on Hilton Head Island.

Crescent Pointe. An Arnold Palmer Signature Course, Crescent Pointe is fairly tough, with somewhat narrow fairways and rolling terrain. There are numerous sand traps, ponds, and lagoons, making for some demanding yet fun holes. Some of the par 3s are particularly challenging. The scenery is magnificent, with large live oaks, pine-tree stands, and rolling fairways. Additionally, several holes have spectacular marsh views. ⊠ *Crescent Pointe, 1 Crescent Pointe, Bluffton* ☎ *843/706–2600* ⊕ *www.crescentpointegolf.com* ⚑ *18 holes. 6773 yds. Par 71. Green Fee: $70–$95* ⚑ *Facilities: Driving range, putting green, pitching area, golf carts, rental clubs, pro shop, lessons, restaurant, bar.*

Eagle's Pointe. This Davis Love III–designed course located in the Eagle's Pointe community in Bluffton is very user-friendly and playable. Eagle's Pointe attracts many women golfers because of its women-friendly tees, spacious fairways, and large greens. It also attracts a lot of amateur golfers, again, because it is very playable. There are quite a few bunkers and lagoons throughout the course, which winds through a natural woodlands setting that attracts an abundance of wildlife. ⊠ *Eagle's Pointe, 1 Eagle's Pointe Dr., Bluffton* ☎ *843/757–5900* ⊕ *www.eaglespointegolf.com* ⚑ *18 holes. 6126 yds. Par 72. Green fee: $55–$79* ⚑ *Facilities: Driving range, putting green, pitching area, golf carts, rental clubs, pro shop, lessons, restaurant, bar.*

Island West Golf Club. Fuzzy Zoeller and golf course designer Clyde Johnston designed this player-friendly course. The natural surroundings at Island West are stunning. There are live oaks, undulating fairways, plenty of wildlife, and marsh views on several holes. Golfers of all skill levels can find success on this course. There are several holes where the fairways are rather generous, while others can be demanding. This is a fun and challenging course for golfers of all handicaps. ✉ *Island West, 40 Island West Dr., Bluffton* ☎ *843/689–6660* ⊕ *www.islandwestgolf.net* ⚐ *18 holes. 6208 yds. Par 72. Green Fee: $35-$45* ⛳ *Facilities: Driving range, putting greens, golf carts, rental clubs, pro shop, lessons, restaurant, bar.*

The May River Golf Club. An 18-hole Jack Nicklaus course, this has several holes along the banks of the scenic May River and will challenge all skill levels. The greens are Champion Bermuda grass and the fairways are covered by Paspalum, the latest eco-friendly turf. A distinction of this classy operation is that caddy service is always required, even if you choose to rent a golf cart, and then no carts are allowed earlier than 9 am to encourage walking so golfers will enjoy the beauty of the course. ✉ *Palmetto Bluff, 476 Mount Pelia Rd., Bluffton* ☎ *843/706–6500* ⊕ *www.palmettobluffresort. com/golf* ⚐ *Reservations essential* ⚐ *18 holes. 7171 yds. Par 72. Green Fee: $175-$260* ⛳ *Facilities: Driving range, putting green, golf carts, pull carts, caddies, rental clubs, pro shop, golf academy/lessons, restaurant, bar.*

Old South Golf Links. There are many scenic holes with marshland and intracoastal waterway views at this Clyde Johnson-designed course. It was named one of the Top Ten New Public Courses by *Golf Digest* in 1992. Reservations are recommended. ✉ *50 Buckingham Plantation Dr., Bluffton* ☎ *843/785–5353* ⊕ *www.oldsouthgolf.com* ⚐ *18 holes. 6772 yds. Par 72. Green Fee: $65-$95* ⛳ *Facilities: Driving range, putting green, pitching area, golf carts, pull carts, rental clubs, pro shop, golf academy/lessons, restaurant, bar.*

PARASAILING

For those looking for a bird's-eye view of Hilton Head, it doesn't get better than parasailing. Newcomers will get a lesson in safety before taking off. Parasailers are then strapped into a harness, and as the boat takes off, the parasailer is lifted about 500 feet into the sky.

Palmetto Bay Parasail. Parasailers go up 500 feet in the air and glide over Palmetto Bay Marina and Broad Creek on a 31-foot parasail boat with Palmetto Bay Parasail. ✉ *Palmetto Bay Marina, 86 Helmsman Way, South End* ☎ *843/686–2200* ⊕ *www.parasailhiltonhead.com.*

H2O Sports. Parasailers glide above Hilton Head and can check out the views up to 25 miles in all directions. ⊠ *Sea Pines, 149 Lighthouse Rd., South End* ☎ *843/671–4386, 877/290–4386* ⊕ *www.h2osportsonline.com.*

SPAS

Spa visits have become a recognized activity on the island, and for some people they are as popular as golf and tennis. In fact, spas have become one of the top leisure-time destinations, particularly for golf "widows." And this popularity extends to the men as well; previously spa-shy guys have come around, enticed by couples massage, deep-tissue sports massage, and even the pleasures of the manicure and pedicure.

There are East Indian–influenced therapies, hot-stone massage, Hungarian organic facials—the treatments span the globe. Do your research, go online, and call or stop by the various spas and ask the locals their favorites. The quality of therapists island-wide is noteworthy for their training, certifications, and expertise.

Auberge Spa at Palmetto Bluff. Dubbed the "celebrity spa" by locals, this two-story facility is the ultimate pamper palace. It is as creative in its names, which often have a Southern accent, as it is in its treatments. There are Amazing Grace and High Cotton body therapies, sensual soaks and couples massage, special treatments for gentlemen and golfers, and Belles and Brides package. Nonguests are welcome. ⊠ *Palmetto Bluff, 1 Village Park Sq., Bluffton* ☎ *843/706–6500* ⊕ *www.palmettobluffresort.com/spa.*

Faces. Faces has been pampering loyal clients for more than 20 years, with body therapists and cosmetologists who do what they do well. It has a fine line of cosmetics and does makeovers or evening makeups. It is open seven days a week. Monday night is geared to guys, who get 15% off services. ⊠ *The Village at Wexford, 1000 William Hilton Pkwy., South End* ☎ *843/785–3075* ⊕ *www.facesdayspa.com.*

★ **Fodor's Choice Heavenly Spa by Westin.** This is the quintessential sensorial spa experience. Known internationally for its innovation and latest in therapies and decor, Westin's Heavenly Spa brand also brings the treatments home. Prior to a treatment, clients are told to put their worries in a Gullah (a sweetgrass burden-basket); de-stressing is a major component here. Unique is a collection of treatments

Fun for Kids

Hilton Head Island is a really fun place for little ones. Check out these kid-friendly sites.

Adventure Cove. With two miniature golf courses and a large arcade, Adventure Cove is sure to please the kids. ✉ 18 Folly Field Rd., Mid-Island ☎ 843/842–9990 ⊕ www.adventurecove.com.

AMF Main Street Lanes. AMF Main Street Lanes offers regular or bumper bowling, and late-night and weekend extreme bowling with lights and music. ✉ 2600 Main St., North End ☎ 843/681–7750 ⊕ www.amf. com/mainstreetlanes.

Black Dagger Pirate Ship. The kids get to put on pirate gear, learn how to talk like a pirate, and set sail to search for underwater treasure. The ship sets sail from Harbour Town. ✉ Sea Pines Resort, South End ☎ 843/363–7000 ⊕ www.pirate-sofhiltonhead.com.

Coastal Discovery Museum. A butterfly enclosure, various hands-on programs for children to learn about Lowcountry animals, guided walks, and much more make this a great destination. ✉ Honey Horn Plantation, 70 Honey Horn Dr., North End ☎ 843/689–6767 ⊕ www.coastaldiscovery.org.

Island Playground. In the Bridge Center right before the bridges to Hilton Head, the Island Playground has giant inflatable slides, a fairy-tale castle, toddler exploration area, and snack counter. ✉ 1538 Fording Island Rd., Bluffton ☎ 843/837–8383 ⊕ www.island-playground.com.

Lawton Stables. Riding lessons and pony rides, in addition to horseback tours through the Sea Pines Forest Preserve, are offered at Lawton Stables. The animal farm (free admission) includes goats, sheep, pigs, and more. ✉ Sea Pines Resort, 190 Greenwood Dr., South End ☎ 843/671–2586 ⊕ www.lawtonstableshhi.com.

Fodor's Choice★ **The Sandbox, An Interactive Children's Museum.** A hands-on place for kids, the museum offers a Learner's Loft, where children can have tea parties or play with a puppet theater, puzzles, games, toys, Legos, and more. In the Builders of Tomorrow exhibit, children dress up like construction workers and construct walls, move giant Lego blocks to the job site, and play with the construction equipment. ✉ 18A Pope Ave., South End ☎ 843/842–7645 ⊕ www.thesandbox.org.

Station 300. The 24 state-of-the-art bowling lanes, score screens, restaurant, and arcade at Station 300 make it a very welcome addition to the Bluffton area. ✉ 25 Innovation Dr., Bluffton ☎ 843/815–2695 ⊕ station300bluffton.com.

8

based on the energy from the color indigo, once a cash crop in the Lowcountry. The full-service salon, the relax room with its teas and healthy snacks, and the adjacent retail area with products like sweetgrass scents are heavenly, too. In-room spa services are available as are romance packages. Major renovations to the spa and hotel should be complete by spring of 2013. ✉ *Westin Resort Hilton Head Island, Port Royal Plantation, 2 Grasslawn Ave., North End* ☎ *843/681–4000* ⊕ *www.westinhiltonhead.com.*

Main Street Inn and Spa. The holistic massages will put you in another zone at this petite facility. It offers deep-muscle therapy, couples massage, and hydrotherapy soaks. In-room spa services are also available. ✉ *2200 Main St., North End* ☎ *843/681–3001* ⊕ *www.mainstreetinn.com.*

Spa Soleil. Therapies and a wide variety of massages and spa services are offered at Spa Soleil. The colors, aromas, teas, and snacks make your treatment a soothing, therapeutic experience. This is an amazing island treasure. ✉ *Hilton Head Marriott Resort & Spa, Palmetto Dunes, 1 Hotel Circle, Mid-Island* ☎ *843/686–8420* ⊕ *www.csspagroup.com.*

TENNIS

There are more than 300 courts on Hilton Head. Tennis comes in at a close second as the island's premier sport after golf. It is recognized as one of the nation's best tennis destinations. Hilton Head has a large international organization of coaches. ■ TIP→ **Spring and fall are the peak seasons for cooler play, with numerous tennis packages available at the resorts and through the schools.**

★ **Fodor's**Choice **Palmetto Dunes Tennis Center.** This facility has 23 clay and 2 hard courts and welcomes nonguests. In 2010, the resort was ranked #7 in the world by Tennis Resorts Online. ✉ *Palmetto Dunes Oceanfront Resort, 6 Trent Jones La., Mid-Island* ☎ *843/785–1152* ⊕ *www.palmettodunes.com.*

Port Royal Racquet Club. The club has 10 clay and 4 hard courts. ✉ *Port Royal Plantation, 15 Wimbledon Court, Mid-Island* ☎ *843/686–8803* ⊕ *www.heritagegolfgroup.com.*

Sea Pines Racquet Club. The club has 23 clay courts, instructional programs, and a pro shop. There are special deals for registered guests of Sea Pines. In 2010, the resort was ranked #16 in the world by Tennis Resorts Online. ✉ *Sea Pines Resort, 5 Lighthouse La., South End* ☎ *843/363–4495* ⊕ *www.seapines.com.*

Shipyard Racquet Club. Play on 4 hard courts, 3 indoor courts, and 13 clay courts at this club. ⊠ *Shipyard Plantation, 116 Shipyard Dr., South End* ☎ *843/686–8804* ⊕ *www.vander meertennis.com.*

Van der Meer Tennis Center. Recognized for its tennis instruction, this club has 17 hard courts, 4 of which are covered and lighted. ⊠ *Shipyard Plantation, 19 DeAllyon Ave., South End* ☎ *843/785–8388* ⊕ *www.vandermeertennis.com.*

ZIP LINE TOURS

ZipLine Hilton Head. Take a thrilling tour of Hilton Head on a zip line over water, marshes, and tall oaks and pines. This company offers seven zip lines, three suspended sky bridges, and a dual-cable racing zip line. Guests are harnessed and helmeted, and must be at least 10 years old and weigh between 80 and 250 pounds. ⊠ *18 Simmons Rd., Mid-Island* ☎ *843/682–6000* ⊕ *ziplinehiltonhead.com.*

SHOPPING

Hilton Head is a great destination for those who love shopping, starting with the Tanger outlet malls. Although they're officially in Bluffton, visitors drive by the outlets on U.S. 278 to get to Hilton Head Island. Tanger Outlet I has been completely renovated and reopened with many high-end stores, including Saks OFF 5th.

MALLS AND SHOPPING CENTERS

Coligny Plaza. Things are always humming at this shopping center, which is within walking distance of the most popular beach on Hilton Head. Coligny Plaza has more than 60 shops and restaurants, including large grocery store Piggly Wiggly, unique gift boutiques, clothing stores, souvenir shops, and more. There are also bike rentals, beauty salons, and free family entertainment throughout summer. ⊠ *Coligny Circle, 1 N. Forest Beach Dr., South End* ☎ *843/842–6050* ⊕ *www.colignyplaza.com.*

★ **Harbour Town, Shops at Sea Pines Center, South Beach Marina.** The three shopping areas in Sea Pines include boutiques, unique gift shops, restaurants, pro shops, and much more. ⊠ *Sea Pines, 32 Greenwood Dr., South End* ☎ *866/561–8802* ⊕ *www.seapines.com.*

8

KID STUFF. Free outdoor children's concerts are held at Harbour Town in Sea Pines and Shelter Cove Harbor throughout the summer months. Guitarist Gregg Russell has been playing for children under Harbour Town's mighty Liberty Oak tree for decades. He begins strumming nightly at 8 in the summer, except on Saturday. It's also tradition for kids to get their pictures taken at the statue of Neptune at Harbour Town. At Shelter Cove, longtime island favorite Shannon Tanner performs a fun, family show at 6:30 and 8 pm Monday through Friday. For more on local events for the kids, visit ⊕ *www.lowcountrychild.com.*

Old Town Bluffton. A charming area, Old Town features local artist galleries, antiques, and restaurants. ⊠ *Downtown Bluffton, May River Rd. and Calhoun St., Old Town, Bluffton* ☎ *843/706–4500* ⊕ *www.oldtownbluffton.com.*

★ **Fodor'sChoice Tanger Outlets.** Reopened in 2011 after extensive renovations, Tanger Outlet I is anchored by Saks OFF 5th and has 40 other stores, many of them upscale. It also has an Olive Garden, Panera Bread, and Longhorn Steakhouse. Tanger Outlet II has more than 60 stores, including Abercrombie & Fitch, Banana Republic, the Gap, Nike, and Loft. There are also several children's stores, including Gymboree, Carter's, and Baby Gap. Dine at Food Network star Robert Irvine's restaurant, Nosh. There are almost always great outlet-wide coupons at www.tangeroutlet. com/hiltonhead. ⊠ *1414 Fording Island Rd. (U.S. 278), Bluffton* ☎ *843/837–5410, 866/665–8679* ⊕ *www.tanger outlet.com/hiltonhead.*

The Village at Wexford. Upscale shops, including Lilly Pulitzer and Le Cookery, as well as several fine-dining restaurants, can be found in this shopping area. ⊠ *1000 William Hilton Pkwy., South End* ☎ *843/686–3090* ⊕ *www.villageatwex ford.com.*

ART GALLERIES
Arts Center of Coastal Carolina. This gallery showcases local artists. ⊠ *Walter Greer Gallery at the Arts Center of Coastal Carolina, 14 Shelter Cove La., Mid-Island* ☎ *843/681–5060* ⊕ *www.artleaguehhi.org.*

★ **Fodor'sChoice Images by Ben Ham.** The extraordinary photography of Ben Ham focuses on Lowcountry landscapes and is very popular with locals. ⊠ *90 Capital Dr., Suite 104, Mid-Island* ☎ *843/842–4163* ⊕ *www.benhamimages.com.*

GIFTS

★ **Markel's.** You'll find unique Lowcountry gifts and a very helpful and friendly staff who are known for wrapping gifts with giant bows at Markel's. Pick up hand-painted wineglasses and beer mugs, Christmas decorations, pottery, lawn ornaments, baby gifts, greeting cards, and more. ⊠ *1008 Fording Island Rd. (U.S. 278), Bluffton* ☎ *843/815–9500.*

Pretty Papers. Fine stationery and gifts are available at Pretty Papers. ⊠ *The Village at Wexford, 100 William Hilton Pkwy., Suite E7, Mid-Island* ☎ *843/341–5116* ⊕ *www.pretty papershhi.com.*

★ **Salty Dog T-Shirt Factory.** It's a rule that tourists cannot leave Hilton Head Island without a Salty Dog T-shirt, but hit this factory store for the best deals. The iconic Salty Dog T-shirts can be seen all over the country and are hard to resist. There are lots of choices for kids and adults in various colors and styles. ⊠ *69 Arrow Rd., South End* ☎ *843/842–6331* ⊕ *www. saltydog.com/stores/shop.*

☾ **The Storybook Shoppe.** Charming, whimsical, and sweet describe this children's bookstore. It has a darling area for little ones to read as well as educational and unique toys and books for infants to teens. ⊠ *41A Calhoun St., Bluffton* ☎ *843/757–2600* ⊕ *www.thestorybookshoppe.com.*

Top of the Lighthouse Shop. The Hilton Head Lighthouse is the island's iconic symbol, and this shop celebrates the red-and-white-striped landmark. ⊠ *Sea Pines, 149 Lighthouse Rd., South End* ☎ *866/305–9814* ⊕ *www.harbourtown lighthouse.com/shop.*

JEWELRY

★ Fodor'sChoice **Bird's Nest.** Local handmade jewelry, accessories, and island-themed charms are available at this popular spot. ⊠ *Coligny Plaza, 1 N. Forest Beach Dr., #21, South End* ☎ *843/785–3737.*

Forsythe Jewelers. This is the island's leading jewelry store. ⊠ *Sea Pines, 71 Lighthouse Rd., South End* ☎ *843/671–7070* ⊕ *www.forsythejewelers.biz.*

Goldsmith Shop. Classic jewelry and island charms are on sale at the Goldsmith Shop. ⊠ *3 Lagoon Rd., South End* ☎ *843/785–2538* ⊕ *www.thegoldsmithshop.com.*

8

BEAUFORT

*38 miles north of Hilton Head via U.S. 278 and Rte. 170;
70 miles southwest of Charleston via U.S. 17 and U.S. 21.*

Charming homes and churches grace this old town on Port Royal Island. Come here on a day trip from Hilton Head, Savannah, or Charleston, or to spend a quiet weekend at a B&B while you shop and stroll through the historic district. Beaufort continues to gain recognition as an art town and supports a large number of galleries for its diminutive size. Art walks are regularly scheduled throughout the year; check out ⊕*www.guildofbeaufortgalleries.com* for more information about the galleries and events. Visitors are drawn equally to the town's artsy scene and to the area's water sports possibilities. The annual Beaufort Water Festival, which takes place over 10 days in July, is the premier event. For a calendar of Beaufort's annual events, check out ⊕*www.beaufortsc.org.*

More and more transplants have decided to spend the rest of their lives here, drawn to Beaufort's small-town charms, and the area is burgeoning. A truly Southern town, its picturesque backdrops have lured filmmakers here to shoot *The Big Chill, The Prince of Tides,* and *The Great Santini,* the last two being Hollywood adaptations of best-selling books by author Pat Conroy. Conroy has waxed poetic about the Lowcountry and calls the Beaufort area home.

To support Beaufort's growing status as a tourist destination, it has doubled the number of hotels in recent years. Military events like the frequent graduations (traditionally Wednesday and Thursday) at the marine base on Parris Island tie up rooms.

GETTING HERE AND AROUND
Beaufort is 25 miles east of Interstate 95, on U.S. 21. The only way to get here is by private car or Greyhound bus.

ESSENTIALS
Well-maintained public restrooms are available at the Beaufort Visitors Center. You can't miss this former arsenal; a crenellated, fortlike structure, it is now beautifully restored and painted ocher.

The Beaufort County Black Chamber of Commerce (⊕*www.bcbcc.org*) puts out an African-American visitor's guide, which takes in the surrounding Lowcountry. The Beaufort Visitors Center gives out copies.

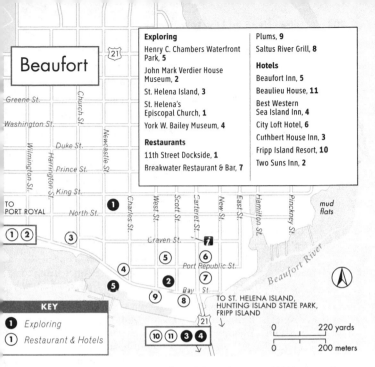

Beaufort

Exploring

Henry C. Chambers Waterfront Park, **5**

John Mark Verdier House Museum, **2**

St. Helena Island, **3**

St. Helena's Episcopal Church, **1**

York W. Bailey Museum, **4**

Restaurants

11th Street Dockside, **1**

Breakwater Restaurant & Bar, **7**

Plums, **9**

Saltus River Grill, **8**

Hotels

Beaufort Inn, **5**

Beaulieu House, **11**

Best Western Sea Island Inn, **4**

City Loft Hotel, **6**

Cuthbert House Inn, **3**

Fripp Island Resort, **10**

Two Suns Inn, **2**

KEY

❶ Exploring

① Restaurant & Hotels

Visitor Information **Beaufort Visitors Center** ✉ *Within Arsenal, 713 Craven St.* ☎ *843/525–8500* ⊕ *www.beaufortsc.org.* **Regional Beaufort Chamber of Commerce** ✉ *1106 Carteret St.* ☎ *843/986–5400* ⊕ *www.beaufortchamber.org.*

EXPLORING

TOP ATTRACTIONS

★ **Fodor's**Choice **Henry C. Chambers Waterfront Park.** Off Bay Street, this park is a great place to survey the scene. Trendy restaurants and bars overlook these 7 landscaped acres along the Beaufort River. At night everyone walks the river walk. ✉ *1006 Bay St.* ☎ *843/525–7000* ⊕ *www.cityofbeaufort.org.*

QUICK BITES. **Johnson Creek Tavern.** There are times when you are as relaxed as a gator in hibernation, when you have just come from the beach and are encrusted in sand, and you want a cold one and maybe some raw oysters. Head to Johnson Creek Tavern and sit outdoors, where you have a long marsh view and the smell of brackish water. Or take a seat inside the sporty bar and dining room, where the ceilings and walls are covered with dollar bills. You may even feel compelled to add a dollar of your own. Ask for the staple gun and try to find an empty spot for your George Washington, as you sample the Frogmore Stew, a Lowcountry classic with boiled shrimp, corn-on-the-cob, potatoes, and sausage. ⊠ *2141 Sea Island Pkwy., Harbor Island* ☎ *843/838-4166* ⊕ *www.johnsoncreektavern.com.*

St. Helena Island. Nine miles southeast of Beaufort via U.S. 21, St. Helena is the site of the Penn Center Historic District. Established in the middle of the Civil War, Penn Center was the South's first school for freed slaves; now open to the public, the center provides community services, too. This island is both residential and commercial, with nice beaches, cooling ocean breezes, and a great deal of natural beauty. It continues to be a stronghold of the Gullah culture, with several African-American–owned businesses in its "downtown" Frogmore, which is actually getting to be quite the tourist magnet. ⊠ *St. Helena Island.*

☾ **York W. Bailey Museum.** The museum at the Penn Center has displays on the heritage of Sea Island African-Americans; it also has pleasant grounds shaded by live oaks. The Penn Center (1862) was the first school for the newly emancipated slaves. These islands are where Gullah, a musical language that combines English and African languages, developed. This is a major stop for anyone interested in the Gullah history and culture of the Lowcountry. ⊠ *30 Penn Center Circle W, St. Helena Island* ☎ *843/838-2432* ⊕ *www.penncenter.com* ⊠ *$5* ☾ *Mon.–Sat. 11–4.*

FARM STAND. Barefoot Farm. Check out this farm stand for perfect watermelons, rhubarb, and strawberry jam. Jacky "Barefoot" Frazier, the owner, is a local celebrity. ⊠ *939 Sea Island Pkwy., St. Helena Island* ☎ *843/838-7421.*

WORTH NOTING

John Mark Verdier House Museum. Built in the Federal style, this house has been restored and furnished as it would have been between its construction in 1804 and the visit by Lafayette in 1825. It was the headquarters for Union forces during the Civil War. ⊠ *Downtown Historic District, 801 Bay St.* ☎ *843/379-6335* ⊕ *historicbeaufort.org* ⊠ *$10* ☾ *Mon.–Sat. 10–4.*

St. Helena's Episcopal Church. The 1724 church was turned into a hospital during the Civil War, and gravestones were brought inside to serve as operating tables. While on church

CLOSE UP

Pat Conroy, Writer, on Beaufort

Many fans of best-selling author Pat Conroy consider Beaufort *his* town because of his autobiographical novel *The Great Santini*, which was set here. He, too, considers it home base: "We moved to Beaufort when I was 15. We had moved 23 times. (My father was in the Marines.) I told my mother, 'I need a home.' Her wise reply was: 'Well, maybe it will be Beaufort.' And so it has been. I have stuck to this poor town like an old barnacle. I moved away, but I came running back in 1993."

A number of Hollywood films have been shot here, not just Conroy's. "The beautiful white house on the Point was called the 'Big Santini House' until the next movie was shot and now it is known as 'The Big Chill House.' If a third movie was made there, it would have a new name.

"One of the great glories of Beaufort is found on St. Helena Island," he says. "You get on Martin Luther King Jr. Boulevard and take a right at the Red Piano Too Art Gallery to the Penn Center. Before making the right turn, on the left, in what was the Bishop family's general store, is Gullah Grub, one of the few restaurants that serve legitimate Gullah food."

He continues: "At the end of St. Helena, toward the beach, take Seaside Road. You will be in the midst of the Gullah culture. You end up driving down a dirt road and then an extraordinary avenue of oaks that leads to the Coffin Point Plantation, which was the house where Sally Field raised Forrest Gump as a boy."

grounds stroll the peaceful cemetery and read the fascinating, historic tombstones. ✉ *505 Church St.* ☎ *843/522–1712* 🌐 *www.sthelenas1712.org* ⏲ *Mon., Tues., and Fri. 10–4; Thurs. 1–4; Sat. 10–1.*

WHERE TO EAT

$$$ **Fodor'sChoice** ✕ **11th Street Dockside.** *Seafood.* Start with the fried green tomatoes or crab-stuffed shrimp. The succulent fried oysters, shrimp, and fish are some of the best around. More healthful options are also available, including a steamed seafood hot pot filled with crab legs, oysters, and shrimp. Everything is served in a classic wharfside environment, where you can eat on a screened porch and have water views from nearly every table. [$] *Average main: $21* ✉ *6 miles southwest of Beaufort, 1699 11th St. W, Port Royal* ☎ *843/524–7433* 🌐 *www.11thstreetdockside.com* ✍ *Reservations not accepted* ⏲ *No lunch.*

CLOSE UP

The World of Gullah

In the Lowcountry, Gullah refers to several things: a language, a people, and a culture. Gullah (the word itself is believed to be derived from *Angola*), an English-based dialect rooted in African languages, is the unique language, more than 300 years old, of the African-Americans of the Sea Islands of South Carolina and Georgia. Most locally born African-Americans of the area can understand, if not speak, Gullah.

Descended from thousands of slaves who were imported by planters in the Carolinas during the 18th century, the Gullah people have maintained not only their dialect but also their heritage. Much of Gullah culture traces back to the African rice-coast culture and survives today in the art forms and skills, including sweetgrass basket making, of Sea Islanders. During the colonial period, when rice was king, Africans from the West African rice kingdoms drew high premiums as slaves. Those with basket-making skills were extremely valuable because baskets were needed for agricultural and household use. Made by hand, sweetgrass baskets are intricate coils of marsh grass with a sweet, haylike aroma.

Nowhere is Gullah culture more evident than in the foods of the region. Rice appears at nearly every meal—Africans taught planters how to grow rice and how to cook and serve it as well. Lowcountry dishes use okra, peanuts, *benne* (a word of African origin for sesame seeds), field peas, and hot peppers. Gullah food reflects the bounty of the islands: shrimp, crabs, oysters, fish, and such vegetables as greens, tomatoes, and corn. Many dishes are prepared in one pot, a method similar to the stewpot cooking of West Africa.

On St. Helena Island, near Beaufort, Penn Center is the unofficial Gullah headquarters, preserving the culture and developing opportunities for Gullahs. In 1852 the first school for freed slaves was established at Penn Center. You can delve into the culture further at the York W. Bailey Museum.

On St. Helena, many Gullahs still go shrimping with hand-tied nets, harvest oysters, and grow their own vegetables. Nearby on Daufuskie Island, as well as on Edisto, Wadmalaw, and John's islands near Charleston, you can find Gullah communities. A famous Gullah proverb says, *If oonuh ent kno weh oonuh dah gwine, oonuh should kno weh oonuh come f'um.* Translation: If you don't know where you're going, you should know where you've come from.

$$$ 🍴 **Breakwater Restaurant & Bar.** *Eclectic.* This downtown restaurant offers small tasting plates such as tuna tartare, rack of lamb, and fried oysters, with mains like lamb meat loaf and filet mignon with truffle demi-glace. The artistic plate presentation is as contemporary as the decor. There's a friendly bar scene, with tapas like pimento cheese, fried shrimp, and crab stack, and an impressive and affordable wine list. [$] *Average main: $23* ✉ *203 Carteret St., Downtown Historic District* ☎ *843/379–0052* 🌐 *www.breakwatersc.com* 🕒 *Closed Sun. No lunch.*

$$ 🍴 **Plums.** *American.* This hip restaurant began its life in 1986 in a homey frame house with plum-color awnings shading the front porch. The namesake awnings facing the riverwalk are still here, but a major renovation has more than doubled its seating, giving it a contemporary open space. An oyster bar that looks out to Bay Street, Plums still uses old family recipes for its soups, crab-cake sandwiches, and curried chicken salad served at lunch, but now it also offers inventive burgers, po'boys, and wraps. Dinner is more sophisticated with creative pairings and artistic plate presentations, particularly in the pasta and seafood dishes. There's live music Tuesday through Saturday, starting at around 10 pm. [$] *Average main: $19* ✉ *904 Bay St., Downtown Historic District* ☎ *843/525–1946* 🌐 *www.plumsrestaurant.com.*

★ $$$$ **Fodor's Choice** 🍴 **Saltus River Grill.** *American.* The hippest eatery in Beaufort, with a classy sailing motif, wins over diners with its cool design, patio, and modern Southern menu. The bar opens at 4 pm, as does the raw bar with its tempting oyster varieties and sushi. Take in the sunset from outdoor seating overlooking the riverfront park. From 5 to 6, the early dining menu is a steal with three courses for $19 and select wines for $5. A flawless dinner might start off with the signature crab-and-lobster bisque, then segue to the seared sea scallops with curry oil, pea puree, and orange salad. The wine list is admirable, and desserts change nightly. [$] *Average main: $30* ✉ *802 Bay St., Downtown Historic District* ☎ *843/379–3474* 🌐 *www.saltusrivergrill.com* 💳 *No credit cards* 🕒 *No lunch.*

8

WHERE TO STAY

Even though accommodations in Beaufort have increased in number, prime lodgings can fill up fast, so do call ahead. The Best Western Sea Island Inn is still the only downtown property with a swimming pool.

$$ 🏨 **Beaufort Inn.** *B&B/Inn.* This coral 1890s Victorian inn charms you with its gables and wraparound verandas; pine-floor guest rooms have period reproductions, striped wallpaper, and comfy chairs, and several have fireplaces and four-poster beds. **Pros:** in the heart of the historic district; beautifully landscaped, green events space; light afternoon refreshments are complimentary. **Cons:** atmosphere in the main building may feel too dated for those seeking a more contemporary hotel; no water views. [$] *Rooms from: $165* ✉ *809 Port Republic St., Downtown Historic District* ☎ *843/379–4667* 🌐 *www.beaufortinn.com* 🛏 *7 queen rooms, 7 queen or king luxury suites, 8 2-bedroom cottages, 1 2-bedroom loft apartment, 2 flats, 1 4-bedroom house* 🍴 *Breakfast.*

$$ 🏨 **Beaulieu House.** *B&B/Inn.* From the French for "beautiful place," Beaulieu House is the only waterfront bed-and-breakfast in Beaufort, a quiet, relaxing inn with airy rooms brightly decorated in Caribbean colors. **Pros:** great views; scrumptious gourmet hot breakfast; about 7 miles from Beaufort historic district. **Cons:** thin walls; hot water can be a problem; a bit off the beaten path. [$] *Rooms from: $179* ✉ *3 Sheffield Ct.* ☎ *843/770–0303* 🌐 *beaulieuhouse.com* 🛏 *4 rooms, 1 suite* 🍴 *Breakfast.*

$ 🏨 **Best Western Sea Island Inn.** *Hotel.* At this well-maintained motel in the downtown Historic District, you are within walking distance of shops and restaurants; guests can see the bay from the front terrace. **Pros:** only accommodation in historic district that is not a B&B; only pool in downtown Beaufort; directly across from marina and an easy walk to art galleries and restaurants; continental breakfast (early) and hot breakfast included. **Cons:** complaints about dim lighting in rooms; not an upscale property. [$] *Rooms from: $145* ✉ *1015 Bay St.* ☎ *843/522–2090, 800/528–1234* 🌐 *www.sea-island-inn.com* 🛏 *43 rooms* 🍴 *Breakfast.*

$$ 🏨 **City Loft Hotel.** *Hotel.* Cleverly transformed into a boutique property, this former motel built in the '60s was bought and resuscitated by the McAlhaneys, a young, hip Beaufort couple, who have infused it with their sense of high-tech, minimalist style. **Pros:** guests can use the adjacent gym around the clock; very accommodating staff. **Cons:** the sliding Asian screen that separates the bathroom doesn't offer full pri-

CLOSE UP

Pat Conroy, Writer, on Fripp Island

"What has Fripp Island meant to me?" Pat Conroy, one of the Lowcountry's famous writers, answered: "The year was 1964. I was living in Beaufort. And when the bridge to Fripp Island was built, I was a senior in high school. My English teacher *and* my chemistry teacher moonlighted as the island's first security guards. It was a pristine island; there were no houses on it yet, and it was as beautiful as any desert island.

"In 1978, my mother moved over there, and all our summers were spent on the island. It was to be her last home. That sealed the island in our family's history. In 1989, I bought a house there, both because it is a private island and thus good for a writer, but also so that our family—my brothers and sisters—could always have a home on Fripp to come to."

vacy; no lobby or public spaces. $ *Rooms from: $179 ✉ 301 Carteret St., Downtown Historic District ☎ 843/379–5638 🌐 www.cityloſthotel.com* *⇨ 22 rooms, 1 suite.*

$$ 🏨 **Cuthbert House Inn.** *B&B/Inn.* Named after the original ★ Scottish owners, who made their money in cotton and indigo, this 1790 home is filled with 18th- and 19th-century heirlooms and retains the original Federal fireplaces and crown and rope molding.**Pros:** owners are accommodating; they and other guests provide good company during the complimentary wine and hors d'oeuvres service; great walk-about location. **Cons:** some furnishings are a bit busy; some artificial flower arrangements; stairs creak. $ *Rooms from: $179 ✉ 1203 Bay St., Downtown Historic District ☎ 843/521–1315, 800/327–9275 🌐 www.cuthberthouseinn.com ⇨ 6 rooms, 3 suites 🍴 Breakfast.*

$$ 🏨 **Two Suns.** *B&B/Inn.* With its unobstructed bay views and wraparound veranda complete with porch swing, this historic home—built in 1917 by an immigrant Lithuanian merchant, whose grandson is now the mayor—offers a distinctive Beaufort experience. **Pros:** most appealing is the Charleston room, with its own screened porch and water views; it's truly peaceful. **Cons:** decor is unsophisticated; it's a bike ride or short drive downtown even though it's located on Bay Street; third-floor skylight room is cheapest but least desirable. $ *Rooms from: $169 ✉ 1705 Bay St., Downtown Historic District ☎ 843/522–1122, 800/532–4244 🌐 www.twosunsinn.com ⇨ 6 rooms 🍴 Breakfast.*

FRIPP ISLAND

$ 🏨 **Fripp Island Resort.** *Resort.* On the island made famous
👶 in *Prince of Tides*, with 3½ miles of broad, white beach
★ and unspoiled sea island scenery, this resort has long been known as one of the more affordable and casual on the island and ideal for families. **Pros:** fun for all ages; the beach bar has great frozen drinks and live music. **Cons:** distance from Beaufort; some of the infrastructure and less expensive units, like the Sun Suites, are dated and even tired from so many children; could use another restaurant with contemporary cuisine. [$] *Rooms from: $121* ✉ *1 Tarpon Blvd., 19 miles south of Beaufort* ☎ *843/838–3535, 877/374–7748* 🌐 *www.frippislandresort.com* 🛏 *210 units* 🍴 *No meals.*

PRIVATE VILLAS ON FRIPP ISLAND

There are more than 200 private villas for rent on Fripp Island (but no hotels). Fripp Island Golf & Beach Resort offers a range of rental options, including homes, villas, and golf cottages, many with oceanfront or golf views.

NIGHTLIFE AND THE ARTS

Emily's Restaurant & Tapas Bar. This fun hangout is populated with locals who graze on tapas while eyeing one of the four wide-screen TVs. The piano sits idle until a random patron sits down and impresses the crowd. The bar is full of local characters. Reservations are suggested. ✉ *906 Port Republic St., Downtown Historic District* ☎ *843/522–1866* 🌐 *www.emilysrestaurantandtapasbar.com* ⏲ *No lunch.*

Hallelujah Singers. The Gullah group, which was founded by Marlena Smalls, performs at Lowcountry venues, foot-stomping, clapping hands, and singing spirituals. ✉ *806 Elizabeth St., Port Royal* 🌐 *www.marlenasmalls.net.*

Luther's. A late-night waterfront hangout, Luther's is casual and fun, with a young crowd dancing to the beats of rock and roll by live bands on Thursday, Friday, and Saturday nights. Luther's also has big-screen TVs, drink specials, and a terrific late-night menu. The decor features exposed brick, pine paneling, and cool 1940s and '50s posters. ✉ *910 Bay St., Downtown Historic District* ☎ *843/521–1888.*

Nippy's Fish. The mood is laid back at this simple café. There's outdoor seating under shade trees and live music—often a vocalist with a guitar—usually on Thursday and Friday night from 6 to 8:30 and Saturday afternoon from 2 to 3. ✉ *310 West St., Downtown Historic District* ☎ *843/379–8555.*

SPORTS AND THE OUTDOORS

BEACHES

★ **Hunting Island State Park.** This secluded park 18 miles southeast of Beaufort via U.S. 21 has 4 miles of public beaches—some dramatically eroding. The light sand beach decorated with driftwood and the raw, subtropical vegetation is breathtaking. The state park was founded in 1938 to preserve and promote its natural existence, and it harbors 5,000 acres of rare maritime forests. You can kayak in the tranquil lagoon; stroll the 1,300-foot-long fishing pier, which is among the longest on the East Coast; and go fishing or crabbing. For sweeping views, climb the 167 steps of the **Hunting Island Lighthouse** (built in 1859 and abandoned in 1933). It costs $2, and kids must be at least 44 inches tall. Bikers and hikers can enjoy 8 miles of trails. **Barefoot Bubba's** (⊠ *2135 Sea Island Pkwy., St. Helena* ☎ *843/838–9222*), less than 1 mile from Hunting Island, rents bikes and kayaks and will deliver them to the park or anywhere in the area. The nature center has exhibits, an aquarium, and lots of turtles; there is a resident alligator in the pond. The campground has 200 sites, about 180 of which are for RVs and tents; 20 are for tents only. Expect to pay about $25 for campsites with electricity, $21 without. **Amenities:** none. **Best for:** solitude; sunrise; swimming; walking. ⊠ *2555 Sea Island Pkwy., off St. Helena Island, Hunting Island* ☎ *843/838–2011* ⊕ *www.southcarolinaparks.com* ⊠ *$5* ⊙ *Park: Apr.–Oct., daily 6 am–9 pm; Nov.–Mar., daily 6–6. Lighthouse daily 10–4.*

BIKING

Beaufort looks different from two wheels. In town, traffic is moderate, and you can cruise along the waterfront and through the historic district. However, if you ride on the sidewalks or after dark without a headlight and a rear red reflector, you run the risk of a city fine of nearly $150. If you stopped for happy hour and come out as the light is fading, walk your bike back "home." Some inns lend or rent out bikes to guests, but alas, they may not be in great shape and usually were not the best even when new.

Lowcountry Bicycles. If you want a decent set of wheels, call Lowcountry Bicycles. For just $5 you can rent bike headlights for your rental bike, which will cost just $8 an hour, $25 a full day, $75 a week. Adult bicycles only are available. ⊠ *102 Sea Island Pkwy.* ☎ *843/524–9585* ⊕ *www.lowcountrybicycles.com.*

CLOSE UP

Sea Monkeys

There is a colony of monkeys living on Morgan Island, a little isle near Fripp Island. If you are in a boat cruising or on a fishing charter and think you might be seeing monkeys running on the beach, you are not hallucinating from sun exposure. The state of South Carolina leases one of these tiny islands to raise monkeys, both those that are used for medical research and also rare golden rhesus monkeys sold as exotic pets. This deserted island and the subtropical climate and vegetation have proved ideal for their breeding. But you can't land on the island or feed the monkeys, so bring binoculars or a long-lens camera.

CANOE AND BOAT TOURS

★ Beaufort is where the Ashepoo, Combahee, and Edisto rivers form the A.C.E. Basin, a vast wilderness of marshes and tidal estuaries loaded with history. For sea kayaking, tourists meet at the designated launching areas for fully guided, two-hour tours.

☼ **A.C.E. Basin Tours.** This outfitter might be the best bet for the very young, or anyone with limited mobility, as it operates a 38-foot pontoon boat tour. A tour with Captain Stan Lawson at the helm costs $35, $15 for kids 12 and under. ⊠ *1 Coosaw River Dr.* ☎ *843/521–3099* ⊕ *www. acebasintours.com.*

Beaufort Kayak Tours. Owner-operators Kim and David Gundler of Beaufort Kayak Tours are degreed naturalists and certified historical guides. Adults pay $40 and children under 18 pay $30 for half-day interpretive/educational trips. The large cockpits in the kayaks make for easy accessibility and the tours go with the tides, not against them, so paddling isn't strenuous. Tours meet at various public landings throughout Beaufort County. ☎ *843/525–0810* ⊕ *www.beaufortkayaktours.com.*

GOLF

Most golf courses are about a 10- to 20-minute scenic drive from Beaufort.

Dataw Island. In a gated community, this island has Tom Fazio's Cotton Dike Course, with spectacular marsh views, and Arthur Hill's Morgan River Course, with ponds, marshes, and wide-open fairways. The lovely 14th hole of the Morgan River Course overlooks the river. You must be accompanied by a member or belong to another private club. To tap into the reciprocal system, one's home-club pro has to call Dataw Island Club to make arrangements. ⊠ *100 Dataw Club Rd., off U.S. 21, 6 miles east of Beaufort, Dataw Island* ☎ *843/838–8250* ⊕ *www.dataw.org* ⅃ *Cotton Dike: 18 holes. 6799 yds. Par 72. Green Fee: $69–$120. Morgan River: 18 holes. 6646 yds. Par 72. Green Fee: $69–$120.* ⌔ *Facilities: Driving range, putting green, pitching area, golf carts, pull carts, rental clubs, pro shop, golf academy/lessons, restaurant, bar.*

Fripp Island Golf & Beach Resort. This resort has a pair of championship courses. Ocean Creek Golf Course, designed by Davis Love, has sweeping views of saltwater marshes. Designed by George Cobb, Ocean Point Golf Links runs along the ocean the entire way. This is a wildlife refuge, so you'll see plenty of it, particularly marsh deer. In fact, the wildlife and ocean views may make it difficult for you to keep your eyes on the ball. Nonguests should call the golf pro to make arrangements to play. One must belong to a private golf club, and its head golf pro must call to arrange a tee time. Both are rated among the top 50 courses in South Carolina. ⊠ *201 Tarpon Blvd., Fripp Island* ☎ *843/838–3535, 843/838–1576* ⊕ *www.frippislandresort. com* ⅃ *Ocean Creek: 18 holes. 6643 yds. Par 71. Green Fee: $75–$99. Ocean Point: 18 holes. 6556 yds. Par 72. Green Fee: $75–$99* ⌔ *Facilities: Driving range, putting green, pitching area, golf carts, pull carts, rental clubs, pro shop, golf academy/lessons, restaurant, bar.*

Sanctuary Golf Club at Cat Island. This is a semiprivate club, so members get priority. Its scenic course is considered tight with plenty of water hazards. The course looks smashing after a major $1 million renovation of greens, tees, bunkers, and even the driving range. Lessons are by a PGA pro instructor. ⊠ *8 Waveland Ave., Cat Island,* ☎ *843/524–0300* ⊕ *www.sanctuarygolfcatisland.com* ⅃ *18 holes. 6673 yds. Par 71. Green Fee $50–$70* ⌔ *Facilities: Driving range, putting green, pitching area, golf carts, pull carts, rental clubs, pro shop, golf academy/lessons, restaurant, bar.*

8

SHOPPING

ART GALLERIES

Bay Street Gallery. A variety of Southern artists who use a variety of mediums to convey the feel of the Lowcountry are featured at Bay Street Gallery, including Lana Hefner, Susan Graber, Denise Choppin, Roger Steele, Jim Draper, Susan West, and Mandy Johnson. ✉ *719 Bay St., Downtown Historic District* ☎ *843/525–1024, 843/522–9210* ⊕ *baystgallery.com.*

The Gallery. One of the best galleries for contemporary art features a litany of artists' exhibitions. There are oils, collages, wood sculpture, jewelry, stained and fused glass, humorous Lowcountry scenes, and whimsical pieces with catchy titles. Pricing is democratic and goes up to high end. ✉ *802 Bay St., Downtown Historic District* ☎ *843/470–9994* ⊕ *www.thegallery-beaufort.com.*

Longo Gallery. The colorful designs of Suzanne and Eric Longo decorate the Longo Gallery. Suzanne creates ceramic sculpture—couples dancing, mothers with children, and even works in concrete, while Eric's whimsical paintings often feature fish. ✉ *103 Charles St., Downtown Historic District* ☎ *843/522–8933* ⊕ *longogallery.com.*

★ Fodor'sChoice **Red Piano Too Gallery.** More than 150 Lowcountry artists are represented at the Red Piano Too Gallery, which is considered one of the best (if not the best) art gallery in the area. It carries folk art, books, fine art, and much more. The gallery is in the Corner Store, the first store in South Carolina to pay people of color with money rather than barter for goods. The gallery is ¼ mile from the National Historic Landmark District of Penn Center, famous as a former school for freed slaves, whose culture is known as "Gullah." Much of the art at the gallery represents the Gullah culture. ✉ *870 Sea Island Pkwy., St. Helena* ☎ *843/838–2241* ⊕ *redpianotoo.com.*

Rhett Gallery. The Rhett Gallery sells Lowcountry art by four generations of the Rhett family, including remarkable wood carvings, as well as antique maps, books, Civil War memorabilia, and Audubon prints. ✉ *901 Bay St., Downtown Historic District* ☎ *843/524–3339* ⊕ *rhettgallery.com.*

DAUFUSKIE ISLAND

13 miles (approximately 45 minutes) from Hilton Head via ferry.

From Hilton Head you can take a 45-minute ferry ride to nearby Daufuskie Island, the setting for Pat Conroy's novel *The Water Is Wide,* which was made into the movie *Conrack.* The boat ride may very well be one of the highlights of your vacation. The Lowcountry beauty unfolds before you, as pristine and unspoiled as you can imagine. The island is in the Atlantic, nestled between Hilton Head and Savannah. Many visitors do come just for the day, to play golf and have lunch or dinner; kids might enjoy biking or horseback riding. On summer Sunday afternoons from 2 to 6, the little tiki hut at Freeport Marina whirrs out frozen concoctions as a vocalist sings or a band plays blues and rock and roll. On weekend nights when there are bands at Marshside Mama's, the hip crowd even boats in from Hilton Head.

The famous Jack Nicklaus signature golf course at Melrose on the Beach is one of the highlights of Daufuskie Island. For tee times, call ☎ 843/422–6963. The island also has acres of unspoiled beauty. On a bike, in a golf cart, on horseback, or in a horse-drawn carriage, you can easily explore the island. You will find remnants of churches, homes, and schools—some reminders of antebellum times. Guided tours include such sights as an 18th-century cemetery, former slave quarters, a "praise house," an 1886 African Baptist church, the schoolhouse where Pat Conroy taught, and the Haig Point Lighthouse. There are a number of small, artsy shops like the Iron Fish Gallery and Silver Dew Pottery.

GETTING HERE AND AROUND

The only way to get to Daufuskie is by boat, as it is a bridgeless island. The public ferry departs from Broad Creek Marina on Hilton Head Island several times a day. On arrival to Daufuskie you can rent a golf cart (not a car) or bicycle or take a tour. If you are coming to Daufuskie Island for a multiday stay with luggage and/or groceries, and perhaps a dog, be absolutely certain that you allow a full hour to park and check in for the ferry, particularly on a busy summer weekend. Whether you are staying on island or just day-tripping, the ferry costs $28 round-trip. Usually the first two pieces of luggage are free, and then it is $10 apiece.

TOURS

Calibogue Cruises runs the public ferries at Freeport Marina. The marina includes the Freeport General store, a restaurant, overnight cabins, and more. A two-hour bus tour of the island by local historians will become a true travel memory. The ferry returns to Hilton Head Island on Tuesday night in time to watch the fireworks at Shelter Cove at sundown.

Daufuskie Discoveries sets you up for adventure, whether it's a three- or six-hour self-guided tour or a two-hour guided tour in one of its gas golf carts. It also offers an eight-hour "Fuskie Beach Day," which includes a round-trip water taxi from Hilton Head Island to 3 miles of secluded beaches, as well as golf excursions, overnight golf cart rentals, a guided cruise on a high-speed water taxi, and charter fishing and dolphin watching with its Unreel Expeditions.

Live Oac, based on Hilton Head, is an owner-operated company that offers Lowcountry water adventures such as nature tours, fishing excursions, and dolphin cruises. On its first-class hurricane-deck boats you are sheltered from sun and rain; tours, usually private charters, are limited to six people. Captains are interpretive naturalist educators and U.S. Coast Guard licensed.

Take a narrated horse-drawn carriage tour of historic Beaufort with Southurn Rose Buggy Tours and learn about the city's fascinating history and its antebellum and Victorian architecture.

Tour Contacts Calibogue Cruises ⊠ *Broad Creek Marina, 18 Simmons Rd., Mid-Island, Hilton Head Island* ☎ *843/342–8687* ⊕ *www.daufuskiefreeport.com* ⊠ *Freeport Rd., Freeport Marina* ☎ *843/785–8242.* **Daufuskie Discoveries** ☎ *843/384–4354* ⊕ *www.daufuskiediscoveries.com.* ⏱ **Live Oac** ⊠ *43 Jenkins Rd., North End, Hilton Head Island* ☎ *888/254–8362* ⊕ *www.liveoac.com.* ★ **Southurn Rose Buggy Tours** ⊠ *1002 Bay St., Downtown Historic District, Beaufort* ☎ *843/524–2900* ⊕ *www.southurnrose.com.*

WHERE TO EAT

★ **Fodor's**Choice ✕ **Old Daufuskie Crab Company Restaurant.** *Sea-*
$$ *food.* Everyone calls this restaurant the Freeport Marina because of its location in the marina. A cold beer may be in order at the colorful bar that plays reggae and rock tunes, especially after a warm-water boat ride. This out-

post, with its rough-hewn tables facing the water, serves up surprisingly good fare. The specialties are deviled crab and chicken salad on grilled, buttery rolls. Many also enjoy the Lowcountry buffet with its pulled pork and sides like butter beans and potato salad. Dinner entrées include shrimp, rib eyes, blackboard specials, and the catch of the day. $ *Average main: $17* ✉ *Freeport Marina, 1 Cooper River Landing Rd.* ☎ *843/785–6652* 🌐 *www.daufuskiefreeport.com* 🕒 *Closed Mon.*

WHERE TO STAY

Because the major resort, now operating under the name Melrose on the Beach, is closed and undergoing renovations, one of the most reliable ways to find accommodations on Daufuskie Island is through a rental agency on Hilton Head Island. Hilton Head Rentals & Golf (🌐 *www.hiltonheadvacation.com*) is efficient and has its own cleaning and maintenance crews right on Daufuskie. They rent out properties in two Daufuskie communities, Bloody Point and Melrose, as well as other cottages and private homes. Sandy Lane Villas, nearly new, is one such fine example. ■ TIP→ **Remember to turn off your outdoor lights if you are staying at an oceanfront lodging. The light can confuse baby loggerhead turtles trying to make it out to sea.**

Should you just want simple digs right where the action is, you can rent a small cabin for $125 a night or a larger one that sleeps eight for $150 a night at Freeport Marina (🌐 *www.daufuskiefreeport.com*). These cabins are bare bones and decades old, but they are painted in Caribbean colors and are just down the crushed-oyster-shell path to the dock.

$$$$ 🏨 **Sandy Lane Villa #2302.** *Rental.* A luxurious, oceanfront low-rise condominium complex, the twin Sandy Lane Villa buildings are a pale yellow with white pillars and arches with decks that look out to the simple boardwalk that leads directly to a nearly deserted beach. **Pros:** clean and nearly new; spacious and private; unobstructed ocean views. **Cons:** not a homey beach cottage; not individualistic like a private mini-manse; it takes 20 minutes. by cart to get to Freeport Marina. $ *Rooms from: $328* ✉ *Sandy Lane Resort, Fuskie La.* ☎ *843/785–8687 reservations, 800/445–8664* 🌐 *www.daufuskievacation.com* 🛏 *3 rooms* 🍴 *No meals.*

8

NIGHTLIFE

Marshside Mama's. A bar, restaurant, and grocery store, this is *the* hot spot on the island, especially on Friday and Saturday nights when bands play everything from blues to bluegrass. The decor and the vibe here are funky and colorful. ⊠ *At the dead end of Old Haig Point Rd., across from a public boat landing, 15 Haig Point Rd., South End* ☎ *843/785–4755* ⊕ *marshsidemamas.com.*

SPORTS AND THE OUTDOORS

🐚 **Seagrass Stables at Melrose on the Beach.** There are trail rides, lessons, carriage hayrides, and romantic drives in a 200-year-old surrey at Seagrass Stables. In general, 45 minutes of riding or instruction costs $65. It also offers a junior equestrian center. ⊠ *10 Ave. of the Oaks* ☎ *843/341–2894.*

Travel Smart
Charleston

GETTING HERE AND AROUND

We're proud of our website: Fodors.com is a great place to begin any journey. Scan Travel Wire for suggested itineraries, travel deals, restaurant and hotel openings, and other up-to-the-minute info. Check out Booking to research prices and book plane tickets, hotel rooms, rental cars, and vacation packages. Head to Talk for on-the-ground pointers from travelers who frequent our message boards. You can also link to loads of other travel-related resources.

You can fly into either Charleston or Hilton Head (which shares an airport with Savannah). Charleston (though not Hilton Head) is reachable by train or bus as well, but you'll certainly need a car if you want to explore beyond Charleston's historic downtown, where it's more convenient to get around on foot. Taxis or pedicabs can take you around the city and may be more convenient than driving, especially if your hotel or bed-and-breakfast offers free parking.

■TIP→ **Ask the Charleston Visitor Center about hotel and local transportation packages that include tickets to major museum exhibits or other special events.**

▮ AIR TRAVEL

Several airlines offer regularly scheduled service to Charleston.

Airlines and Airports
Airline and Airport Links.com. You'll find links to many of the world's airlines and airports here. ⊕ www.airlineandairportlinks.com.

Airline-Security Issues
Transportation Security Administration. Check in for answers to almost every question that might come up, particularly regarding security issues. ☎ 866/289–9673 ⊕ www.tsa.gov.

AIRPORTS
Charleston International Airport is about 12 miles west of downtown. Charleston Executive Airport on John's Island is used by private (noncommercial) aircraft, as is Mount Pleasant Regional Airport.

Airport Information
Charleston Executive Airport ✉ 2742 Fort Trenholm Rd., Johns Island ☎ 843/559–2401. **Charleston International Airport** ✉ 5500 International Blvd., North Charleston ☎ 843/767–7000 ⊕ www.chs-airport.com. **Mt. Pleasant Regional Airport** ✉ 700 Faison Rd., Mount Pleasant ☎ 843/884–8837 ⊕ www.mountpleasantairport.com.

GROUND TRANSPORTATION
Several cab companies serve the airport. Green Taxi (⇨ *Taxi Travel*), with new hybrid vehicles and a minivan, charges between

$20 and $35 for an airport run. The basic taxis, like Yellow Cab, average about $25. Charleston International Airport Ground Transportation arranges shuttles, which cost $12 per person to downtown. You can be picked up by the same service when returning to the airport by making advance reservations with the driver. If you want to add a little excitement to your life, call Star Limousine Service. They have the largest and most varied fleet in town. Choose from many vehicles, including a stretch limo or a vintage Rolls-Royce. YCC Charters has London-style cars that can seat five and can accommodate passengers in wheelchairs. The cars are available by reservation only.

Airport Transfers Charleston Downtown Limo ✉ *209 Meeting St., Historic District* ☎ *843/723-1111* ⊕ *charlestondowntownlimo.com.* **Charleston International Airport Ground Transportation** ✉ *5500 International Blvd., North Charleston* ☎ *843/767-7026* ⊕ *www.chs-airport. com/Transportation-and-Parking/ Subpage-1.aspx.* **Star Limousine Service** ✉ *1934 Summerville La., North Charleston* ☎ *843/745-6279, 877/460-5166* ⊕ *www.astarlimo. com.* **YCC Charters** ✉ *7281 Cross County Rd., North Charleston* ☎ *843/216-2627.*

FLIGHTS

Charleston International Airport is served by American Eagle (American Airlines), Delta, JetBlue, Southwest, United Express, and US Airways.

Airlines American Airlines ☎ *800/433-7300* ⊕ *www.aa.com.* **Delta Airlines** ☎ *800/221-1212 for U.S. reservations, 800/241-4141 for international reservations* ⊕ *www. delta.com.* **JetBlue** ☎ *800/538-2583* ⊕ *www.jetblue.com.* **Southwest Airlines** ☎ *800/435-9792* ⊕ *www. southwest.com.* **United Airlines** ☎ *800/864-8331 for U.S. reservations, 800/538-2929 for international reservations* ⊕ *www.united. com.* **US Airways** ☎ *800/221-1212* ⊕ *www.usairways.com.*

▌ CAR TRAVEL

You'll need a car in Charleston if you plan on visiting destinations outside the city's Historic District or plan to take trips to Walterboro, Edisto Island, Beaufort, or Hilton Head.

Although you'll make the best time traveling along the South's extensive network of interstate highways, keep in mind that U.S. and state highways offer some delightful scenery and the opportunity to stumble upon funky roadside diners, leafy state parks, and historic town squares. The area is rural, but it's still populated, so you'll rarely drive for more than 20 or 30 miles without passing roadside services, such as gas stations, restaurants, and ATMs.

GASOLINE

Gas stations are not hard to find, either in the city limits or in the outlying areas. Prices are characteristically less expensive than up north. Similarly, outside Charleston, in North Charleston and the suburbs, gas is usually cheaper than at the few gas stations downtown.

PARKING

Parking within Charleston's Historic District can be difficult. Street parking can be aggravating, as meter readers are among the city's most efficient public servants. Some parking garages and lots, both privately and publicly owned, charge around $2 for the first hour and then $1 for each additional hour; the less expensive ones charge a maximum of $10 to $12 a day if you park overnight. ■TIP→ **The garage at 63 Mary Street, between King and Meeting streets, has a special rate of $2 an hour for overnight parking or anytime after 5 pm until 8 am the next morning.** Some private lots now charge as much as $10 per day as a flat rate, whether you are there one hour or six hours. Most of the hotels charge a fee to valet-park your car. Nevertheless, if you have a car, it's usually best to park it and simply take pedicabs, taxis, or shuttles around the Historic District. Save the car for trips outside town.

RENTAL CARS

All of the major car-rental companies are represented in Charleston, either at the airport or in town. Enterprise has both an airport and a downtown location, good prices, and will pick you up.

Contacts ACE Rent-a-Car
☎ 888/861–7695 ⊕ www.acerentacar.com. **Avis** ☎ 843/767–7030, 800/331–1212 ⊕ www.avis.com. **Budget** ☎ 800/527–0700, 843/767–7051 ⊕ www.budget.com.

Dollar Rent A Car ☎ 843/552–1400, 800/800–4000 ⊕ www.dollar.com. **Enterprise** ☎ 843/767–1109, 800/261–7331 ⊕ www.enterprise.com. **Hertz** ☎ 843/767–4552, 800/654–4173 ⊕ www.hertz.com. **National** ☎ 843/767–3078, 800/468–3334 ⊕ www.nationalcar.com.

RENTAL CAR INSURANCE

Everyone who rents a car wonders whether the insurance that the rental companies offer is worth the expense. No one—including us—has a simple answer. If you own a car, your personal auto insurance may cover a rental to some degree, though not all policies protect you abroad; always read your policy's fine print. If you don't have auto insurance, then seriously consider buying the collision- or loss-damage waiver (CDW or LDW) from the car-rental company, which eliminates your liability for damage to the car. Some credit cards offer CDW coverage, but it's usually supplemental to your own insurance and rarely covers SUVs, minivans, luxury models, and the like. If your coverage is secondary, you may still be liable for loss-of-use costs from the car-rental company. But no credit-card insurance is valid unless you use that card for *all* transactions, from reserving to paying the final bill. It's sometimes cheaper to buy insurance as part of your general travel insurance policy.

ROADSIDE EMERGENCIES

Discuss with the rental-car agency what to do in the case of an emergency, as this sometimes differs between companies. Make sure you understand what your insurance covers and what it doesn't. It's a good rule of thumb to let someone at your accommodation know where you are heading and when you plan to return. Keep emergency numbers (car-rental agency and your accommodation) with you, just in case.

ROADS

Interstate 26 traverses the state from northwest to southeast and terminates at Charleston. U.S. 17, the coastal road, also passes through Charleston. Interstate 526, also called the Mark Clark Expressway, runs primarily east–west, connecting the West Ashley area, North Charleston, Daniel Island, and Mount Pleasant.

▌ BOAT AND FERRY TRAVEL

Boaters—many traveling the intracoastal waterway—dock at Ashley Marina and City Marina, in Charleston Harbor. The Charleston Water Taxi is a delightful way to travel between Charleston and Mount Pleasant. Some people take the $10 round-trip journey just for fun. It departs from the Charleston Maritime Center. Do not confuse its address at 10 Wharfside as being near the area of Adger's Wharf, which is on the lower peninsula. The water taxi departs daily every hour from 10 am to 7 pm. It also offers dolphin cruises and harbor boat rides.

Boat and Ferry Contacts
Ashley Marina ✉ *73 Lockwood Dr., Medical University of South Carolina* ☎ *843/722-1996* ⊕ *www.theharborageatashleymarina.com.* **Charleston City Marina** ✉ *17 Lockwood Dr., Medical University of South Carolina* ☎ *843/723-5098* ⊕ *www.charlestoncitymarina.com.* **Charleston Water Taxi** ✉ *Charleston Maritime Center, 10 Wharfside St., Upper King* ☎ *843/330-2989* ⊕ *www.charlestonwatertaxi.com.*

▌ PUBLIC TRANSPORTATION

The Charleston Area Regional Transportation Authority, the city's public bus system, takes passengers around the city and to the suburbs. Bus 11, which goes to the airport, is convenient for travelers. CARTA operates DASH, which runs buses that look like vintage trolleys along three downtown routes. All trips are free on DASH. CARTA buses go to James Island, West Ashley, and Mount Pleasant. From Mount Pleasant you can catch CARTA's Flex Service to the beach at Sullivan's Island for $3.

Contacts CARTA ✉ *36 Johns St., Daniel Island, North Charleston* ☎ *843/747-0922* ⊕ *www.ridecarta.com.*

▌ TAXI TRAVEL

Fares within the city average about $5 per trip with the regular cab companies. The newer Green Taxis, using hybrid vehicles (and one minivan), run $7. Other taxis include Yellow Cab, available 24 hours a day.

Bike-pedaling companies will take you anywhere in the Historic District for $4.50 per person per 10 minutes. It is a fun way to get around in the evening, especially if you are barhopping. They stay available until the bars close. Three can squeeze into one pedicab.

Contacts Charleston Bike Taxi ✉ *1 Pinckney St., Historic District* ☎ *843/532–8663* ⊕ *www.biketaxi. net.* **Charleston Rickshaw Company** ✉ *Downtown historic district* ☎ *843/723–5685* ⊕ *www.charles tonrickshaw.net.* **Green Taxis** ✉ *334 E. Bay St., #254, Historic District* ☎ *843/819–0846* ⊕ *www.charles tongreentaxi.com.* **Metro Limo-Taxi** ✉ *5437 Tee St., North Charleston* ☎ *843/572–5083.* **Yellow Cab** ✉ *2019 Cherry Hill La., Midtown* ☎ *843/577–6565* ⊕ *www.yellow cabofcharleston.com.*

▌ TRAIN TRAVEL

Amtrak has service from such major cities as New York, Philadelphia, Washington, Richmond, Savannah, and Miami. Taxis meet every train; a ride to downtown averages $25.

Contacts Amtrak ✉ *4565 Gaynor Ave., North Charleston* ☎ *843/744– 8264, 800/872–7245* ⊕ *www.amtrak. com.*

ESSENTIALS

■ COMMUNICATIONS

INTERNET

Most area lodgings have in-room data ports or in-room broadband, and some have wireless connections in the rooms or public areas. Internet cafés are rare, but many coffee shops, including Starbucks, have wireless available for free or a minimal fee. The FedEx Kinko's branch on Orleans Road has computers you can use for 20¢ a minute, as does the downtown branch.

Contacts Cybercafes ⊕ www.cybercafes.com. **FedEx Kinko's** ⊠ 73 St. Philip St., Radcliffeborough ☎ 843/723–5130 ⊕ www.fedex.com ⊠ 873 Orleans Rd., West Ashley ☎ 843/571–4746 ⊕ local.van.fedex.com/sc/charleston/office-1572.

PHONES

The area code in Charleston is 843.

■ EMERGENCIES

Medical University of South Carolina Hospital (MUSC) and Roper Hospital have 24-hour emergency rooms. Rite Aid Pharmacy, across from MUSC, closes at 10 pm daily; on weekends the pharmacy counter closes at 6 pm.

Emergency Services Emergency Services ☎ 911.

Hospitals Medical University of South Carolina Hospital ⊠ 171 Ashley Ave., Medical University of South Carolina ☎ 843/792–2300 ⊕ www.muschealth.com. **Roper Hospital** ⊠ 316 Calhoun St., Upper King ☎ 843/724–2000 ⊕ www.rsfh.com.

Late-Night Pharmacy Rite Aid Pharmacy ⊠ 261 Calhoun St., Upper King ☎ 843/805–6022 ⊕ www.riteaid.com.

■ HOURS OF OPERATION

Like most American cities, Charleston businesses generally operate on a 9-to-5 schedule. Shops downtown will often open at 10 am and close at 6 pm, with some conveniently staying open until 7; around the market area, clothing stores stay open as late as 9, and the fresh-made-candy shops and souvenir stores may stay open even later.

■ MAIL

The main post office is downtown on Broad Street, and a major branch is at West Ashley. To ship packages, FedEx Kinko's has a downtown branch and another at West Ashley. The UPS Store has locations in Mount Pleasant and West Ashley.

Post Offices Downtown Station ⊠ 83 Broad St., South of Broad ☎ 843/577–0690 ⊕ www.usps.com. **West Ashley Station** ⊠ 78 Sycamore St., West Ashley ☎ 843/766–4031 ⊕ www.usps.com.

Parcel Shipping FedEx Kinko's
✉ 73 St. Philip St., Radcliffeborough ☎ 843/723–5130 ⊕ www.fedex.com ✉ 873 Orleans Rd., West Ashley ☎ 843/571–4746 ⊕ local.van.fedex. com/sc/charleston/office-1572. **UPS Store** ✉ 1000 Johnnie Dodds Blvd., Mount Pleasant ☎ 843/856–9099 ⊕ www.theupsstorelocal.com/2130 ✉ 1643 Savannah Hwy., Floor B, West Ashley ☎ 843/763–6894 ⊕ www.theupsstorelocal.com/2114.

▌ MONEY

As in most cities, banks are open weekdays 9 to 5. There are countless branches in the downtown area, all with ATMs.

CREDIT CARDS
Reporting Lost Cards
American Express ☎ 800/528–4800 ⊕ www.americanexpress. com. **MasterCard** ☎ 800/627–8372 ⊕ www.mastercard.com. **Visa** ☎ 800/847–2911 ⊕ www.visa.com.

▌ SAFETY

Charleston is considered a very safe, midsize city. You can feel quite secure in the downtown Historic District (from Broad Street, to Upper King Street, Mary Street, and slightly beyond) even until midnight during the week and later on weekends. In neighborhoods where there is public housing (especially off upper King Street in the direction of Spring Street), you would not want to walk around carefree, either by day or night. A lot of late-night street crime is directed at those

who drink too much, making themselves easy marks for robbery. Do lock your car doors, and do not leave valuables in sight. Full shopping bags, luggage, and laptops will be particularly tempting in hard economic times.

■TIP➔ **Distribute your cash, credit cards, IDs, and other valuables between a deep front pocket, an inside jacket or vest pocket, and a hidden money pouch. Don't reach for the money pouch once you're in public.**

Contact Transportation Security Administration (TSA). ☎ 866/289–9673 ⊕ www.tsa.gov.

▌ TAXES

In Charleston, sales tax on most purchases is 7.5%. Hotels are taxed at 12.5% (11.5% in Mount Pleasant). In restaurants, the tax is 9.5% for food, beer, and wine (14.5% for liquor); however, in Mount Pleasant, food, beer, and wine are taxed at 8.5%, liquor at 13.5%.

▌ TIPPING

In fine dining restaurants, it is customary to tip 15% to 20%. In less expensive, family restaurants, 15% is the norm. For taxis, a tip of 10% to 15% is typical. Passengers are often more generous to pedicab drivers, as they are pedaling those bicycles hard.

▌ TOURS

Tours in Charleston run the gamut, from aerial tours to city and ecotours, and also numerous boat and harbor trips; in a city that is known as a walker-friendly destination, walking tours are numerous and popular. A large percentage of tourists opt for a horse-and-carriage tour, mostly on large wagons with a dozen or so other visitors, but private horse-and-buggy trips by day or night are definitely a romantic option. Whatever you choose, it is a good way to orient yourself in the city and best taken at the beginning of your stay.

AIR TOURS

Flying High Over Charleston provides aerial tours of the city and surrounding areas. A 60-minute, 50-mile tour is $190; a 40-minute, 30-mile tour is $150.

Contacts Flying High Over Charleston ⊠ Atlantic Aviation, 6060 S. Aviation Ave., 211A, North Charleston ☎ 843/569-6148 ⊕ www.flyinghighovercharleston.com.

BOAT TOURS

Charleston Harbor Tours offers tours that give the history of the harbor; it's the oldest harbor tour boat company (since 1908) in Charleston and gives a good narrated tour of the harbor; however, these tours do not stop at Fort Sumter. Spiritline Cruises, which runs the ferry to Fort Sumter, also offers harbor tours and dinner cruises ($49–$55). The dinner cruises leave from Patriots Point Marina in Mount Pleasant and include a three-course dinner and dancing to music by a local radio DJ. Each table has a water view. Sandlapper Tours has tours focused on regional his-

tory, coastal wildlife, and nocturnal ghostly lore; you must make reservations by phone in advance since there is no ticket office where the harbor tours depart. All harbor cruises range between $22 and $30. On the authentic, 84-foot-tall schooner *Pride* (capacity 49 people), you can enjoy a diesel-free sail and the natural sounds of Charleston harbor on a two-hour harbor cruise, a dolphin cruise, a sunset cruise, romantic full-moon sails, and special events; tours range from $34 to $55.

Contacts Charleston Harbor Tours ⊠ Charleston Maritime Center, 10 Wharfside St., Upper King ☎ 843/722-1112, 800/344-4483 ⊕ www.charlestonharbortours.com. **Sandlapper Tours** ⊠ Charleston Maritime Center, 10 Wharfside St., Upper King ☎ 843/849-8687 ⊕ www.sandlappertours.com. **Schooner Pride** ⊠ Aquarium Wharf, 360 Concord St., Upper King ☎ 800/344-4483, 843/722-1112 ⊕ www.schoonerpride.com. **Spiritline Cruises** ⊠ Aquarium Wharf, 360 Concord St., Upper King ☎ 843/881-7337, 800/789-3678 ⊕ www.spiritlinecruises.com.

BUS TOURS

Adventure Sightseeing leads bus tours of the Historic District. The Historic Charleston Foundation pairs local guides with visiting tour groups. Doin' the Charleston, a van tour, makes a stop at the Battery. It leaves from the Visitor Center, but will pick up passengers from their downtown hotel 30 minutes before the tour. Native Charlestonian Marvin Katzen is a seasoned guide, journalist, and actor with Doin' the Charleston. Sites and Insights is a van tour that covers downtown and nearby islands and focuses on Black history. Al Miller, the premier guide, will even sing "Summertime" while giving the Porgie & Bess Tour. Similarly, Gullah Tours, which leave from the Visitor Center, focuses on sights significant to African-American culture. Tour guide Alfonso Brown is fluent in the Gullah language. Chai Y'All shares stories and sights of Jewish interest.

Contacts Adventure Sightseeing ⊠ *1090 Fort Sumter Dr., Historic District* ☎ *800/722–5394, 843/762–0088* ⊕ *www.touringcharleston.com.* **Chai Y'All** ⊠ *Downtown historic district* ☎ *843/556–0664.* **Doin' the Charleston** ⊠ *375 Meeting St., Market area* ☎ *843/763–1233, 800/647–4487* ⊕ *www.dointhecharlestontours. com.* **Gullah Tours** ⊠ *375 Meeting St., Market area* ☎ *843/763–7551* ⊕ *www.gullahtours.com.* **Historic Charleston Foundation** ⊠ *Ticket office, 108 Meeting St., Market area* ☎ *843/723–1623 main office, 843/722–3405 ticket office* ⊕ *www. historiccharleston.org.* **Sites and Insights** ☎ *843/762–0051* ⊕ *www. sitesandinsightstours.com.*

CARRIAGE TOURS

Carriage tours are a great way to see Charleston. The going rate is $22 for an adult. Carolina Polo and Carriage Company, Old South Carriage Company (where drivers wear mock Confederate uniforms), and Palmetto Carriage Works run horse- and mule-drawn carriage tours of the Historic District. Each tour, which follows one of four routes, lasts about one hour. Most

carriages queue up at North Market and Anson streets. Carolina Polo and Carriage, which picks up passengers at the Doubletree Guest Suites Historic Charleston on Church Street, has a historically authentic carriage that is sought after for private tours and wedding parties. Palmetto offers free parking at their big red barn and has combo tickets for harbor tours.

Contacts Carolina Polo and Carriage Company ⊠ *Lobby of DoubleTree hotel, 181 Church St., Downtown historic district* ☎ *843/577–6767* ⊕ *www.cpcc.com.* **Old South Carriage Company** ⊠ *14 Anson St., Downtown historic district* ☎ *843/723–9712* ⊕ *www. oldsouthcarriagetours.com.* **Palmetto Carriage Works** ⊠ *8 Guignard St., Downtown historic district* ☎ *843/723–8145* ⊕ *www.palmet tocarriage.com.*

ECOTOURS

Barrier Island Ecotours, at the Isle of Palms Marina, runs three-hour pontoon-boat tours to a barrier island. Coastal Expeditions has half-day and full-day naturalist-led kayak tours on local rivers. Coastal Eco Tours offers a wide variety of two- and three-hour water tours of the Lowcountry.

Contacts Barrier Island Ecotours ⊠ *Isle of Palms Marina, off U.S. 17, 50 41st Ave., Isle of Palms* ☎ *843/886–5000* ⊕ *www.nature-tours.com.* **Coastal Eco Tours** ⊠ *Isle of Palms* ☎ *843/568–8427* ⊕ *www. coasteco.com.* **Coastal Expeditions** ⊠ *514-B Mill St., Mount Pleasant* ☎ *843/884–7684* ⊕ *www.coastal expeditions.com.*

PRIVATE GUIDES

To hire a private guide to lead you around the city, contact Charleston's Finest Historic Tours. Janice Kahn has been leading customized tours for more than 38 years. She is well versed in subjects such as architecture, art, literary landmarks like those in Pat Conroy's *South of Broad*, and African-American history. She can give tours walking, in a private car, or as a step-on-guide for charter bus groups.

Contacts Charleston's Finest Historic Tours ⊠ *Tour meets at Charleston Visitors Center, 375 Meeting St., Downtown historic district* ☎ *843/577–3311* ⊕ *www.historictoursofcharleston. com.* **Janice Kahn** ⊠ *Downtown historic district* ☎ *843/556–0664.*

WALKING TOURS

Walking tours on various topics—horticulture, slavery, or women's history—are given by Charleston Strolls and the Original Charleston Walks. Bulldog Tours has walks that explore the city's supernatural side. Listen to the infamous tales of lost souls with Ghosts of Charleston, which travel to historic graveyards. They have expanded their offerings to include a sunset cruise and a culinary tour. They explore culinary strongholds where you can watch food artisans at work while sampling and shopping along the way.

Let Mary Coy, a fourth-generation Charlestonian and former teacher, bring the history and architecture of Charleston's back alleys and noble streets to life on her two-hour Charleston 101 Tour. Pay attention—there may be a quiz at the end.

Culinary Tours of Charleston is a foodie adventure that stops at a variety of restaurants in the Historic District, where you'll experience the area's rich culinary history and Southern hospitality.

Contacts Bulldog Tours ⊠ *40 N. Market St., Downtown historic district* ☎ *843/722–8687* ⊕ *www.bulldogtours.com.* **Charleston 101 Tours** ⊠ *Tours start at the Powder Magazine on Cumberland St., one block from the City Market, Downtown historic district* ☎ *843/556–4753* ⊕ *www.charleston 101tours.com.* **Charleston Strolls** ⊠ *40 N. Market St., Market area* ☎ *843/766–2080* ⊕ *www.charlestonstrolls.com.* **Culinary Tours of Charleston** ⊠ *40 N. Market St., Market area* ☎ *843/722–8687, 800/918–0701* ⊕ *www.bulldogtours.com.* **Ghosts of Charleston** ⊠ *184 E. Bay St., French Quarter* ☎ *800/854–1670 Office, 800/979–3370 reservations* ⊕ *www.tourcharleston.com.* **Original Charleston Walks** ⊠ *45 S. Market St., Market area* ☎ *843/408–0010* ⊕ *www.charlestonwalks.com.*

▌ TRIP INSURANCE

Comprehensive travel policies typically cover trip cancellation and interruption, letting you cancel or cut your trip short because of a personal emergency or illness. Such policies also cover evacuation and medical care in case you are injured or become ill on your trip. Some also cover you for trip delays because of bad weather or mechanical problems as well as for lost or delayed baggage. Another type of coverage to look for is financial default—that is, when your trip is disrupted because a tour operator, airline, or cruise line goes out of business. Generally you must buy this when you book your trip or shortly thereafter, and it's available to you only if your operator isn't on a list of excluded companies.

Expect comprehensive travel insurance policies to cost about 4% to 7% or 8% of the total price of your trip (it's more like 8%–12% if you're over age 70). Always read the fine print of your policy to make sure that you are covered for the risks that are of most concern to you. Compare several policies to make sure you're getting the best price and range of coverage available.

■TIP→ **Okay. You know that you can often save on trips to warm-weather destinations, like the Carolina Lowcountry, by traveling during hurricane season. But there's also a chance that a severe storm will disrupt your plans. The solution? Look for hotels and resorts that offer storm/hurricane guarantees. Although they rarely allow refunds, most guarantees do let you rebook later if a storm strikes.**

Insurance Comparison Sites
Insure My Trip.com ☎ 800/487–4722 ⊕ www.insuremytrip.com.
Square Mouth.com ☎ 800/240–0369 ⊕ www.squaremouth.com.

Comprehensive Travel Insurers
Allianz Travel Insurance
☎ 800/284–8300 ⊕ www.allianz travelinsurance.com. **CSA Travel Protection** ☎ 800/873–9855 ⊕ www.csatravelprotection.com. **HTH Worldwide** ☎ 610/254–8700 ⊕ www.hthworldwide.com. **Travelex Insurance** ☎ 888/228–9792 ⊕ www.travelex-insurance.com. **Travel Guard** ☎ 800/826–4919 ⊕ www.travelguard.com. **Travel Insured International** ☎ 800/243–3174 ⊕ www.travelinsured.com.

▌ VISITOR INFORMATION

The Charleston Area Convention & Visitors Bureau runs the Charleston Visitor Center, which has information about the city as well as Kiawah Island, Seabrook Island, Mount Pleasant, North Charleston, Edisto Island, Summerville, and the Isle of Palms. The Historic Charleston Foundation and the Preservation Society of Charleston have information on house tours.

Contacts **Charleston Visitor Center** ✉ 375 Meeting St., Market area ☎ 843/853–8000, 800/868–8118 ⊕ www.charlestoncvb.com. **Historic Charleston Foundation** ✉ 40 E. Bay St., Downtown historic district ☎ 843/723–1623 ⊕ www.historiccharleston.org. **Preservation Society of Charleston** ✉ 147 King St., Downtown historic district ☎ 843/722–4630 ⊕ www.preservationsociety.org.

INDEX

PHOTO CREDITS

NOTES